KING LEOPOLD II.

Photo: Géruzet Frères, Brussels.

KING LEOPOLD II.

In the uniform of a Lieutenant-General, with the Grand Cordon of the Order of Leopold.

KING LEOPOLD II.

His Rule
IN
BELGIUM AND THE CONGO

.. BY ..

JOHN DE COURCY MacDONNELL

*WITH 40 FULL-PAGE PLATES FROM PHOTOGRAPHS,
GENEALOGICAL TABLE, AND MAP.*

NEGRO UNIVERSITIES PRESS
NEW YORK

Originally published in 1905
by Cassell and Company, Ltd., London

Reprinted 1969 by
Negro Universities Press
A DIVISION OF GREENWOOD PUBLISHING CORP.
NEW YORK

SBN 8371-2657-6

PRINTED IN UNITED STATES OF AMERICA

CONTENTS.

CHAPTER I.
The King's Policy 1

CHAPTER II.
King, Parliament, and People, 1865–1890 14

CHAPTER III.
Belgium and the Foreign Powers 54

CHAPTER IV.
Belgian Expansion 88

CHAPTER V.
The Opening of the Geographical Conference of 1876 . 93

CHAPTER VI.
Slave Hunting in the Congo—Resolutions of the Conference 98

CHAPTER VII.
The International Association — King Leopold's First African Enterprise 107

CHAPTER VIII.
Diplomatic Victories 119

CHAPTER IX.
The Recognition of the State's Supremacy . . . 132

CHAPTER X.
The Congress of Berlin 141

CONTENTS.

CHAPTER XI.
The Suppression of the Slave Trade 152

CHAPTER XII.
The Congo Law and the Natives' Future 162

CHAPTER XIII.
The Congo Missions 181

CHAPTER XIV.
The Progress of the Independent State 233

CHAPTER XV.
Crime, Controversy, and Justice in the Independent State 272

CHAPTER XVI.
Belgium, 1890–1905 308

CHAPTER XVII.
The Future Empire 373

LIST OF ILLUSTRATIONS.

	FACING PAGE
KING LEOPOLD II. . . . . *Frontispiece.*	
KING LEOPOLD AS DUKE OF BRABANT, 1853	4
PLACE DE LA BROUCKÈRE AND THE BOULEVARD DE LA SENNE . . .	8
M. BEERNAERT, LT.-GENERAL BRIALMONT, M. CHARLES ROGIER, AND M. FRÈRE-ORBAN	20
PALAIS DE LA NATION, BRUSSELS	40
HÔTEL DE VILLE, BRUSSELS	52
TYPES OF THE BELGIAN ARMY (*from paintings by Maurice Romberg*) . . .	70
THE BELFRY, BRUGES	74
GENEALOGICAL TABLE	84
THE KING'S PALACE, BRUSSELS	96
A NATIVE CANOE ON THE ARUWIMI—NATIVE BRIDGE OVER THE LUFU . .	98
NATIVES PREPARING RUBBER—NATIVE WOMEN MAKING FLOUR . . .	104
COUNT DE SMET DE NAEYER—BARON DHANIS—BARON LAMBERMONT . .	128
ARMS OF KING LEOPOLD—ARMS OF THE INDEPENDENT STATE . . .	134
NATIVE STREET, BASOKO—CONSTRUCTION OF NATIVE STOREHOUSE, TURUMBU	154
RUINS OF ARAB MOSQUE—NATIVE DWELLING, AND IMPROVED NATIVE DWELLING, BAFUMU	160
TAILORING PUPILS—NATIVE TEACHER AND HIS CLASS	184
TRAPPIST WITH THE CHILDREN OF A FARM CHAPEL—NATIVE CATECHIST PREACHING	194
STATE STATION AT THE EQUATOR—TRAVELLING THROUGH THE FOREST, KATANGA	202
COTTAGES OF THE WHITE RESIDENTS, COQUILHATVILLE—OFFICE OF THE GOVERNMENT SURVEY STAFF, BOMA	210
SHIPBUILDING AT LEOPOLDVILLE—LAUNCH OF A STEAMER	214
THE CHURCH AND MISSIONARIES' HOUSE, KISANTU	220
AGRICULTURE AT KISANTU—GIRLS' SCHOOL GROUP	230
AUTOMOBILE ROAD NEAR KWANGO—STEAM MOTORS	234
SCENES ON THE CATARACTS LINE	240
PLOUGHING AT EALA—STUD FARM, EALA	246
THE KITCHEN GARDEN, LOFOI—CULTIVATED FIELDS, LOFOI	250

LIST OF ILLUSTRATIONS.

	FACING PAGE
Natives Preparing Rubber—Collecting Rubber	252
Natives Sawing Timber—Shaping Timber by Hand	256
Cattle at Stanleyville—Stable at Eala—Cattle at Vankerckhovenville	260
A Clearing in the Bamboos—Drying Rubber	268
Mouth of the Lilo—Inspection of Jesuits' Agricultural School.	280
The *Force Publique* on the March	286
Rubber Creeper Nursery, Lowa—Field of Sweet Potatoes on the Aruwimi	298
Ostriches and Dromedaries at Uere—Breaking-in Baby Elephants	302
Port of Matadi—State Pier at Boma in '96	306
Dimanche des Rameaux	316
Mineur au Répos—La Remonte des Mineurs	324
Unloading Potatoes, Liége	352
Palais de Justice, Brussels	368
The Quays, Antwerp	376

KING LEOPOLD II.

CHAPTER I.

THE KING'S POLICY.

OF all the occurrences in the nineteenth century which changed the map of Europe and the government of European states, those which made Belgium an independent kingdom and gave to that country princes of the House of Saxe-Coburg were pre-eminently fortunate. The sturdy Belgians, revolting against bigotry and oppression, won their own freedom, and have none but themselves to thank for it; but they owe gratitude to the shifting interests of foreign politics which led the Powers to suggest to them that their choice of a ruler should fall on Prince Leopold. In him Belgium had a King whose reputation was deserved as that of the wisest prince in Christendom. The results of King Leopold I.'s prudent and far-seeing counsels made themselves felt in many lands; England, through Queen Victoria, the King's niece and his disciple in statecraft, owes almost as much to King Leopold I. as Belgium does. And Belgium owes great things to her first King. The greatest of all the debts of gratitude she owes him is that due for the care he so wisely bestowed on the education of his son and successor, King Leopold II.

When Leopold I. was called to the throne of Belgium, and throughout his reign, the power of the middle classes was at its height. Parliamentary oratory was then, too, at its most popular period; and in his reign cheap newspapers came, bringing with them cheap wisdom and cheap philosophy. In those days every newspaper reader imagined himself, quite seriously, to be a statesman, and the ideal of statesmen in monarchical countries lay then in constitutional government under a king who, as their axiom phrased it, reigned but did not rule. Politicians' axioms are seldom otherwise than delusive, and this political axiom of the nineteenth century impregnated with nonsense the minds of men in all classes—from those professedly wise to those admittedly simple. The middle class felt all-powerful by its votes, and the newspapers paraphrased the axiom into meaning that they ruled, while the king reigned; and middle class philosophers and historians repeated their paraphrase for them until all the world seemed to believe in it.

Nothing is more absurd than this theory. In a constitutional monarchy the king's place is well defined, but the king's place is ever that of a ruler, and his first duty is to rule. If he be a weak man his rule will be feeble, if he be a vicious man his rule will be bad; but, strong or feeble, a king cannot but fix his imprint on his country, and he it is who himself produces for his reign its result, good, bad, or indifferent, according to his abilities and his will.

Whatever the limits of the constitution, it is inevitable that on many, and these the most vital, points of government the king's voice must be most powerful in the councils of his country. The history of the nineteenth century, now opening to the world, proves that this was so, even when the middle-class power was at its highest; and beside the proof of history, common-sense shows that it must be so, as long as kings remain. In a free country, during a single reign, thousands of politicians, hundreds of ministers, come and go, each with an individual policy and a separate aim of his own, each with other interests than those of politics, and each with little training in the deep game of statesmanship. The king alone remains unchanging, and of all who share or seek to share in the government, he alone is the one whose sole business preoccupation is government, and he is the only one whose education has been that of statesmanship. He is, in fact, a highly-trained specialist at the head of half educated amateurs. This being so, he reigns and rules. The Liberal doctrinaires who surrounded King Leopold I. during a great part of his reign puffed themselves out with different theories which that wise King left undisturbed while he guided them, and all his other ministers, with the firm hand of a ruler confident in himself, too wise to be misled, too patriotic to be affronted; and instilled a knowledge of statecraft into his eldest son, his successor, on whom he had bestowed the title of Duke of Brabant.

The Duke of Brabant, who was born on April 9th, 1835, came of age in 1853, and at once entered the Belgian Senate. His character was then already formed, and his future policy was already fixed in his mind. That policy was, doubtless, elaborated more fully as time advanced; but so great was it from the moment of its inception that neither his far travels as a young prince, nor his wide knowledge of men as king, can have deepened or enlarged it.

The young prince was ambitious for his country's good, as men should wish every future ruler to be. His ambition was of the highest, but it was all centred in Belgium. He alone, of all the Belgians of that time, saw that Belgium could only remain free by becoming great; and his resolve was to lead Belgium to greatness—a resolve impossible of accomplishment in the eyes of the Belgian statesmen themselves of the time, who saw in their country no more than a small State existing on tolerance in the midst of powerful empires but, nevertheless, a resolve which history will show to have been accomplished, thanks to the genius and perseverance of the prince and the energy of the people he led.

The men of the new generation which was succeeding to that of the patriots who had made Belgium free were as contented with their fathers' work as they were proud of it. Knowing nothing of the secret policies of the great States surrounding their country, which again and again threatened to sweep that independence away, the majority of them relied for the maintenance of their freedom on the guarantees of the Powers. These men felt no need of expansion for themselves, and expected none for their descendants. Freedom, well ordered, was their goddess, and their debates and struggles were upon the question of the particular mould of freedom into which young Belgium should be forced. If the earlier generation which won the independence of Belgium had looked for much to the constitution of the United States when mapping out the charter of Belgian liberty, the generation which followed moulded its policy in a great degree on that of English Liberalism, and loved to shape its Parliamentary procedure on that of England, in copying which its leaders felt that they were giving proof to the world that Belgium possessed a solidly founded and a perfected form of government. To these excellent politicians the entry of the Duke of Brabant into Parliament as an hereditary senator was momentous chiefly from its resemblance to the entry of the Prince of Wales into the House of Lords, a resemblance which was intentionally heightened by the duke taking his seat, not on the cross-benches, for in the semicircle of the Belgian Senate there are no cross-benches, but on a seat arranged exactly in the middle of the house so as to be equidistant from the seats of each party.

To the Duke of Brabant his entry into Parliament

From a painting by De Keyser.

KING LEOPOLD II.
When Duke of Brabant, 1853, in the uniform of a Colonel of Grenadiers.
(*An unpublished portrait.*)

had quite another significance. It was to him a sign that the time had come for his participation in the government of the country over which he was one day to rule. He threw himself at once into the performance of what he rightly conceived to be his duty, and men learned that in the young prince a thinker, an orator, and a patriot had arisen in the Belgian Parliament. The Duke of Brabant's action as a member of the Senate was no idle parade. In the Senate he commenced the labour which as king he has achieved, and the nature of which, in its every aim, he unfolded while yet senator and heir-apparent.

King Leopold II. found Belgium, when he came to the throne, a small state; under his rule it has become a strong, and in many respects a great kingdom. He has provided it with the means of expansion, and placed empire within its grasp. To him the boast of that Emperor who found his city of brick and left it marble may seem the boast of an almost pitiably mean achievement; yet if King Leopold had no other claim on his people than that of a builder, his name would live in reverence in Belgium. It is no exaggeration to say that there is no town in Belgium so small or so insignificant that it does not bear the imprint of his hand. Above all, as was but fitting, he has laboured, planned, and contrived for the improvement of his capital. Its noble suburbs, its wide arteries, its cleanliness, and its health; the beauty of its modern quarters, which are no blots beside the splendour of its mediæval glories, are all alike due to the King's forethought and his initiative; and it is worthy of remembrance that his first important speech as Duke of Brabant was made to the Senate for the adoption of measures for the beautifying of Brussels.

On December 19th, 1860, the Duke of Brabant introduced into the Senate a motion for the institution of a prize of 10,000 francs for the best plan for the embellishment of Brussels. Seven months later he returned to the subject of the decoration and utility of the great towns, and spoke in the Senate of the necessity of undertaking public works for the improvement of Ghent, Antwerp, Namur, Mons, Liége, Charleroi, and Verviers, as well as the capital. " Everywhere," said the Duke of Brabant in this speech, " the embellishment of towns advances step by step with the increase of public welfare "; but it is to be noted it was not of embellishment alone that the young prince thought or spoke of in his speech to Parliament. " The working populations have a right to our full solicitude," he said; " we must exert ourselves to improve their dwellings and give them light and air." These would be trite words now; they were not so in 1860 to the plutocrats of the Belgian Senate, whose policy towards the working classes was, in all things material, one of *laissez-faire*. The Belgian ministry and Parliament was swayed at the time this speech was made, and for a full quarter of a century later, by the will of a great Liberal statesman whose policy in all things, excepting those relating to spiritual affairs, was one of *laissez-faire* and *laissez-passer*; but, much as he admired that minister, *laissez-faire* or *laissez-passer* was never a policy of King Leopold's in any domain of politics; while he remained a senator he continued to return to these economic questions and in his speeches urge their solution on the Parliament; and when he became king he adopted the still more efficacious means of dragging to light the evils which needed remedy in his speeches to local authorities and his public conversations with local officials, of personally taking the lead in the movements for their remedy, and of never allowing the public to lose sight of them until they were remedied.

The questions of internal economy were far from being the only ones on which the Duke of Brabant sought to influence the Belgian Senate. His policy for

THE KING'S POLICY.

the development of Belgium was also urged by him on the Senate. In that policy the extension of the trade of the Belgian ports held a foremost place, side by side with a scheme which he never relinquished, but the development of which is only now beginning : one for the formation of a Belgian mercantile marine.

It is impossible to treat the public life of the King of the Belgians other than as a whole, so closely are later acts and earlier words interwoven, so certainly is the effect produced to-day traceable to the cause originated by him long decades past. With King Leopold there is no such thing as haste, no grasping of what is opportune, no acceptance of makeshifts, no patience with half measures. All such things the King is content to leave to lesser men who trade in politics. The King of the Belgians is a strong man, physically as well as mentally. He has probably known himself for a strong man all his life ; but even were he physically a weakling, and possessed of the same strong mind that he has, it is probable that his actions would have been marked by the same indifference to the passage of time in the pursuit of the ends for which he strove.

In a speech which he made to the Belgian Senate in 1904, when that body presented him with an address congratulating him on the birth of the second son of Prince Albert, he showed why such indifference to the fleeting moment possesses him. " The extreme importance of the principle of hereditary monarchy," said the King, " lies in the fact that it allows monarchs to pursue designs of distant ends. Human life is very short ; the life of a nation may be very long. The King, my father of great memory, always longed ardently to see the country possessed of one or more exterior dependencies. This sage counsel has perhaps been carried out under the second reign. Our ports, many of our public works, the embellishment and the sanitary improvement of our towns, will see many reigns preside over their development. They have been commenced under the founder of the dynasty, and each reign will deposit its stone or stones on the national edifice which can and must be raised unceasingly.

"Certainly, we are progressing ; but, in spite of all our efforts, the actual reign will be far from seeing the realisation of all the patriotic designs of our first king. The basis of our maritime commerce is not yet laid."

Pride in the attainment of lofty aims lies in every sentence of this speech, although its closing words speak of work hardly as yet begun. That work, the foundation of the maritime commerce of Belgium, has been pushed forward since this speech was made ; and it seems as though Belgian traders, being at last roused to a perception of their interests in the matter, a Belgian mercantile marine will be now created. The rousing of the trading interests is the result of ceaseless effort on the King's part, in letters, speeches, and conversations from the time of his entry into public life until the present moment. His first speech on the matter was made more than forty years ago in the Senate, while he was still Duke of Brabant ; and then his words on the importance of Belgian shipping were the same as his words of this year. "I wish," he said, "that at the stations of Antwerp and Ostend, where the Belgian railways stop, all were not finished for us ; but that, on the contrary, a new and large way of national activity would open itself out at these places. I wish that these stations, the termini of to-day, would soon become the starting points of numerous steamers which would prolong our railways over seas. Gentlemen, you will not long permit that, alone amongst nations possessing ports and a maritime frontier, we shall remain tributary to foreigners for the greater part of our exports. There is a great work of extension and emancipation to accomplish. That work is worthy of all the friends of progress."

Belgian parliamentarians forty years ago saw the

GENERAL VIEW OF THE PLACE DE BROUCKÈRE AND THE BOULEVARD DE LA SENNE.

Photo: Neurdein Frères, Paris.

neighbouring countries—England, France, Germany, and Holland—rather than the sea washing the Belgian coast. The most advanced leaders kept their eyes fixed on their boundaries, and had no thought of extending their energies or their country's influence beyond them; it needed the Prince, full of patriotic zeal, to point out the horizon to his countrymen, and to teach them of the boundless possibilities which lay for Belgium beyond it. It is true, as King Leopold II. said in his speech to the Senate, that his father, the first king, ardently desired to see the country possessed of exterior dependencies. King Leopold I. even made some attempts to realise this desire; but his attempts were frustrated by the action of his ministers, who declared the realisation of his wish to be impossible; and while the germ of the colonial idea was doubtless implanted in the mind of King Leopold II. by his father, its growth is due to the latter's own serious study, and to the investigations he personally made in foreign and distant lands. For the first movements which King Leopold II. made to impress on his countrymen the necessity of founding Belgian colonies, we must again go back to the time when he was Duke of Brabant.

The Duke of Brabant was married shortly after coming of age to the Archduchess Marie Henriette of Austria, and the first years after his marriage were spent by him in travels with the duchess in Africa and Asia, in Algeria, Morocco, and Tunisia, in Egypt and Nubia, in India and in China. Every country in Europe was already familiar to him, and to him every country, either in its present condition or in its relics and memories of the past, repeated the same lesson—a lesson he summed up and sought to spread, where its spreading would be most fruitful, by a present he made on the return from his travels to the Liberal statesman to whom reference has already been made. This present consisted of a stone carried back by the prince from the ruins of an ancient Grecian monument, and bearing an inscription which he had caused to be engraved on it : " *Il faut à la Belgique des colonies.*"

In the mind and the speeches of the Duke of Brabant, as in his mind and speeches since he became king, the interests of Belgian trade and commerce were inseparably united to those of Belgian expansion—that expansion which could only come through colonisation. The close commercial alliance which now exists, through King Leopold's exertions, between Belgium and China, was urged on the Belgian Senate by the King while Duke of Brabant, in 1858. In 1860, from his place in the Senate, he urged the Belgian manufacturers to carry samples of their goods to distant lands, and to seek their customers in their homes, rather than to sit quietly in Belgium waiting for custom to come to them ; and in 1861, in a great speech to the Senate, enunciated the policy which was to guide him—and, through him, Belgium—throughout his reign. In this speech he laid stress on the necessity which existed for industry to create exterior markets for itself ; in it he pictured the encumbrance of the markets of Europe, and the profits to be gained by spreading commercial activity in the distant countries of Asia, of Oceania, and of Africa ; and said that emigration, instead of impoverishing a nation, helped to propagate its influence. He recalled the efforts of the Compagnie d'Ostende, which, founded in 1722, carried the Belgian flag into distant seas and ports, and created a powerful commercial movement ; and, finally, he cited the lessons of history to prove that " settlements and colonies have not only always well served the commercial interests of nations, but it is even to these foundations that the majority of them owe their past or their present grandeur " ; and, turning to the example of England, he recalled the fact—significant above all others for Belgium—that, " reduced to itself alone, it is only a nation of twenty-eight million inhabitants, but with its colonies it counts more than two hundred millions, and everywhere on the globe finds itself at home."

These lessons, which the ardent Prince preached with such zeal, were long in sinking into the minds of his hearers. So long, that any other than he would have abandoned his self-imposed labour in disgust at the slowness of the chiefs of industry to grasp what was so obviously for their interest. King Leopold, however, is one whose zeal for Belgium, and whose confidence in its future, has never wavered: he is one who has never turned back from any work for his country, and never lessened his exertions, however tedious his labour, and however uncertain of fructification that labour might appear to others to be. His action on the question of a Belgian mercantile marine shows how determinedly he pursues his ends. It was never out of season for him to refer to it, and every means a king could use was used by him to give it prominence. The King's letters, as well as his speeches, are full of the subject. In 1889, in a royal letter to the Belgian Chamber, there was, for instance, the following passage:—

"I have never ceased to call the attention of my co-patriots to the necessity of turning their views towards the countries across the ocean. History teaches that the countries with restricted territories have a moral and material interest in spreading out beyond their narrow frontiers. More than any other, a manufacturing and commercial nation such as ours must exert itself to secure outlets for all its workers; those with capital, with brains, and with strength."

Again, in October, 1898, addressing the delegates of industry and commerce at Antwerp, the King said:—

"We have been the first on the Continent to construct railways; let us understand how to prolong them by lines of navigation. May the Belgians at length interest themselves in the most important industry of sea transport."

Perhaps the most striking illustration of how King Leopold seizes on every occasion to press home these subjects, which he looks upon as of the first importance, is found in his replies, given in January, 1903, to the addresses from Parliament. Referring to the allusion in the address of the Senate to the newly-discovered coalfields in Limbourg, the King said:

"There is another source of riches which my fellow-citizens, I regret to say, have not learned how to profit by up to the present. It is the sea. The land frontiers are more and more closed to us by protective tariffs; the maritime frontier remains always open, and no one has the power to close it. Our industry, profiting by these new mineral riches, should be able to take a modest but a useful and profitable place beside the other nations which dispute the empire of the sea."

On the same day, in his reply to the address from the Chamber, the King again dwelt upon the subject, speaking as follows:—

"I hope this treasure will be made profitable as soon as possible; but let us not lose sight of the fact that while the frontiers are closing against us everywhere we have at the side of the sea an admirable frontier, and our fine coast can be utilised for the exportation of our new mineral riches."

Thus, for forty years and more, as prince and king, has King Leopold forced these matters, of the first import to them, upon the attention of the merchants and manufacturers of Belgium. What he undertakes for the country he has sworn to achieve, as he told the Senate, either by himself or through his dynasty. Most of his projects, lofty as they are, and distant from realisation as they once seemed, have been, or are being, attained within his own reign. The

THE KING'S POLICY.

foundation of a Belgian marine has now been laid. Within the last year in the ports of the country companies have been formed for the establishment of lines of Belgian steamers, the Belgian flag has been hoisted on vessels of established lines, and training-ships for Belgian sailors have been fitted out. As has been shown, it was not the commerce of Belgium with foreign countries only that King Leopold had in mind in his appeals to the Belgians to found a mercantile marine; his dream from the first was one of Belgian colonies, in which the life of Belgium might expand, and from which fresh glory and new wealth might be brought to rich and glorious Belgium. That dream of the young prince in his ardent youth is realised to-day when the King's steamers ply between the chief Belgian port of Antwerp and the great colony he has founded on the Congo.

CHAPTER II.

KING, PARLIAMENT, AND PEOPLE, 1865-1890.

KING LEOPOLD ascended the throne of Belgium on December 17th, 1865, on which day he made his solemn entry into Brussels, and took the oath to observe the Belgian constitution. The entry of the King into the ancient capital of Belgium was a brilliant pageant. Not only were the heads of the Belgian Government, of the army, and of the Church massed around him, but there were also in the King's train princes of the great houses of Europe to which King Leopold was allied by blood and marriage: the King of Portugal, the Crown Prince of Prussia, Prince Arthur of England, the Duke of Cambridge, the Archduke Joseph of Austria, Prince George of Saxony, the Duke of Saxe-Coburg-Gotha, and a crowd of other foreign princes, as well as the Envoys Extraordinary of all the Powers. The Belgians love pageants. From the earliest days of their history they have loved them, and from the earliest days the most solemn and the most important, as well as the most splendid of all their civic pageants, were those which took place on the entries of their princes into their cities. These " Joyous Entries," as they were called, were in ancient Belgium, a land of cities and of civic government, the counterparts to the enthronement of the rulers in other states. They were not only the occasions of the cities throwing open their gates to their sovereigns and surrendering their keys to them, but they were also the occasions of the burghers coming face to face with their ruler for the first time after each new accession; and, as such, they were occasions invariably seized on in these ancient times by the citizens to wring the concession of new rights from the princes if they were weak, or at least to obtain from them the ratification of their existing charters in return for their submission and tranquillity. When King Leopold II. ascended the throne, the cities had already surrendered their power to the Parliament, whilst their ancient charters were represented by, and to no small extent embodied in the constitution of the country. Under these circumstances, the joyous entry of King Leopold into Brussels might easily have passed off as nothing more than a pleasing ceremony, marking only the interchange of goodwill between the King and his subjects.

Such it was undoubtedly ; but it was more. Amongst the words of praise and thanks and compliment, of sorrow at the late King's death and eulogy of his actions, and of hope and promise for the future, which were inevitable to the occasion, King Leopold uttered some sentences which struck the keynote of his life's policy and of his whole future action as ruler. Undistracted by the brilliant concourse around him, with no thought of using the citizens of Brussels as a stage mob to whom he could address rounded phrases for the admiration of the listening kings and princes of foreign lands, the King of the Belgians went directly and at once to the needs of the citizens, and called for their fulfilment.

"I hope," he said, having spoken of the improvements effected in Brussels during the reign of his predecessor, "that very long before the entry of my successor the capital will receive new embellishments, and, notably, that it will no longer suffer from the emanations of an unwholesome river." Probably few, besides the King and the citizens, amongst the crowds that heard them paid any attention to the closing words of this sentence ; yet they were the most pregnant that King Leopold spoke on that day on which he uttered several weighty speeches. They indicated the greatest need of the inhabitants of the poorer quarters of Brussels, and they had the full effect on the council of the municipality which the King intended they should have. Before long the Senne was vaulted over where it ran through the city, and instead of its muddy shores, its open sewers and its sluices, which were festering places of disease and horror, and of every filth, a noble central boulevard was built; but more important even than this particular effect of the King's recommendation was the light his words threw on the relations which were to prevail in future between King Leopold and the local administrations and the people of Belgium. The *rôles* were changed; in future it was not to be the burgomasters or aldermen who fought for the people's cause; it was the King who was himself to advance it, and of his own initiative, and to insist, prevailing over official greed and over official egotism, that the measures needed for the public weal should be executed without delay.

While King Leopold has intervened directly in this manner in local affairs from the first moment of his reign, wherever there was an evil to be abolished or a good to be furthered, it must not be thought that he ever sought to interfere with or ignore the great central authority of Parliament. On the contrary, he has prided himself throughout his reign on ruling as a strictly constitutional sovereign, and if he holds an exalted idea of kingship, and jealously maintains the prerogatives of the crown, he has always declared with truth that he looked to Parliament for his strength, and that it is the Constitution which makes the power, and not the weakness, of the king. To the Parliament on this day of his accession, when he had taken the oath as king, he made a notable speech; and, although the speeches to Parliament of constitutional rulers reflect more generally the desires of the ministry than the thoughts of the monarch, there was much in this speech which marked it out as being in very truth the

King's own words, while there can be no doubt but that every phrase in it expressed the real feelings of the King. "I promise Belgium," said King Leopold, "a King, Belgian in heart and soul, whose whole life will belong to it. The first King of the Belgians to whom Belgium has given the day, I am associated in all the patriotic feelings of my country from my infancy. Like it, I have followed with joy that national development which makes all the sources of force and of prosperity teem in its womb. Like it, I love those great institutions which guarantee order at the same time as liberty, and are the most solid bases of the throne. In my thoughts the future of Belgium is always blended with my own, and I have always considered it with that confidence which is inspired by the right of a free nation, honest and courageous, which desires its independence, which has known how to conquer it, and has shown itself worthy of, and which will know how to protect, it."

The assembly cheered these and the succeeding words of King Leopold, and the King continued : "It has been delightful for me to recognise in these spontaneous manifestations the unanimous accord of the population. On my side I have never made a distinction between Belgians ; I include all devoted to their country in a common affection. My constitutional mission places me outside the war of opinions, leaving it to the country itself to decide between them. I desire ardently that their dissidences may be always tempered by that spirit of national fraternity which unites all the children of the Belgian family at this moment around the same flag.

"Gentlemen, during the first thirty-five years Belgium has seen itself accomplish things which have been rarely realised by a single generation in a country of the extent of ours. But the edifice, the foundations of which were laid by the Congress, can raise itself higher, and will raise itself higher again."

King Leopold's speech was received with an enthusiasm such as is not common in Belgium. In those days the Belgian members of Parliament, elected by a monetary franchise, did not directly represent the people, but an incident which occurred as the King left the chamber showed that he spoke truly in referring to the unanimous accord of the population, and proved that the people welcomed the commencement of his reign as ardently as the politicians. In the Rue Ducale there was massed a body of thousands of workmen, representing the workmen's associations, and these men presented King Leopold with a wreath bearing the inscription, " You have been crowned before the two chambers ; allow the people to crown you in their turn."

When King Leopold II. ascended the throne a Liberal Government was in power in Belgium. Nearly twenty years was past since the union formed by all the parties in the country to throw off the Dutch yoke and to uphold Belgian independence was broken, and for the greater part of these twenty years the Government of Belgium had been in the hands of the Liberal party. That party, formed from a bourgeois oligarchy, and having little but its name in common with the Liberal parties of English-speaking lands, was destined, as King Leopold's reign advanced, gradually to lose its power before the advent of the Democracy to the suffrage, and the spread of the principles of a truer liberalism than it possessed. Founded on the principle of antagonism to the Church, the State as an all-powerful government was the ideal of this party. It would have been more correctly described, as one of the most clear-minded and able of the Belgian Liberals of the present day —M. Wilmotte—points out in his work " *La Belgique morale et politique,*" as a Statist party ; but the most correct description of all for it would be that of a Bureaucratic party. Centralisation of all administrative

power, great and small, was its constant object ; and
since centralisation was the thing of which Belgium as
an independent country stood most in need in the
period which followed the founding of the Belgian
kingdom, the constant return of this party to power
in that period was fortunate for Belgium, even though
much in the doctrines of the party was wrong, and
though many of its actions were deplorable.

The Liberal party in the days when it held office
never represented more than a tittle of the Belgian
people ; its largest, if not its whole following lay
amongst the class which possessed parliamentary votes,
and the parliamentary franchise was held by no more
than two per cent. of the population in the time of
the Liberals' ascendency. Its too virulent anti-clericalism was continually checked, not only by the
moderating influence of King Leopold I., but by the
great mass of public opinion in the country which,
though long voteless, could never be without influence
on the political movement. The party was thus, in
spite of itself, generally forced to confine its legislative
action to the welding together of the different local
bodies into a uniform mass, such as would substitute
a national for a parochial spirit in the minds of the
local functionaries ; yet was prevented from giving these
local bodies the anti-religious character it desired.

It was fortunate in the early days of the Liberals'
ascendency, when they were filled with a desire to
tear down all the religious institutions of the country,
that Belgium was ruled over by King Leopold I., who
was both a Protestant and a Freemason, and who
could not, therefore, be accused of subserviency to
Rome in the action he took for the preservation of
religious rights ; and it is still more fortunate for
the country in the later period, when the power of
the Liberals was declining, and when the greatest
danger which the country ran was that of a too great

clerical reaction, that it has been ruled over by King Leopold II., a Catholic prince, whom none could accuse of anti-Catholicity, whose wise moderation led him at all times to curb the manifestation of violent party spirit in the Governments of the country, and the real Liberalism of whose views caused him to protect the freedom of the institutions of the country from whatever side it was attacked.

It is beyond doubt that King Leopold has owed much to his early intercourse with Walthére Frère-Orban, the greatest of the Liberal statesmen of Belgium, who was Prime Minister when King Leopold ascended the throne, and who was the Liberal statesman—alluded to in the previous chapter—for whom King Leopold, while Duke of Brabant, manifested an admiration, and on whom he impressed the need of colonies for Belgium.

The policy of Frère-Orban was stained by the virulent anti-clerical hatred of his party, which drove the members of that party into actions against their opponents as bigoted and illiberal as those of the most reactionary cleric on the other side could be ; there was much in it that would seem strangely narrow to a liberal thinker of our day ; it was not without its contradictions ; it was entirely wanting in a perception of the duties of the State to the labourer. " Every regulation of labour is a form of servitude," he declared in 1869, when rejecting an appeal for a law on the labour of women and children in manufactories. " If that regulation is absolute, it is slavery. If it is partial, it is servitude." But in spite of all these things, as far as it went it was the highest Liberalism in Belgium of the time, and King Leopold, with the genius of a ruler, knew how to draw from it all that was best and most noble.

It is impossible to write of the history of Belgium in the reign of King Leopold II. without treating of what King Leopold I. called the sterile war of parties

M. BEERNAERT.
Minister of State and President
of the Council of Ministers (1884-1894).

LIEUT.-GENERAL BRIALMONT.

M. CHARLES ROGIER.

M. FRÈRE-ORBAN.
Minister of State. President
of the Council (1861-69, 1878-84).

on religious questions. The whole of the interior history of the country throughout the King's reign up to the time of the return of the Catholic party to power in 1884, and the introduction of an era of social legislation, centres round the battle between Church and State—a battle forced on the country by the Liberals, and one which may be said to have resulted, through the wisdom of the country at large and the action of the restraining influences which have been cited, in a victory, not for one political party or the other, but in that of both Church and State, each victorious in its own proper province.

The Belgian Constitution, framed by the National Congress of 1830, secured the freedom of religion, of education, of the press, and of association to the Belgians. Formed by an assembly in which the Catholics were in a majority, it went to what extreme churchmen considered to be an improper length in providing for the supremacy of the State with regard to the performance of the marriage rite, as to which it laid down that "the civil marriage must always precede the nuptial benediction," and even with regard to the freedom of religion which bigots have always held to mean freedom of error; but there were few extreme churchmen in the Congress or out of it in Belgium then, or later, and the great mass of the Belgian Catholics have never complained or found reason to complain, or, indeed, do otherwise than rejoice at the Liberal clauses of their Constitution, which they have from the first regarded, to quote the phrase of Pope Leo XIII. with reference to it, not as a truce to be ended, but as a fundamental pact to be loyally adhered to.

If the Catholics had reason to rejoice at the independence and liberality of their spokesmen in the Congress, which secured the personal liberties of the Belgians of every creed, they had, however, as the years went on, much cause to regret the far-carried desire of providing for the inclusion of all parties in the future Parliaments of Belgium which these same spokesmen and representatives of theirs manifested in voting for a high monetary suffrage. The monetary suffrage, of from twenty florins as a minimum and one hundred florins as a maximum, paid in direct taxes—the florin being equivalent to two francs and ten centimes—was made the qualification of future parliamentary electors to the Chamber in order that the preponderating mass of Catholic farmers, peasants, functionaries, and professional men should not deprive the trading classes of the cities who held Liberal principles, and were tinged with Voltaireism, of their share in the government. The Catholic members of the Congress knew that this was so. It was announced openly to the Congress that the high monetary suffrage was introduced "in order to hinder the influence of what they call a party (the Catholics) in the elections"; but although some of the Catholic leaders pleaded for the rights of the small tax-payers, "who, in the day of peril, exercised the privilege of danger at the price of their blood," they joined in fixing the franchise at a monetary suffrage, and in decreeing that it could not be revised without a vote of a two-thirds majority of Parliament. This vote of the Congress illustrates the essentially fair and moderate character of the Belgian nature, which tends towards a recognition of the rights of all; but while it fulfilled its end in giving representation to the various parties then existing in the country, it soon became evident that the Parliament elected on that franchise was a Parliament representative of one class instead of the whole nation; and as time advanced, and with increased riches and improvements in the manner of living, a more enlightened and more vigorous democracy arose, the parliamentary franchise, instead of being expanded with the growth of the people, was made more and more oligarchic, until the Crown remained the only barrier between the people and the unchecked sway of the moneyed middle class. It is true that the parliamentary qualification, fixed at the commencement nearly at the maximum allowed by the Constitution, was reduced, in a moment of panic in 1848, to the minimum figure of twenty florins, in spite of Frère-Orban's opposition to its reduction ; but this minimum had proved long before King Leopold II. began to reign in 1865 to be an insurmountable obstacle to the participation of the great body of the Belgian people in the exercise of the parliamentary franchise, and, nevertheless, the Liberals continued throughout the King's reign up to the year 1893, to use all their power, not for the widening, but for the clipping and the narrowing of the electorate.

As the desire spread for a share in the government, through the exercise of the franchise, and as no sign became apparent of a revision of the existing law, the extraordinary sight was seen of large numbers of people trying by every means possible to increase the amount of taxes they paid, and even resorting to tricks to draw the imposition of taxes on them. Thus, a tax being placed on horses kept for luxury—that is, for riding or driving—and on horses kept for " mixed " purposes —riding or driving and tillage—while there was no tax on horses kept exclusively for tillage, the farmers of many localities were in the habit of turning their tillage horses into taxable horses of the " mixed " class by borrowing a saddle, and using it in turn for a ride on each of their horses. Instead of being induced by such occurrences to lower the franchise, the Liberals indignantly protested that the Catholics connived at them, and exerted themselves to make such connivance impossible, by exempting from that particular tax all the farmers whose taxes without it did not reach the minimum necessary for the franchise. While other countries were extending their franchises, the Liberals in Belgium continued to pass restrictive acts up to the moment of their final fall from power. Thus, by laws passed in 1878 and 1879, they reduced the number of the parliamentary electors in the country from 125,069 to 116,090, the population of the country being at the time five and a half millions, and being continually increasing.

The war, then, which was so long waged in Belgium between the opponents and the defenders of religious teaching and influence, and which was confined to Parliament and the polls, was not a war between the inhabitants of the country at large, but between the different sections of the middle class. It was a war, although it made much noise at all times, which hardly attracted the attention of the great mass of the people until, as happened at various times throughout its duration, one party or the other attempted to subvert or undermine the broad and sufficient liberties inscribed on the Constitution.

It is not strange that in its war against the Church the Liberal party gained a strong following amongst the middle class inhabitants of the towns, nor that the Church party was strongest in the country districts. Town life, in which men may live for years without a single serious thought, leads easily to indifferentism; while country life, in which the worker is forced to long self-communing, draws men into the habits of thought and introspection from which mysticism is bred.

While indifferentism is a state of mind into which descent is easy, it is one in which few men can long remain who are surrounded by the servants of a Church militant; and between the rude assaults of the priests, who attacked them on moral grounds, and the strenuous invitations of the Liberals, who appealed to them on political grounds, it is not difficult to guess which side the greater mass of indifferent citizens joined.

The Liberals declared they did not attack religion, but Clericalism—the interference of the priest in politics ; and by many amongst them, leaders as well as followers, this declaration was honestly believed to be true. Nevertheless, the matters which they forced to the front of the parliamentary battle, and on which they legislated, were those in which morality was directly concerned, and which more often than not affected the very existence of religious institutions, and even of religious belief. Under such circumstances, it was a mockery to call on the priests to stand aside from the political arena, and a falsehood to say that they were unjustified in entering it.

The fiercest battles between the Catholics and the Liberals, if the great fights of 1879 and 1884 on the question of primary education be excepted, were already fought when King Leopold II. ascended the throne. The application of a law placing the distribution of all charitable bequests in the hands of Government appointed committees, and annulling the special clauses of the wills of the donors of money for charitable purposes, was commenced by the Liberals in 1847, and an attempt to modify this practice by the Catholics in 1857 had led to popular clamour and the fall of a Catholic ministry. The law on secondary education, which substituted the authority of the State for that of the Communes in the public schools of the intermediate class, and struck the first blow at the teaching of religion in these schools, had been passed in 1850 ; the practical release of the cemeteries from religious control in 1860 ; the law on the bourses of education, which transferred to the official schools the foundations instituted for religious education, had been carried in 1863 ; nevertheless, throughout the whole of the first twenty years of the reign of King Leopold II. the parliamentary warfare continued on the battle ground of religion and morals.

It might seem strange that this was so in Belgium, where the Constitution of the country itself protected the freedom of religion and education, and at the same time protected every citizen from religious constraint or interference, even to the extent of prescribing the official observance of religious holidays, and decreeing the full right of each individual to do as he chose at every time and every day of the year, on Sunday or on Monday, to idle or labour, to scoff or worship, as his inclination, his habit, or his necessity led him; and where, moreover, the ministers of every religious cult were regarded as being on an equal standing before the law, and were paid the stipends by the State on an equal ratio without regard for the religion to which they belonged or the principles they taught; but the strangeness of the long war for liberty in a land already free disappears before the fact that the war was in reality almost entirely one of politicians fighting for power, and not one of the people striving for freedom. A party must have either a policy or a rousing war cry in order to exist; and although there were things in Belgium which could be improved or needed reform, economical or administrative, the gross selfishness, the timid fear for the safety of its money, which has ever been the most characteristic mark of the middle class, prevented those who called loudest for Liberalism from agreeing to the adoption of any policy of reform which could affect their interests in the slightest degree. The Liberals refused to adopt reform of the franchise as their policy; they refused to adopt a policy for the regulation of the hours or conditions of labour; they refused to adopt economic legislation for the working class; they refused to reform the law on military service, though that law was at once iniquitous and insufficient, since all its burthens fell on the people and all its exemptions were for the middle class—there remained no policy for the party but that of anti-Clericalism.

Attempts were made, in the very month of the accession of King Leopold II., by some of the more enlightened of the Liberal party to constitute a party of real Liberal reform instead of the anti-Clerical party. These Liberals, to quote the words of a leading Liberal politician, Count Goblet d'Alviella, in " Cinquante Ans de Liberté," " thinking that the Liberals attached too much importance to the religious question, wished to seek in the democratic questions, which had a superior importance in their eyes, the touchstone, and in some sort the new axes of parties. . . They said : The question of electoral reform is of a very different importance from that of the privileges of the clergy. Suppose the first to be settled, the latter will disappear in some way. Would the exaggeration of the influence of the clergy be feared in a State in which all the citizens were instructed and in possession of their rights ? On the contrary, the solution of the Clerico-Liberal question would not bring any direct amelioration to the masses. And as to our eyes that amelioration is the capital end of politics, we are always with those who work seriously for it, without thinking of the colour of the flag which they wave in accessory questions." These views were sound, as the later history of Belgium itself proves, where the moral influence of the clergy in a free and educated State has helped on instead of hindering the march of social and economical progress ; but sound reasoning could not prevail over the selfish conservatism of the great mass of the Liberal party, and anti-Clericalism continued to be the only policy of the party.

Summing up the situation of his party in the work just quoted, Count Goblet d'Alviella says : " The essential principle of the Liberal party is found in the absolute independence of the civil power as regards the churches. There is seen, however, in this party a tendency to act in contrary senses on the ground of democratic reforms—the Conservative element, and the Progressive element. The alliance between these two shades, easy when it is a question of snatching power from the Catholics, generally maintains itself after the victory just as long as the new majority follows the course of its anti-Clerical reforms. But a moment arrives when the moderate element, satisfied to hold the power, seeks to arrest itself in the realisation of the common programme. The advanced members, on the contrary, claim its integral execution. The Ministry, which generally represents the medium between the different shades of the majority, refuses to advance without the support of its right wing. The left wing then, to mark its discontent better, puts forward its democratic programme. Division slips into the ranks of the party, stirred up by the tactics of its adversaries. The majority is dislocated, and the Catholics resume the direction of affairs."

It is noteworthy that in this examination of the tactics of his party, Count Goblet d'Alviella does not consider for a moment the possibility of the adoption by the party as a whole of the democratic policy put forward by its left, or Radical, wing. The truth is, that there is much more of a Conservative than of a Liberal element in the party which is known in Belgium as the Liberal party. Indeed, the one question of anti-Clericalism apart, its action has been wholly Conservative; and it is a fact, however strange, that in estimating what the party has done for Belgium its anti-Clericalism may be left out of the question. Although anti-Clericalism lay at the bottom of all its policy, this party—a great party, in spite of its faults—never succeeded in all the years in which it seemed to shape the destinies of Belgium, in damaging the position of the Church, or in lessening the moral influence of religion, and this even though the party sought, after the manner of those who brought foreign armies into their countries to rid themselves of tyrants, to pull down one church by raising up another in the place of it, and to use ministers of Christ for the overthrow of Christianity.

The fact that the party on which the defence of religious interests in Belgium has always rested bears the name of the Catholic party has given a colour to the idea that it was the power of Rome, and that alone, the Liberal party attacked in its anti-Clerical campaign; but, although the less honest amongst the Liberals have been ready to foster that idea, it is false. The Liberal party is a party of Free Thinkers, which believes Christianity to be false and superannuated, and aims at banishing the Christian belief from men's minds; and when it encourages the advance of any Christian sect in opposition to that which has the greatest hold in the country, it does it to weaken the one, not to strengthen or establish the other. This is admitted by the Liberal statesman from whom I have just twice quoted, who, recording the fact that members of the Liberal party subscribed to the erection of a Protestant church in a rural district of Belgium, adds " the greater number of them did not dissimulate their hopes of seeing many analogous attempts of multiplying themselves in the country. Many, on the reproach being cast at them that they propagated a religion without believing in it, even asked themselves if they could not find amongst the diverse forms of Protestantism a church which would permit them to preach the example without impairing the integrity of their free examination." And he adds this deliberate statement : " Belgian Protestantism sufficiently large to include, beside the most conservative orthodoxies, pastors who deny the direct revelation of the Scriptures, and even the divinity of Christ, offered them with regard to this a solution advantageous and sure."

This happened in the earlier portion of the reign of King Leopold II., when many Liberals declared themselves Protestants ; but the party soon abandoned its pretence of religion, finding its attempt to undermine Christianity as signal a failure as were its attempts to overturn the Church by direct assault. Owing to the opposition of the people whose children were to be taught, and to the restraining influence of the Crown, the party failed to banish religious education from Belgium, which was its aim in re-modelling the school system ; but although it failed in its aim, it succeeded in centralising and equalising the school system of the whole country, and in centralising the administrative authority, thus hastening the educational rise of the people and the strengthening of the national feeling in them. It is here their glory lies, and it is for these achievements that the Belgians must remember with satisfaction the legislation effected by the Liberal party during its long exercise of power.

The Liberal party refused to accept the principles of compulsory education, which it declared to be a violation of the rights of individual liberty, and instead of compulsion it instituted a system of official and semi-official bribery, by which to draw the children into the State schools and away from the private schools. The instruction in the State schools was not only made free, but also the children of these schools were provided with free meals and free clothes when they belonged to the poorer classes, and given prominent places at all civic festivals and celebrations, to the exclusion of the children educated in the private schools. The party did not at first seek to alter the law on primary education which had been established by the unanimous vote of all parties in 1842, and which made religious education a part of the educational programme, the ministers of every cult being authorised themselves to instruct or provide for the religious and moral instruction of the children of their cults at stated times within the hours of school.

Its first attack on the giving of religious instruction in the State schools was contained in its law on intermediate education, passed in 1850, in which the teaching of religious education ceased to be provided for in the programme of the schools, but which provided for the invitation of the ministers of cults to give religious instruction to the pupils of the schools, and decreed that rooms should be placed at their disposal in which they could give such instruction should they accept the invitation. The intention of this law, which was to banish religious education from the schools, was frustrated by the accord which arose between the advocates of religious teaching and the heads of the schools, and which was ratified by what was known as the Convention of Antwerp, made in 1854, which provided that while religious instruction should be given by the ministers of religion, care should further be taken to use no school books adverse to the religious beliefs of the children, and that the lay teachers of the schools should inculcate the children with " the principles of morality and the love of Christian duties." Although the education of the State schools was thus prevented from being antagonistic to Christian education, the law of 1850 was, nevertheless, the commencement of a complete change of the Belgian educational system, since it removed the direction of education from the Communes and the clergy, and placed it directly in the hands of the State.

M. Wilmotte, describing the change which it effected, says, " Without having it too apparent it was, with regard to this, a complete revolution. . . For a local and familiar conception of instruction, breaking with an old tradition, it substituted a powerful machine, actuated by a single motor, the complicated machinery of which supposed a bureaucratic organisation and the constitution of a State corps, that of prefects and professors, strangers to the town where they taught, and withdrawn from all dependence on the locality. At the same time the unity of the programme was to have the effect of passing the same wheel over all the mentalities without taking count of individual particularities, or of the native varieties of the provincial spirit, with their pettiness and meannesses, equally dear to the middle class mediocrity and in general to all conservatisms."

Great as was the change this law effected, it failed to satisfy any portion of the Liberal party from the moment it became apparent that it had failed to introduce the anti-religious education which the party desired into the State schools. From that moment the Radical wing of the party clamoured for its revision; but although Frère-Orban admitted almost from the first, and emphatically from 1866, that he hoped to carry out its revision, it was not until 1870, when the Liberals were in opposition, that the complete neutralisation of education in the State schools of every grade was inscribed on the Liberal programme, and not until 1879 that the Liberal party, on its return to power, succeeded in amending the law in accordance with this programme.

In the meantime, another side of the education question, and one even more difficult of settlement in accordance with its desires—that of higher education—occupied the attention and the energies of the Liberal party. The country was possessed of four universities when King Leopold II. ascended the throne: the two State universities of Liége and Ghent, the Catholic university of Louvain (founded by the clergy), and the Liberal university of Brussels (founded by the Freemasons). Since the Constitution of Belgium proclaimed the freedom of education, and the principles of the Liberal party bound it to respect individual liberty, it did not seem easy for the State to interfere with the actions of the independent universities. Nevertheless, the earlier chiefs of the Liberal party declared that it was the duty of the State " not only," says M. Wilmotte, " to exercise a final control, but also to interfere, every instant, in the manufacture of future lawyers, doctors, etc." In its desire to act on this principle, the Liberal Government drove all the universities of the country into a deplorable situation ; and even when some of the pretensions of the Government were relaxed, and the final examinations only were sought to be controlled, the situation of the universities and of their students was but little improved. While the freedom of instruction was left to the universities, the right of granting the only legally recognised degrees and diplomas in the country was given to a body appointed by the Government consisting of—to again quote the Liberal historian, M. Wilmotte—" combined juries, on which, like the fantastic beings ' which howled at being coupled ' in the poetry of Victor Hugo, professors incarnating antithetical doctrines were grouped two by two, and fulfilled the function of tormentors and tormented at the same time." It was to put an end to this situation that Frère-Orban and the more liberal members of the Liberal party joined with the Catholic Government then in power in 1876 to restore to the universities the free exercise of their functions. The law of 1876, which, completed and modified in its details in 1890, is still in force, provided for the exercise of a judicious supervision over the universities by a central committee appointed by the State, the duty of which it is to see that the education of the universities is sufficient, and that their examinations are *bonâ-fide ;* but, notwithstanding this protection of the rights of the State, there were those amongst the Liberal party who held that their leader had abandoned the principles of the party in voting for the law. Frère-Orban made it clear, however, in more than one speech, that neither in his intention nor in his vote had he abandoned or drawn back from his policy of centralising all the administrations of the country, and turning out all the functionaries and officials from the same Government mould. "You can be a lawyer, a doctor, an engineer, or an apothecary," said he; "but that will not make you a magistrate, or a notary, or a doctor of a hospital or an institution, or an engineer of the mines department or of the bridges and roads. The State will reserve to itself the right of electing its own. . . It will be the business of the State to invest its schools with the duty of forming those who are preparing for the magistracy, the notariat, the functions of doctor and pharmacist of the civil and military administrations, of the services of hospitals and institutions."

These were no idle words. The Liberals returned to power in 1878 and remained in office until 1884, and during the period between these years they showed, says the Liberal historian, "an implacable logic in the choice which they made, according an exclusive preference to those educated in the public schools," and "reducing the favour granted in 1876 to the free establishments to the minimum imposed by the Constitution of the country"; or, in other words, allowing the private schools and the independent universities to teach their pupils according to the stipulation in the Constitution for the freedom of education, but deliberately and completely barring the students of these institutions from any employment whatever under the State or under the local administrations; and to understand the full import of this action it must be remembered that the great bureaucratic or Statist party had already, by successive laws, turned every possible organisation in the country—railways, canals, hospitals, alms-houses, charitable boards, and such like, as well as the magistracy and the notariat, in addition to the ordinary local bodies and practically the communal councils — into Government departments.

The action of the Liberal Government in giving what M. Wilmotte quaintly calls "an exclusive preference" to the pupils of the State schools in the appointment of all the officials of the country, high and low, reduced the liberty of education to a farce, and was, in fact, a practical repeal of the principles of the equality of all Belgians and of freedom of education inscribed in the Constitution; but the revolutionary nature of the action of the Government, like that of the law of secondary education, "was not too apparent," and it did not at first attract sufficient attention in the country to cause an outburst of popular opinion in defence of the Constitutional liberties. The public indignation at the Liberals' exclusiveness was slow in growing; nevertheless the action of the Liberals in making public employment an appanage of public education was one of the causes which led to the downfall and the continued exclusion from power of the Liberals.

The first fall from power of the Liberals, in the year 1870, was caused, not by indignation in the country against any special measure of the Government, but because the country was weary of the Government's ceaseless and sterile war against the Church, and impatient of its neglect of the material interests of the people. The measures which the Liberal Government had passed up to that time, modified as they had been in deference to the growing public opinion of the country, and as yet wanting in the strength of absolute compulsion in the matter of education—a thing which the respect for individual liberty (which the Liberal party still professed, in spite of its Stateism) prevented the party from adopting—were in no way detrimental to the public good. On the contrary, although the Liberal party had sinned grievously in refusing to adopt many necessary reforms—such as those of the suffrage, of the regulation of military service, and of labour laws— where its Government had legislated its legislation was good, marking an advance in the right direction, and consolidating the interests of the kingdom.

The Catholic party, backed by the weight of public opinion, had already succeeded in depriving the laws made by the Liberals of their anti-religious sting, and the greatest danger to be feared on the return of the Catholics to power in 1870 was that of a Clerical reaction. The Catholics had been returned to power on the same narrow suffrage as the Liberals, and they were, of course, directly representative of the same narrow class. The years which followed their advent to office were years of trouble for the Catholic world, the years in which Pope Pius IX., deprived of the temporal power, launched denunciation after denunciation against Liberalism, and in which Catholics all the world over preached, argued, and intrigued for the Papal cause. There were reactionary Catholics in Belgium then, more papal than the Pope, and it seemed possible that the Catholic party, allowing itself to be swayed by the voices of the most fanatical amongst these, and at the same time following the example of the Liberals in ignoring the voices of the voteless masses, would set to work to pull down the Government edifice which the Liberals had built, and bind the country to the chariot wheels of Clericalism. Such a thing could not come to pass in a Parliament really representative of the spirited and independent Belgian nation; but it was possible in a Parliament elected by a narrow and a selfish class, as the Parliament of Belgium then was. The danger, beyond all doubt, was there; it is impossible to know now to what extent it might have grown, or to estimate the harm to Belgium, and to Catholicity itself, which it might have done, for at the first moment of its appearance a power showed itself in the State strong enough and determined enough to crush it in the bud. This was the King.

The first actions of the Catholic Government on its

return to office in 1870 were marked by a reactionary tendency against which rumblings of popular discontent were soon heard. These rumblings broke out into public clamour in the next year; but it was the voteless democracy which made the loudest uproar, and the Ministry manifested an intention of proceeding on its course undeterred by the expression of public opinion amongst those who had no votes, and oblivious of the fact that voters were joined with non-voters in crying out for no retrogression. It was King Leopold who at this juncture insisted on the obvious wish of the nation being deferred to, and who, in doing so, inaugurated a new era in Belgian politics: that in which the middle class was no longer to be the dictator, but in which the country was to be governed by the accord of King, Parliament, and People.

King Leopold insisted on the withdrawal from the Cabinet of the ministers who were disapproved of by the country. His determined action, in making it clear that he would allow of no legislation contrary to the clearly manifested desires of the country, put an end, not only for the moment, but for ever, to any attempt to utilise the narrow franchise as a means of forcing distasteful or coercive measures on the country, and during the continuance of the Catholic administration not one backward step was taken. It was inevitable that a Catholic Government elected by the middle class should be mainly Conservative; and on certain points—such as those of labour legislation—the Catholics seemed to be still as blind to the necessities of the country as the Liberals; but on other matters—such as those of the extension of the franchise and the substitution of personal service in the army for the abominable system of replacements by which the well-to-do could buy their exemption from military duty—the Catholic Government showed an enlightened and a reforming spirit. Nevertheless, although these matters came before the Parliament, nothing could be done at the time in face of the selfish opposition of the middle class, whose interests, supported on these points by the whole of the Liberal representation, and a portion of the Catholics, outweighed the policy of the Government. Asked, when it approached the end of its tenure, what his party had done, the Catholic Prime Minister was able to say nothing more than " We have existed."

The return of the Liberals to power in 1878 was marked by the recommencement of the attack on religious education. The King's speech opening the Parliamentary session announced the introduction of a series of measures for the transformation and development of public instruction, placing it under the exclusive supervision of the State, measures which it would require more than one session to complete. The nature of the proposals the Government intended to make was soon known, and the voices of the Catholic clergy were raised so loudly in protest that the Government felt it necessary to bring their action under the notice of the Holy See even before it had introduced its measures into Parliament. It was on this occasion that Pope Leo XIII. made the declaration already referred to regarding the Belgian Constitution. " It is a pact," he said to the Secretary of the Belgian Legation at the Vatican ; "it must be loyally observed ; and since it has given the Belgians a half-century of peace, I do not see the reason for making changes in it, or even for desiring them." The Pope's counsel of moderation had the effect of causing to draw back those who had advanced too far, and the result of the attempt of the Government to have the Belgian clergy silenced by Rome was to bring about a more close union between the Belgian Catholics than existed before for the purpose of defending the free education of the country. The Bill reforming elementary education was introduced in January, 1879, and carried the same year. It completed the work of centralising the education of the country, which had been begun in the law on secondary education. The schools were placed under the supervision of the department of the newly-created Ministry of Public Instruction, and the authority of the Communes over them was whittled away. It was enacted that the masters of the primary schools could only be chosen from amongst the students of the normal schools of the State, and religious education was excluded from the teaching of the pupils of the normal schools. The teaching in the primary schools was secularised in the most complete fashion, although it was provided that the ministers of the different cults might give religious instruction in the school buildings, out of school hours, to such pupils as desired it.

Out of the passing of this law, and the events which followed it, there has grown the admirable school system which prevails in Belgium to-day. From the moment of its introduction the Catholics resolved to remove their children from the schools from which religious education was banished, and they set themselves to work with so much ardour that at the close of the vacation almost every commune in the country was in the possession of a Catholic school. The great opponent of religious education—Count Goblet d'Alviella —declares with justice that this work did honour to the activity and generosity of the Belgian Catholics, and says of it, " We do not know an example, above all in a matter of education, of such a considerable result attained by the resources alone of private initiative."

The Catholic clergy had recourse to the strongest measures to prevail on the parents of their religion to withdraw their children from the State schools and place them in the Catholic schools ; and so loud were their attacks on the Government for the institution of the system of neutral education that the Government, on the refusal of the Pope to interfere with them, withdrew the Belgian ambassador from the Vatican, and broke off diplomatic relations with the Holy See. Moreover, if the Catholic clergy put forth the whole weight of their immense moral influence to prevent the Catholic children of Belgium from attending the Government schools, the teaching in which, while professedly neutral, they had perfect reason for believing would be in future, as long as the Liberal Government remained in power, distinctly hostile to Christian belief, the Liberals, on their side, exerted themselves with no less ardour, utilising to the last possible degree the whole material influence of the Government, of the local bodies, and even of the charitable boards—the supreme authority over which their centralising policy had placed in the hands of the Government—to force the children of the people to frequent these schools. The Catholic bishops launched anathemas against those who sent their children, without good cause and sufficient precaution, to the schools in which religion was not taught; the Liberal authorities refused all employment to those who were educated outside of these schools, and withdrew all aid from those whose children frequented the schools of the Catholics: in Antwerp alone 2,789 families being deprived of succour by the Bureau de Bienfaisance on the pretext that, since their children attended private schools, they were evidently beyond the need of public assistance.

The war of education continued throughout the whole of the Liberal administration, until it threatened not only to break the peace of families, but to ruin the prosperity of the country. The Government completed its scholastic legislation by a new law on secondary education similar to its law on primary education. Although the Catholics had established no less than 3,300 new free schools in the course of the year which

Photo: Neurdein Frères, Paris.

PALAIS DE LA NATION, BRUSSELS.

followed the passing of the education law, the Government continued to fill the country with new official schools, and to maintain them with full staffs of teachers, even where not a single pupil, or only those of the teachers' own families attended, or were likely to attend them, and to meet the cost of these new official establishments an imposition of additional taxation, amounting to thirty millions of francs, was found necessary. When this stage of excess was reached the Liberals had at last gone too far. The electoral body itself rose against them, and in 1884 they fell from power, so discredited that, notwithstanding the traditions which centred around their name, notwithstanding the great things the party—even in its last years of office—had done for Belgium, notwithstanding the ability and the patriotism of many of their leaders, they have never, in the long years which have elapsed between then and now, been able to regain a tittle of their lost authority, or, in a country where Liberalism was all the time striding forward with sturdier and more sturdy footsteps, to give their imprint to a single lasting movement.

The return of the Catholics to power was not marked at this juncture by any cessation of the civil discord. Instead of an era of peace it seemed fated to lead to an exterminating warfare, more fierce even than that the Liberals had carried on, one in which the Catholic Government, made ruthless alike by the bigotry of some of its leaders and the knowledge that the weight of the great mass of public opinion in the country, and that of the moral support of the Church, lay at its back, would throw itself on the institutions the Liberal Government had founded, tear them down, and raze to the ground every vestige of the fabric their predecessors had built up. It is beyond doubt that—at least in the supreme matter of education—this was what the most powerful members of the new Catholic Cabinet desired and intended to do.

The Catholics were returned to power on a definite programme containing three clauses : educational reform, electoral reform, and the re-establishment of provincial and communal autonomy. Each of these reforms—and the first two in a greater degree—was desirable and even necessary ; but what is called reform can be turned into retrogression, and there were those in the Catholic counsels who were bent on forcing a retrograde movement, not only beyond the point from which the last Liberal ministry had started, but even beyond the boundaries set by the Constitution ; and so great was the general disgust at the Liberal excesses, that it seemed likely the country would follow them, for a time, in their retrogression, to the damage of Belgian liberty and the prolonged disturbance of the country's peace. Immediately on the assembly of Parliament in the autumn of 1884, a law was passed restoring the authority over the public schools to the communal councils, permitting the granting of public funds to the private schools on their submission to supervision by the State, and making the teaching of religion to children compulsory on their parents' wish ; and this law, which restored religious teaching to its place in the education of the State, was completed by another law passed within a few days of it, which made the teaching of religion and of Christian morality compulsory in all the normal schools of the State and all the primary schools, public or " adopted," to which public funds were granted.

These laws undid at a stroke the whole of the anti-Clerical legislation of the Liberals on education. Since they re-established the freedom of education, and protected the rights of parents to have their children taught whatever creed they desired, it is impossible for those who respect freedom of education and who remain Christian to do otherwise than approve of them ; but the Belgian Liberals of 1884 had advanced far beyond desiring really neutral education—if such a thing can be had in any school in which thinking men and not phonographs are used as teachers—what they wanted was an education which should be the negation of Christianity. On the passing of the new laws they raised the loudest outcries in all the towns of Belgium where they still had a following sufficiently large ; and in Brussels itself they organised meetings and even riots, with the admitted intention of pulling down the Government.

In attacking these laws, they were attacking merely laws of amendment which their own doctrinaire excess had made necessary to bring the laws into line with the needs and the desires of the people ; and in attacking them their cause was as bad as the means they took to advance it, but nevertheless they were making a fight at the same time for true Liberalism and even for liberty. The speeches of the members of the Catholic Cabinet most directly responsible for these laws, and the actions of the chief supporters of these ministers, showed that the laws which they had just passed were not intended to be final ones, but that it was their intention to push the cause of religion in the schools farther and still farther, until by their enactments they had effectively deprived the country of the rights of liberty of conscience and freedom of religious instruction which were inscribed in the Constitution of the country, which the Pope himself admonished them they should loyally respect, but which to them represented no more than a detestable tolerance of the " right of error."

The situation throughout Belgium at this moment was full of danger. It seemed as if nothing could save the country from a new rule of bigots : of Catholic bigots, which would be bad ; or of anti-Christian bigots, which would be infinitely worse. The reasonable Catholics, the moderate men on every side—that is,

the great majority of the nation—had already, with
the passing of the revision laws, got all they desired
with regard to public and private teaching and the protection of religious education, and wished for nothing
more than to have the Parliament proceed to legislate
on the long-neglected matters of social welfare and
labour rights ; but the majority of the citizens of Belgium were still voteless, and the fanatics cried down
the moderate members on either side in Parliament and
in the electors' organisations. At this juncture it was
the King who saved the country from the unnumbered
woes which threatened it, and turned the direction of
the legislature to the path of social and economic
progress which it has followed ever since with golden
profit to Belgium and all the inhabitants of Belgium.

During the turmoil the municipal councils of the
great towns met and expressed themselves adverse to
the reactionary ministers, and during the same period
communal elections held all over the country gave the
communal electors an opportunity of also registering
their views, which were no less adverse. The communal
electors were not, generally, as yet parliamentary voters,
for it had been found possible to extend the communal
franchise ; but they none the less represented the
public opinion of the country, and this public opinion
the King insisted should be respected. The King called
for the resignation of the obnoxious ministers, and
transferred the portfolios of office to moderate Catholic
statesmen who represented the real will of the country.
At that moment bigotry was crushed, and oligarchy
with it ; and from that moment the liberty and prosperity of Belgium have spread and flourished under the
united culture of King, Parliament, and People.

The Catholics came to power in 1884, says a Liberal
historian, with their hands full of grievances and their
heads stuffed with projects. These grievances, he tells
us, were all of an intellectual order. They put them

by when the King insisted on the withdrawal of the irreconcilables from the Ministry; what their projects were, and how they have carried them out since their hands were freed, shall be told in another chapter. It is sufficient to say here that already in 1884 they had recognised and resolved to conquer the social evils of the time, and that their laws made between 1884 and 1890 marked the commencement of the great work of legislation for the protection of the labourer, and in the interests of the working class which the same party —still in power—has carried on unceasingly since then.

Much has been written of the differences of the two races—Flemish and Walloon—which unite to form the Belgian people; much might also be written of the characteristics they have in common, of their bravery, of their unconquerable independence, of their honesty; but that of all the things they have in common which must be dwelt on most, which serves most to unite and to strengthen them, is their untiring labour. It is their ceaseless and ever-willing labour, the labour of freemen working for themselves and their own, which has made their nation and preserved it; that labour which, through all the centuries, produced rich harvests from their soil, golden outputs from their looms, whatever battles raged around them; which enabled them to rear and sustain their hardy race, and to make Belgium at once the most prosperous and the most populous of countries.

The history of the people, then, during all the time that the Catholic zealots and the doctrinaire Liberals fought for the mastery of their souls and their minds, can be summarised in this one phrase—they laboured. In all those years, as in the centuries that went before, they laboured and they thought. They knew then, as they had known when dukes and counts, prince-bishops and emperors, reigned over them, what their strength was and what were their rights; and, as their forefathers had so often done in the past, they showed that they would allow none of their cherished rights to be trampled on when one party or the other tried to interfere with them or to override their newly made constitution. The people of Belgium had never been without means of their own of asserting their rights. It was not in the reign of King Leopold II. that they found their voice for the first time ; but this King's reign marks a great change for them, nevertheless, for King Leopold has been the first of all their sovereigns to listen willingly to their voice, and to teach his ministers that it must be heard when truly and properly expressed. And he has been the first, moreover, as was shown in the commencement of this chapter, to teach men in office that not only must the people's griefs be remedied, but that their wants must be sought out and supplied.

The laws which the Catholic ministry passed from 1884 onwards showed an awakening to the needs of the country and the age. Military service was made less oppressive in 1884, and two years later an attempt to introduce personal service was made ; a law relieving Flemish-speaking citizens from the necessity of pleading in French in the law courts was passed in 1886, in which year also a Flemish academy was established ; a commission to inquire into the condition of labour was appointed that year, and councils of labour and industry to arbitrate between employers and workmen were appointed in 1887 ; a law for the protection of children engaged in strolling occupations was passed in 1888 ; and a law for the conditional condemnation of criminals —equivalent to a First Offenders Act—was passed the same year. But the first great Act for the economic benefit of the working man was passed in 1890 as a lasting memorial of the twenty-fifth anniversary of King Leopold's reign, and it was due to the King's initiative and to the King's benevolence.

When the date of the twenty-fifth anniversary of the accession of King Leopold to the throne drew near all Belgium began to look forward to the celebration of that event, which everyone in the country recognised should be marked in an impressive manner. Many—and chief amongst them the public officials of the country—high and low, were eager for public ceremonies and gorgeous pageants, which would at once prove to the world the Belgians' respect for their King, satisfy the love of the public for spectacles and festivities, and ensure a shower of decorations and promotions on the heads of official organisers. It was King Leopold himself who, while welcoming the exhibition of the people's loyalty, taught the Government and the country how to spend the public money better than on a passing show, and how to erect a memorial to him which would speak more truly of his virtues and his aims than the highest eulogy that man could write, and be more worthy than the greatest work of art. He did this by suggesting that the money which Parliament had announced its intention of voting for the public celebration of his jubilee should be devoted, instead, to the foundation of a fund for the assistance of disabled workmen and their families. The King's wish was made known in a letter which he wrote to the Minister of the Interior on November 1st, 1899, and which was communicated to the Chambers on January 18th, 1900.

This letter, by which there was inaugurated the great work of social legislation and effort which is the glory of Belgium in the second part of the reign of King Leopold, is assuredly one of the most important and one of the greatest documents which have emanated from this King, whose pen has planned and signalled the achievement of so many great undertakings.

It was as follows :—

Brussels, November 1st, 1899.

DEAR MINISTER,—

I am extremely sensible of the sentiments which you express in your letter of October 31st. Please thank the council very sincerely on my behalf.

During a period of time already long—thirty years as senator, twenty-five years as constitutional head of the State—the principal end of my life has been to increase the prosperity and the security of Belgium. The constant anxiety for the economic conditions of a country where products and men accumulate to excess within narrow bounds, has led me to desire for it a more vast field of expansion, capable of furnishing the means of developing an active fecundity in the labour by brain and hands of all its children. Personally struck by that which is accomplished in this direction by the efforts of all the nations of Europe around us, I have sought to give my compatriots the means of attempting enterprises of the same nature, which could assure to the Belgian people a future worthy of its past and of its days of grandeur. The country has not appeared indifferent to the accomplishment of this design, and I have now well founded hopes that the epoch is not far distant when it will gather largely from its fruits.

If I have always favoured, with all my force, the pursuit of new openings which are indispensable to our industrial activity, and on which so many of our co-citizens depend—some to make their capital fructify, others to obtain a remunerative salary for their work—I must preoccupy myself in the same degree with the workers who, because of accidents, can only provide for their existence with difficulty, if at all.

I know all that is done for them; all that many of our great institutions do for this end. I know also what has been the remarkable development for some years of the societies of mutual succour, and I hope that a larger legislature will soon come to encourage more and more the spirit of forethought and solidarity. But how many unfortunate individuals—often undeservedly so—there are to succour; how many workers incapable of working, and wanting necessities!

Great catastrophes always create a generous outburst, even beyond the frontiers, and the recent catastrophe of Antwerp has furnished a new proof of this which has vividly affected me.

It is not the same for isolated accidents, which too often pass unperceived.

Some years ago the Sauveteurs Belges, that phalanx of four thousand of the pick of the citizens, of whom so many have often devoted themselves to succour their kind, established a fund for the assistance of injured workmen. Their first funds came from the profits of a military tournament, from public reunions organised in the interest of the work, and from private subscriptions. It is to a permanent fund of the same sort, but administered or controlled by the State, that I ask you to remit the sums which it was the intention of the Cabinet to solicit in view of the celebration of the twenty-fifth anniversary of the inauguration of my reign. The interest could be distributed to those injured by a commission, the work of which I would be careful to follow.

Perhaps the provincial and communal authorities who would have shared your arrangements would be willing also, by the intermediation of this fund, to bring to injured workmen the sums they intended to spend in rejoicings. Even then the property of this fund would be still modest, but an endowment would be acquired by it, and new gifts would permit it, beyond doubt, to extend the basis of its work.

Besides, it is not at all a question of substituting it for private initiative and the spirit of charity, which will be always more fecund than all the official institutions. It is an auxiliary rôle which I would wish to be filled by this new fund.

Private people, I have a hope, would interest themselves in this Red Cross in favour of unfortunate workmen. There is there an action to perform at once patriotic and fraternal, capable of strengthening the social ties ; a work of union, of neighbourly love to pursue, specially on the part of those who possess, with regard to those whose co-operation is a vital element of production and, consequently, of public prosperity.

Acts of this kind give birth to more resignation on the one hand, more confidence on the other, and our multiplied industries would be able under these conditions to conquer a domain ceaselessly enlarging for national labour all over the globe.

I ardently hope that all the authorities who have the extreme goodness to think of my anniversary will be kind enough to celebrate it in this way. No resolution on their part would touch my heart more directly ; there is none for which I would be more thankful to all those willing to help in it and to lend it their aid.

I hope to see the Fund for Injured Workmen enrich itself

during my reign, and its resources grow to the point of enabling it to make the families of the sick and infirm participators in its benefits.

Receive anew, and transmit to the Council, the assurances of my vivid gratitude. Tell it my wish. Lend me your concurrence and your aid in this, and believe me,

My dear Minister,
Yours very affectionately,
LEOPOLD.

As a result of this letter, the two millions of francs which the Belgian Parliament had intended to spend on street decorations, on the dressing of pageants, and on feasts were handed over to a commission of five members appointed by the King for the assistance of injured workmen. The public and private support which the King called for was, in a measure, given, and the total of the fund rose to nearly two and a half million francs. The interest of this money has been continually expended since then in grants to injured workmen, and has proved sufficient to bring aid to over five thousand cases a year. Never, surely, was there a better, or a more disinterested, project devised by a ruler than this one—Red Cross work, as King Leopold called it, for the wounded of labour. For years the fund has remained the mainstay of many a stricken household, and the influence of King Leopold's appeal to the Belgian Parliament for a larger legislature to encourage the spirit of forethought and solidarity did not end with the formation of this workmen's fund. It is to be traced in much of the subsequent legislation of the Belgian Chambers, and the great law on employers' liability, recently passed, which makes noble and enlightened provision for the protection of workmen, may with truth be said to be the direct outcome and the crowning result of the movement set on foot by the King in 1890.

Although at the King's wish the public money was turned to a better purpose than one of civic junketting, the Belgian nation was not prevented from celebrating the twenty-fifth anniversary of its sovereign's accession with fitting dignity. *Te Deums* were sung in all the churches of the country, public rejoicings were held in each of the great centres, and in the capital, on a throne erected in the open air before the royal palace, in sight of thousands of the citizens, and surrounded by the officers of Church and State, the King received and replied to addresses from the representatives of the nation, of the army, of the great administrative bodies, and of the communes. The words of the addresses and of the King's reply were such as were fitting on a great anniversary to the successful ruler of a prosperous people ; and though the proud boast of the King that " Belgium has conducted her destinies with success and proved once more that peoples have the histories they merit " may cause those to pause whose countries are still sunk in misery, still dominated by foreigners, though they hold the spirit of independence as fiercely as the Belgians have for ever done, and though they are no less blessed than Belgium with teeming soil and high-aspiring sons, these words ring true. The history of Belgium does truly prove that the smallest nation, arising from centuries of cruel or stupid misgovernment, can win for itself stability and prosperity, and plant itself in a foremost position, provided that its people are willing to labour and its chief is fit to lead, and that they possess, chief and people, like those of Belgium of our time, the determination to do, and the nobility to dare.

Belgium in 1890 was no longer a puppet of the Powers. The spirit of the nation was fully aroused ; great aims were set before it ; its horizon was extended, and the King had taught the people that even beyond the horizon there lay fields for rich and glorious enterprise. The State of the Congo was then already firmly established, much of its possibilities were manifest, and King Leopold's speeches on the presentation of the congratulatory addresses to him naturally bore many references to his great African enterprise, on which, he declared, he had embarked in order to secure to Belgium the essential elements of prosperity. The history of the Congo is told in later chapters; it need not be touched on in this chapter, which treats of the interior history of Belgium, further than to note that the sense of the responsibility and the importance of the great colony, which the King had made and which he announced he had bequeathed to Belgium, served already to stir the pulses and widen the intellects of the people. This chapter cannot be ended in a more fitting manner than by telling of how King Leopold turned to the municipal council of Brussels on the twenty-fifth anniversary of his accession, as it is told in the commencement of the chapter he did on the day of his accession itself, not only to testify his love for his native city, but also to give proof of his practical interest in the welfare of the citizens.

Instead of receiving the address from the communal council of Brussels with the other addresses presented to him at the palace, the King preferred to go specially to the Hôtel de Ville on the next day, and to receive the address of the representatives of the citizens in the ancient hall in which the Provisional Government which drew up the charter of Belgian liberties had sat; and, further, he used the occasion of the presentation of this address to make a pronouncement in which he defined his policy and his conception of the duties of a constitutional ruler. Having replied in set terms to the set terms of the address, he turned to the burgomaster, and spoke directly to the head of the municipality.

"Besides this address," he said, "the Burgomaster has thought it his duty to make me a speech. I wish to

HÔTEL DE VILLE, BRUSSELS.

Photo: Ed. Nels, Brussels.

thank him for what has been affectionate in it. The Burgomaster has acknowledged that I am outside parties, devoted to all the Belgians. You know that for me this sentiment will be extinct only with life itself. You have said that the accomplishment of constitutional duties was sometimes a delicate mission. I believe, gentlemen, it is not possible to accept this compliment absolutely. It seems to me, on the contrary, that the constitutional mission—as all other missions which one seeks to fulfil honestly—is easy. It is sufficient to do one's duty.

" My co-patriots know that I have no other ambition than to serve my country well. The parties succeed each other in power. They have the right, respectively and successively, to the same loyalty. It will never be wanting to them. You have recalled some scenes of our history. I think willingly of those which have marked this place, the origin of our independence. It is here itself, I think, Monsieur le Burgomaster, that the Provisional Government sat. That is another motive which made me desire to be present here on the occasion of this anniversary. You have spoken of the Gueux and their wallet. I need not assure you, although you have recalled also the spontaneity with which the Gueux offered to carry it for their Sovereign, that I will never ask you to go as far as that. That which I ask you, which I ask of all, is to work hand in hand for the prosperity and the embellishment of Brussels, and for the maintenance of the independence and the prosperity of the Belgian Fatherland."

CHAPTER III.

BELGIUM AND THE FOREIGN POWERS.

THE situation of perpetual neutrality which Belgium assumed in 1830 at the dictation of the Great Powers in return for their recognition of her independence does not place her outside of European politics, or leave her unaffected by the changing play of the great game of nations. The neutrality imposed on Belgium was an armed neutrality. In accepting it she renounced aggression; but in doing so she accepted the position of the Warden of the Peace of Europe, and in this noble position she is bound to maintain herself, by her treaties as well as in her own self-interest. This fact must be borne in mind, for in it lies the key to the whole policy of King Leopold II., as did that of the policy of his father, King Leopold I.

The Great Powers, assembled at the Congress of London in 1830, laid it down as an axiom, preliminary to recognising the independence which the Belgians had won by their war against Holland, that, "united to Holland, and making an integral part of the kingdom of the Low Countries, Belgium is bound *to fulfil her part of the European duties of that kingdom.*" And in another protocol, made early in the following year, on February 19th, 1831, they declared that the separation of Belgium from Holland released that country from none of the obligations towards Europe which she had shared when a part of the Dutch kingdom. "Every nation has its rights, but Europe has also its rights," said this protocol. "Belgium finds the treaties which regulate Europe made and in vigour; she is bound to respect them, and cannot infringe them. The events which give birth to a new State do not give it the right to alter the system into which it enters, any more than it follows that the changes taking place in an ancient State authorise it to believe itself released from its ancient engagements."

These declarations marked the determination of the Powers to oblige Belgium to uphold the position of armed and embattled watchfulness against foreign aggression, in which the country had been maintained by the desire—and, in part, at the expense—of the Great Powers since 1814. Belgium accepted the responsibility thus thrust upon her without hesitation or demur, although, had the Belgian Government so desired, it might have rejected the accuracy of the propositions laid down in the protocol of February, 1831, by declaring that the treaties imposed on Belgium by right of conquest in 1814 could not be held as binding on Belgium —no longer conquered, but conquering—in 1830. Having accepted the authority of the Great Powers, Belgium consented to have her attitude with regard to foreign countries regulated by them, and accepted their declaration that " the five Powers have it only in view to assure Belgium an existence in the European system, which will guarantee at once its own welfare and the security of other States." This existence was secured to Belgium by the Seventh Article of the Treaty of London, made on November 15th, 1831, and repeated in the Seventh Article of the Treaty of April 15th, 1839, by which the long continued negotiations of the Powers were at length concluded, and which recognised Belgium as an independent and perpetually neutral State.

The treaties of the Great Powers bound them individually as well as collectively, to defend the neutrality of Belgium should it be attacked from any side ; and there were many in Belgium who would have been willing to find a sufficient guarantee for their country's safety in these promises,—to dismantle their fortresses and turn their swords into ploughshares. It was at first the interests of the Great Powers in maintaining Belgium as a buffer State, which prevented any policy of disarmament being adopted; but long before the accession of King Leopold II., Belgium was given proof that the adoption of such a policy would entail the certain violation of her peace, and the almost certain loss of her independence. Fresh and startling proof of this was given on the very morrow of King Leopold's accession; and since then, throughout the King's reign, there has hardly been a year in which additional proof of the fact has not been found in the open or covert actions of neighbouring States.

Even as an armed Power, Belgium has never been wholly free from attempts on her independence, made either by threat or bribe, on the part of one or other of the Powers which are bound by solemn treaties to defend that independence. The history of the attempts on the liberty and neutrality of Belgium previous to the accession of King Leopold II., instructive though it is, is foreign to this work. It is sufficient to note here that when King Leopold ascended the throne, he did so with the knowledge of the fact that Belgium, for her freedom as well as her strength, should rely on herself alone, and with the recollection of the solemn warning of Lord Palmerston, given in the House of Commons on June 8th, 1855, ten years before his accession, when he said, "I know that obligatory treaties have guaranteed the neutrality of Belgium, but I am hardly disposed to attach great importance to declarations of this kind. The history of the world clearly attests that when a war breaks out and one of the belligerent parties has an interest in throwing its army into neutral territory, the declarations of neutrality are never respected by themselves." With such clear warnings as he had before him, it was, without a possibility of doubt, King Leopold's duty not only to maintain Belgium fortified as a buffer State in the interests of the foreign Powers, but also to raise the home defences and the army to the strongest point possible, and to keep them at it in the interest of Belgian freedom itself.

No one in Belgium, excepting the King and his most trusted advisers, knew of what vital and pressing importance the fulfilment of this duty was at the moment of his accession. At that moment secret plans were being laid by the Emperor Napoleon III. for the conquest of Belgium by France. The annexation of Belgium by France was an aim of the Emperor's which he never relinquished, and for which he never ceased to work. Even before he became Emperor, while he was Prince-President, Napoleon formed a project for annexing Belgium with the connivance of England, who was to be paid for her assistance by being placed in possession of Antwerp ; and the refusal of England to enter into a conspiracy for the overthrow of Belgian independence had no other effect than that of causing Napoleon to defer the execution of his project, and to seek for assistance with regard to it in another direction. The designs of the Emperor of the French on Belgium can have at no time been a secret to the Belgian King or his Cabinet; but the people, easily led to believe what is most pleasing and least burthensome, were lulled into forgetfulness, and a misplaced belief in their security from French attacks, by the friendly protestations of the Emperor at the time of King Leopold's accession—at the very time, in fact, when Napoleon was laying his most elaborate plans for their overthrow.

A letter which the Emperor Napoleon addressed in June, 1866, to M. Drouyn de Lhuys, and which was published as a political manifesto, awakened diplomatists to a knowledge of some of the danger which threatened Belgium, and the action of the Emperor after the battle of Sadowa added to their anxiety. But it was not until four years later that the people of Belgium, in common with the rest of the world, were made aware that in the months of July and August, 1866, the Emperor Napoleon had carried on negotiations with the Prussian court through his representative, M. Benedetti, as the outcome of which France proposed a secret treaty to Prussia which provided that France would not oppose the federal union of the Confederation of the North with the South German States, and that in return Germany should secure the surrender of Luxembourg and Belgium to France; and which, in its Fourth Article, bound Prussia to give active assistance to France in any attempt on Belgium. "On his side," it was laid down in that Article, "his Majesty the King of Prussia, in case his Majesty the Emperor of France shall be led by circumstances to cause his troops to enter Belgium, or to conquer it, will accord the assistance of his arms to France, and he will sustain her with all his forces on land and sea against and opposite all the Powers which, in this eventuality, shall declare war against her."

This secret treaty was not accepted by Prussia; but the fact that the Emperor Napoleon proposed it is sufficient to show in what imminent danger Belgium stood. Although the secret of the proposed treaty was kept for the time being, it was clear that the Emperor had formed some designs on Belgium, and it was thought that these consisted of a desire to regain the ancient frontiers of France as they had been in 1814. The suspicion of such a desire was sufficient to excite the patriotic fears of Belgium; but the Emperor Napoleon found no difficulty in denying that he entertained it, probably shaping his denial on the fact that a lesser aim does not include the greater.

The Belgian people were again lulled into false security by the solemn disavowal of France, published in the *Moniteur*, of any pretensions against her ancient fortresses of Philippeville and Marienbourg; but the disavowal of the French Government was of small importance beside the new manifesto of the Emperor, published on September 16th, 1866, this time in the form of a circular from M. de la Valette, in which the Emperor Napoleon, while recognising the *faits accomplis* in Germany, formulated the theory of the suppression of small States in favour of great agglomerations. From this moment the designs of the Emperor of the French could be no longer a secret to anyone. It is interesting to note how King Leopold replied to this open challenge on the part of his powerful neighbour. The King of the Belgians turned in the first place to his own people— to Belgium, whose independence he had to defend; and, in the second, to Belgium's ally, England. In neither case was he disappointed.

The action of King Leopold, at this moment of a great crisis, was, perhaps, the most immediately beneficial to Belgium of his long life of able statesmanship for Belgian interests. The Emperor Napoleon was desperate; to stay his falling power he would dare anything in which success seemed possible, and success in which would cause the French people to rally around his throne. His long-projected scheme of a Belgian annexation recommended itself more than ever to him, even though the King of Prussia had given him vague answers instead of definitely accepting the secret treaty he had proposed. If Napoleon could settle himself firmly in Belgium, and obtain the command of the Belgian fortresses, even at the cost of a war with Prussia and the other German States, his position would be infinitely better than if he remained at peace over a people already sickening of his rule—or so he thought. Could he have convinced himself that England would stand by without offering any very effective assistance to Belgium, and, above all, that Belgium herself would make no great effort to resist annexation, it is almost certain that, all the treaties of neutrality notwithstanding, his armies would have put an end to Belgian peace, and with it, in all probability, whoever were the ultimate conqueror, to Belgian liberty.

In addition to these reasons, the attitude of England was not sure; a skilled diplomatist might always hope to find some plausible cause for quarrel and some opportune moment which might prevent the adverse interference of a third party in his quarrel; but if the attitude of England was uncertain, the condition of Belgium itself seemed to be most favourable to the Emperor's designs. The most popular and the most advanced of the Belgian politicians distinguished themselves in Parliament and in the Press in the years 1865 and 1866 by crying out for a reduction of the military expenses of the country, and even by advocating " a good gendarmerie instead of the eighty thousand men who absorbed unproductively the best part of the Budget."

It almost seemed at the time as though the Belgians were willing to disarm themselves. Had the Emperor been allowed to fall into the delusion which the reading of Belgian speeches and newspaper articles made easy, the worst results might be feared for the country. To provoke acrimonious debates on military defence in a Parliament dominated by the more selfish bourgeois element, which showed itself more ready to appoint a commission to inquire into the means of reducing the military expenditure than to make a demonstration of its resoluteness to defend the country, would have only been to aggravate the danger. Yet the King knew that Belgian patriotism and Belgian bravery were as ardent and as fierce as ever. His knowledge of this enabled him to read France the lesson she needed without giving the misguided politicians of anti-military tendencies a chance of striking a discordant note, and without giving anyone cause to say that he had interfered in the affairs of the kingdom more than his constitutional rights entitled him to do.

The opportunity King Leopold sought of showing to the world the real feelings and determination of the Belgians and of their most powerful ally was found by him in an exchange of simple courtesies with a newly formed and minor branch of the British army—the volunteers. The British volunteers visited Belgium in October, 1866. They were received by the citizen soldiers of Belgium, the Guarde Civique, and, indeed, by the whole population, with a welcome which left no possibility of doubt at home or abroad as to the patriotic ardour of the Belgians or the friendship of their allies. Writing of the event a few years afterwards, M. van de Weyer, the Belgian statesman who had filled the posts of Prime Minister of Belgium and of Minister to England, said of it, " The enthusiasm with which the English volunteers were received at Brussels, the cordial manifestations of which they were the object, accentuated the solidarity of the two peoples, and gave to the demonstration an imposing and significant character. On the morrow of the fêtes security sprang up again in our exterior relations ; and the King, in opening the legislative session the following month, declared that Belgian neutrality would remain in the future that which it had been in the past—sincere, loyal, and strong."

These occurrences warned the Emperor of the French that the moment was still distant when he could hope to make a swift conquest of Belgium by arms, and he turned again to the more devious paths of diplomacy. In the commencement of 1867 he negotiated with the King of Holland for the cession of the Grand Duchy of Luxembourg. Prussia still held the fortress of Luxembourg, and on learning the proposals of the Emperor, that country not only opposed its veto to them, but disclosed the negotiations with regard to the Grand Duchy to Europe by making an appeal for its protection to the powers signatory to the Treaty of 1839. This action had the result of bringing the affairs of Luxembourg into prominence and making a settlement of its position necessary. Belgium was involved in the settlement, it being suggested by Austria that it should be handed over to Luxembourg in exchange for the Belgian cantons which had been in the possession of France before 1814, which should be returned to France. Belgium, which had no desire to surrender any of her territories, refused to accept this suggestion; whereupon the Government of the Emperor Napoleon again renewed its false protestation that it desired no aggrandisement of territories, and called only for the withdrawal of the Prussians from the Grand Duchy; and finally, as the result of a new congress held in London, at which Belgium was represented, the matter was settled by the erection of Luxembourg into an independent and neutral State on the model of Belgium.

In spite of all his declarations to the contrary, the Emperor Napoleon continued to seek means for the annexation of Belgium. It is a curious fact that the next means by which he sought to accomplish his object were amongst the very things which the anti-militarists of Belgium cited as a proof that peaceful brotherhood of nations had come through freer commerce and improved means of communication to put an end for ever to war or aggression. While the Radical members of the Belgian Chamber were pressing for the reduction of the military budget, and eloquently explaining that an army was no longer necessary, since " the fall of the last economical barriers, which alone seemed to prevent Europe from transforming itself into a vast workshop organised on the double principle of the division of labour and the association of effort . . . and the prodigious scope of communications which tend to equalise manners and customs everywhere . . . all these symptoms of a growing cosmopolitanship permit

BELGIUM AND THE FOREIGN POWERS. 63

belief in the efficacious intervention of public opinion, when it would be necessary to prevent the absurd and ruinous explosion of a new war amongst civilised States," agents of the Emperor Napoleon were actually in Brussels intriguing for the establishment of a customs union and the purchase of the principal lines of Belgian railways, which would have, for their real effect, the result of delivering Belgium, bound hand and foot, to France.

The eloquence and the persistence of the Radicals obtained the appointment of a commission to inquire into the military charges of Belgium; but the wisdom of the King and of the people, whose desire was to defend the liberty of Belgium at any cost, prevailed over the dictates of petty economy; and, as a result of the commission and the representations made to it, the army budget was increased and the war-footing of the army raised to a hundred thousand men.

The astuteness of the Emperor Napoleon had enabled his puppet, the Compagnie de l'Est, to enter into conventions with the Belgian railway companies Grand-Luxembourg and Liégeois-Luxembourg, which placed these great strategic lines, which ran right through the Belgian territories, in the possession of France; and here, again, the wisdom of the Belgian Government undid what the guilelessness or private greed of the shareholders would have done to the detriment of Belgium. No sooner was the convention between the railway companies made known than the Premier declared to the Belgian Chamber that the Government would never ratify such a sale; and when the railway companies, regardless of this declaration, proceeded to complete their contract, a special Act of Parliament was passed to enable the Government to prevent the handing over of the ownership or control of the Belgian lines to any foreign body. France protested against this Act, as was to be expected, and went so far as to threaten a rupture if it was enforced; but Belgium was firm in maintaining her rights: France had to withdraw her pretensions. Thus, when the moment of the great struggle came, and the Franco-Prussian war broke out, Belgium found herself, not only with her peace preserved, but with her neutrality inviolate, her independence strengthened, and her forces armed for the defence of her rights.

The wisdom of King Leopold in stirring the patriotic ardour of the people to the fullest, and by its means keeping the armed strength of the country at the highest point possible, was proved by an incident which took place towards the close of the war. When the French army saw itself repulsed towards the gorge at the end of which the town of Sedan stood, a council of war was called, over which the Emperor Napoleon presided; and at this council the question was discussed of the army throwing itself into Belgium in order to attempt to gain Lille by marching through the provinces of Namur and Hainaut. This movement would have been executed, and Belgium would have been invaded by the armies of each of the powers, and its neutral soil would have been given over to all the horrors and the dangers of war, had not one of the French generals cried out at the council, "Invade Belgium! That would be to draw seventy thousand more enemies upon us!"

Belgium came forth from the great trial of the Franco-Prussian war triumphant in every way, and with her independence secured more firmly than ever. Not only had she made her neutrality respected by the resolute display of her own strength, but she had given proof beyond the possibility of question of the fact that she knew how to preserve, and was resolved to preserve, that neutrality in the most impartial manner.

In insisting on Belgium forming herself into a buffer State, armed against aggression from all sides, the Great Powers had been sensible that there lay a spot of serious weakness in their scheme. They insisted on Belgium erecting fortifications against every foe, but no ingenuity had enabled them to provide that when the moment came it would be impossible for Belgium to hand over these fortresses to any foreign belligerent whose cause she favoured. The only safeguard against such an action on the part of Belgium lay in the threat of the united vengeance of the Powers for any infringement of her neutrality; but none knew better than the Powers themselves how empty such a threat might come to be, and how little weight Belgium would be likely to attach to it if she chose to throw in her cause with any conquering nation.

So impressed were the Powers most concerned with this fact that for a long time, in every provision for warfare, the German States—which believed Belgium to lean secretly towards France—counted Belgium as a hostile country, and made their plans as though the fortresses of Belgium were in the hands of their enemies. Belgium dissipated this fear by her action during the great war between France and Prussia, when she proved that her forts, like her army, stood for Belgium alone. From that time no man has dared to say that Belgium is, or is likely to become, a province of France; and from that time no sane and honest man in Belgium has thought or said that his country's armed strength does other than stand for peace and for security.

The fall of Napoleon III. removed the danger which threatened Belgium from his policy of war and extension. After the war, eight thousand French soldiers were found to have taken refuge in Belgium. Questions of a difficult nature arose with regard to these, and to the trade in arms and ammunition; but in regulating them Belgium was again able to give proof of her perfect neutrality, while at the same time revealing, by her treatment of the wounded and desolate, the abundant charity which is never wanting on Belgian soil. The peace which fell on Europe after the Franco-Prussian war was a peace of fatigue ; it was in no way the peace of nations resolved to live for ever in perfect brotherhood, which the Radicals of the disarmament party persuaded themselves, and tried to persuade the people. Belgium was still surrounded by armed and envious nations, nations in which hate was for long henceforth added to jealousy. It behoved Belgium to be more than ever on the watch, and ready to defend her peace.

Some countries seem marked out by destiny to be the political storm-centres of the world. Of such Belgium had been from the Middle Ages down to the nineteenth century, when its plains were again and again swept by the armies of Europe. With the assertion of the Belgians' supremacy on their own soil, and the proof of their determination to uphold that supremacy by force of arms, this was changed ; and Belgium, standing between the great nations of England, France, and Germany, and serving as a protection for each, has, in our time, instead of a storm centre, become a peace centre of Europe. This change, and the high function of the Belgian King as the preserver of peace, was most fittingly recognised by the selection of Brussels, in 1874, as the headquarters of the conference which regulated the international laws of conflicts and laid the foundations of the Peace Convention. Belgium has many times since then been so recognised as the common meeting ground of nations bent on peace and the furtherance of humanitarian ends ; and the high manner in which Belgium filled the noble *rôle* of Peace, and the far-extending charity assumed by her and acknowledged as hers, was accentuated by the fact that the greatest and most important of these congresses—the Geographical Congress and the Anti-Slavery Congress—were not only held in Brussels, but were initiated and summoned by King Leopold himself.

Nevertheless, Belgium's peace amidst embattled

nations rests upon her armed strength alone. Proof of the watchful jealousy with which foreign countries regarded her, and were ready to snatch at pretexts for interfering in her affairs, was given in the very year of the Congress of Brussels, 1874, by a dispute which arose between Germany and Belgium with regard to the pastorals of the Belgian bishops. Although Belgium had given proof of the correctness of her peaceful and neutral attitude by recognising the *fait accompli* of the establishment of the kingdom of Italy, and although King Leopold had refused to accede in the slightest degree to the petition which the Belgian bishops addressed to him to raise his voice in favour of the temporal power of the Holy See, the German Government chose to find a cause for international complaint in the denunciations of the anti-Catholic actions of that government, which the Catholic bishops of Belgium made in their pastoral charges. The Belgian Government replied to the representations of Germany that the Belgian clergy were not functionaries of the Government, and that it was impossible to interfere with the free expression of their opinions otherwise than by giving them advice ; and with the diplomatic expression of regret for any excess of language, the incident was closed. It was of importance, however, as showing the critical position in which Belgian liberties, even that of freedom of speech, stood ; and as affording Belgium an opportunity of recalling to Germany, and the rest of Europe, not only what Belgian liberties were, but what Belgium had done for the solidification and preservation of European peace. To close the incident, the Belgian Minister for Foreign Affairs—the Count d'Aspremont-Lynden—wrote on February 26th, 1875, to the German Minister at Brussels :

" Belgium, independent and neutral, has never lost view of her international obligations, and she will continue to fulfil them with all her intelligence. To acquit herself of this task she finds the most sure support in her institutions, which, sprung—if one may say so—from the entrails of her past and appropriate to the character of the country, have stood, during close on to half a century, the test of events, and have become the indispensable conditions of her existence. It is these institutions which at home have enabled her to resolve all the difficulties which arise in the Government of a free people, and which have fixed the constitutional monarchy on an immovable basis. Their influence has not been less beneficial abroad. The undersigned must leave to others the care of seeking to what extent Belgium has aided the strengthening of the monarchical principle, the development of the parliamentary system which is to-day universally adopted, and, in fine, to the fundamental problem of all modern government—the conciliation of order and liberty; but expresses the firm conviction that, in spite of individual digressions, and of abuses always and everywhere possible, the Belgian nation could not have taken a better way to arrive at, and to occupy worthily and usefully, the place which is assigned to it in European order. The liberties guaranteed by its Constitution, far from being a cause of feebleness for the Government, are an element of force for it, and give it, over a people accustomed from the most distant time to manage their own affairs, a persuasive action a thousand times more heeded and more efficacious than would be that of restrictive laws. It is to that system that Belgium owes having kept, at moments of revolutionary commotion, an attitude for which Europe has seemed to be grateful; it is, thanks to it, that, in another order of interests, and by paralysing the designs of the International, of which the doctrines brought to light have succumbed before the good sense of the population, she has contributed her

BELGIUM AND THE FOREIGN POWERS.

part in conjuring the perils which menaced the very foundations of society; and it is still thanks to that system that she has been able to resist at home every temptation and every exaggeration."

The downfall of Napoleon III. removed from Belgium —for the time being, at least—the danger of an invasion undertaken with a view to the annexation of the whole country. Against that danger the fortification of Antwerp—a strong position into which the Belgian army could retreat, or from under cover of which it could carry on operations against an invading foe while waiting for the aid of foreign arms promised to the country in the case of invasion by the Treaty of London— had been considered sufficient. With the changed conditions which followed the close of the Franco-Prussian war, the protection of the forts of Antwerp was seen to be no longer enough. The danger lay thenceforward in an invasion of Belgium by foreign forces, not with the definite intention of overturning Belgian liberties, but in order to further a quarrel foreign to Belgium: in an invasion of Belgium, in fact, by France or Germany during a new war between these countries. Such an invasion seemed inevitable in the event of any such war breaking out, should Belgium not be in a position to prevent it; and to provide means for resisting such an invasion—or, rather, to fortify the country so strongly that no such invasion would be contemplated—has been the constant pre-occupation of the King and the heads of the Belgian army since the downfall of Napoleon.

Both France and Germany have covered their frontiers with defences since the great war; and it long since became clear to those versed in military tactics who studied the actions of these Powers that, in the event of a new war, the Germans would be almost certain to fling the right wing of their army into Belgium in order to traverse that country by the valley of the Meuse, unless that valley were as strongly defended as the

French frontier, or unless France had anticipated her by securing the Belgian passes with her army. It became, therefore, most desirable to fortify the district.

Whatever those individuals might think who deluded themselves with beatific visions of a peaceful millennium, the King and his advisers knew too well the danger which would exist for Belgian independence in the most casual occupation of their country by a foreign army. They remembered that the promises of France and Prussia to respect Belgian neutrality at the commencement of the war in 1870 were made conditional on Belgium putting itself in a position to protect that neutrality effectively. An attitude of disarmed peace would never be sufficient to save Belgium from the horrors of war, or the danger of foreign occupancy. Indeed, such an attitude, being practically one of a refusal to fulfil the part of her "European engagements," which were made binding on Belgium by the Treaty of London, would of itself offer an excuse for foreign occupation, and a reason for the refusal of foreign aid; and, besides, those who governed Belgium were too fully impressed of the truth of the words of M. Van de Weyer when he said: "To speak of the guarantee of law, to oppose the respect for law to the covetousness of victorious armies, on this old soil of Belgium, which carries along the whole length of her frontiers so many sad vestiges of the most revolting abuse of force, is to hold strange illusions."

The rapid increase in the armed strength of their continental neighbours, even in the midst of profound peace, forced the question of the perfecting of the defences of Belgium more every day on the King and his military advisers; but the mass of the inhabitants, and those responsible for the government of the country outside of the army, allowed themselves to be beguiled by the pacific assurances which came from every side,

CAPTAIN OF GRENADIERS.

GUNNER, HORSE ARTILLERY.

CAPTAIN OF GUIDES.

TYPES OF THE BELGIAN ARMY.

without noticing the warlike preparations which these assurances cloaked, until they were awakened to the realities of the situation by the outspoken declarations of England, and the clear warnings addressed to Belgium from that country. The Belgians learned, with something like alarm, by authoritative statements in the English Press in 1886, they should no longer count on the aid of an English army in the event of a European war, since the English land forces, not having grown in proportion to the increase of the armies of the great continental Powers, could no longer be held to be sufficiently strong to contend with these armies on continental soil.

In the face of such declarations, the Belgian Parliament could no longer remain blind to the necessity of perfecting the defences of the country, and the plans for the fortification of the districts of the Meuse which had been made at the King's desire in 1882 were adopted in 1886. In 1889 the fortification of the Meuse was perfected by a line of forts erected between the strongly fortified centres of Namur and Liége.

With the perfection of the fortifications of the country, there was necessary the perfection of the Belgian army. King Leopold, being amongst those who rightly hold that army service is the best education for citizens and the surest guarantee for the preservance of the virility of a nation, has always shown himself an open advocate for the system of general army service, and an equally open and determined foe of the mean and unequal system of substitution by which the lazy or cowardly rich can buy exemption, while the poor are forced to serve in the army. The King's views on army service are those of the great body of the nation, as none can doubt who have studied the question in Belgium, and who know the patriotism and the bravery of the Belgians—a patriotism and bravery as strong in the small bourgeoisie of the cities and towns as in the peasantry or the nobles, and as clearly manifested in the ranks of the civic guards—in which every male citizen is bound to serve, without exception—as in those of the army itself. Nevertheless, the Belgian Parliament, then dominated by the middle class, allowed itself, in the egotistical interest of its class, to remain partisan of the system of substitutes; and, while showing itself willing to vote the funds necessary for the erection of fortifications, it rejected a proposal for the institution of personal service in July, 1887.

On this King Leopold felt it his duty to appeal to the patriotism of the Belgians, and he seized the occasion of a great festival at Bruges, when he unveiled a monument to two of the ancient heroes of the country—Pierre de Coninck and Breydel—to make a stirring address to the people. This was the King's appeal, made at Bruges on August 15th, 1887, in which, speaking for himself, he called on the country to share his enthusiasm and his patriotism in discharging its duties for the defence of Belgium :—

" I have responded very willingly to your invitation to join with you for the inauguration of these statues which recall such grand souvenirs.

" It is nearly six hundred years since Flanders passed through one of the hardest trials of which her annals make mention. Invaded by strangers, torn by factions, abandoned by all, separated from her princes kept in captivity, and put in an impossibility of doing anything to be useful for it, it seemed vowed beyond redemption to ruin and servitude. It was then that Pierre de Coninck and Jean Breydel appeared like a living protestation against the discords which enervate, against the weaknesses which are suicidal at the most sombre hours. They did not doubt either the right of their country or its force.

" Puissant by courage and faith, they infused into

the souls of their fellow citizens the heroic ardour which animated them.

"Workmen and bourgeois of Bruges, of Ypres, of Ghent, and of Courtrai went proudly under their conduct to face, one against three, the shock of one of the most formidable armies of feudalism, and to bring back from it that beautiful victory of the Golden Spurs which, while it saved the independence and the liberty of Flanders, resounded far in Europe as a signal of affranchisement.

"Let us bow with respect before the images of these great citizens. Let us render homage in them to the civic and warlike virtues of our valiant ancestors. In erecting this expressive bronze, in glorifying the sentiments and the acts of which it is the symbol, the Flemish proclaim that the same sentiments animate them, that they are capable of the same acts, that neither to-day nor ever will they cease to be worthy sons of the Flanders of 1302.

"What reflections, gentlemen, pervade the spirit here! What a contrast strikes it from all sides! The rude and energetic fighters of the fourteenth century —in these places full still of their memory—did they ever foresee the lot reserved for their distant posterity? To the agitations, ardent but fecund, of that tormented epoch, the most entire independence has succeeded, the most extended liberty, a peace which has lasted for more than fifty years. Our cities are reconciled, our provinces are united. After the morselling and the divisions of the Middle Ages, after the centuries of foreign dominion, the Belgian people has reconquered its historic individuality. In the full exercise of its sovereignty it has chosen, in 1830, the institutions which it desired; since then it has not ceased for one day to be master of its free destinies. Belgium has never known a situation comparable to that she possesses.

"But good fortune entails grave responsibilities; prosperity has its dangers, the prolonged enjoyments of peace have their perils, the excesses of security which they engender have often cost dear to those who have abandoned themselves to them.

"The life of nations is a combat; it is the Divine decree. The dangers which formerly menaced your powerful communes, in their bosoms as around them, which so often compromised their existence or their grandeur, have not all disappeared. General civilisation has made a considerable step. It has transformed the state of things, but its agents have remained the same. The political oscillations of the world, distributed over a vaster surface, rendered slower and more regular, are by so much more irresistible in their redoubtable effects and in their consequences. Wars have become fulminating; those whom they surprise are lost.

"Let it suffice, then, gentlemen, that I repeat in face of this monument the pressing appeal of the chronicler who has sung of the exploits of our ancestors. The Lion of Flanders must not sleep. The noble heritage of which you are justly proud will subsist, and it will not cease to grow in cultivating forever virile sentiments, in cherishing the sacred fire of patriotism, of which I have such generous models before my eyes.

"All liberty is born and perishes with independence. This is the lesson written on every page of our history.

"Great causes are united. In the memorable days when your intrepid soldiers fought under the walls of Courtrai, nobles, bourgeoise, and workmen merged themselves in the same ranks, joining their arms, pouring out their blood in a sublime transport, and their priests were beside them to sustain the living and bless the dead. Let us elevate our minds, gentlemen, to the height of these great examples; let us all here take upon ourselves the solemn obligation like those heroes,

Photo: Neurdein Frères, Paris.

THE BELFRY, BRUGES.

BELGIUM AND THE FOREIGN POWERS. 75

of never recoiling before any sacrifice to maintain in all time the rights of the Fatherland, and to assure it destinies worthy of its glorious past."

This stirring speech of the King's had the natural effect of rousing the popular enthusiasm, and of strengthening at once the general determination to maintain the national defence in the highest possible state of efficiency, and the general detestation of the system which allowed the purchase of substitutes for army service. Of all the utterances made by the rulers of constitutional countries in recent times, none can have produced a greater or more lasting effect on the people to whom it was addressed than the "Bruges speech," as it is called. The manner in which it was received all over the country gave ample proof—if proof were wanting—that King Leopold knew his people to their core, and was thoroughly in touch with them. From the moment the Bruges speech was uttered, the system of substitutes for the army service was doomed. That compulsory service did not immediately take its place is due neither to King nor people. Two things have combined to retard it: the selfish objection to army service on the part of a certain section of the well-to-do middle class, out of which soldiers have never been drawn except on compulsion; and the existence of a strong admiration for "English customs" on the other. Of the two the latter is the strongest reason.

There is a strong section of the older and most influential members of the Catholic party in Parliament which, in common with the doctrinaire Liberals, still holds fast to the belief that the perfection of all things in human government is to be found in England. This section, more powerful at the present time in the Chamber than in the country, continually advocated the formation of an army on the English method of voluntary enlistment, and, although the King again raised his voice in favour of compulsory service in a speech addressed to general officers of the army in 1897, the Belgian Parliament was prevailed on to adopt measures for the encouragement of voluntary service, in the place of direct Acts for the suppression of substitution.

As we advance it becomes more and more apparent that King Leopold's views on compulsory service are correct. Nevertheless, the older Conservatives cling to the idea that an army of volunteers is possible, and they succeeded in having the army laws remodelled in 1902 on this basis. They and their supporters hold that the new law has not yet existed long enough to have had a fair trial; but to all except those of what is really a small party, it is evident that the new army scheme has proved a failure as far as voluntary enlistment is concerned. Indeed, except in the minds of impracticable theorists, no other result was possible, and those who advocate a volunteer army need only look to England to learn why it is impossible under the conditions of the present time.

The fact is, that in Belgium young men see clearly that under the short service rules the army leads to nothing, and that to become a volunteer soldier is to take up a profession which a man must quit for good and all as soon as he has learned it, and after he has spent the best years of his life in learning it. As a profession young men will not become soldiers in these days, and no amount of pay or bounty money will tempt them to do so, but these same young men, who will not become soldiers for insufficient gain, are willing to take their turns at soldiering, in common with the rest of their fellow citizens, for their country's cause. In no period of modern history was patriotism a more vivid sentiment than it is to-day, and in no country does it flourish more strongly than in Belgium. The Belgians are determined to hold their own by every means they can, and the most popular measure of the Belgian legislature will be that which at length places

BELGIUM AND THE FOREIGN POWERS.

the army on the only just and sufficient footing possible—that of compulsory service.

In the close of the year 1904 King Leopold's views with regard to the national defence of his country were again put prominently forward. In reply to a letter tendering his resignation, from the Minister for War, General Cousebant d'Alkemade, who for some time had been suffering from ill-health, the King wrote as follows :—

DEAR MINISTER,—

You have written to me that the state of your health obliges you to offer me your resignation.

This communication causes me double pain. I regret to know you are suffering, and I regret that you wish to quit the War Office. Allow me to refuse your resignation, and to induce you to regulate your service in such a manner as will allow of your returning frequently to the country. Your resignation would be very inopportune ; it would neither serve the army nor the country. It was against your own will and at my pressing request that you undertook the labour of the War Office. The situation was difficult, and certainly very thankless. You accepted it out of devotion ; you know the tendencies you have encountered ; you know that a certain number of members of Parliament demand not only an exaggerated diminution of the length of service, but also the reduction of the annual contingent.

The realisation of these ideas would have been a disaster from the national point of view. You have contributed to its prevention, and I thank you for doing so.

The forces of which the country would dispose in the case of mobilisation have been augmented, and should be provided with good artillery.

It must be hoped that the country will understand some day that its independence must, above all, be assured by itself. I persist in believing that personal service would be useful for the national defence ; but it should not be united to a new reduction in the length of service, for that would lead quickly, and perhaps without its being wished, to the armed nation—that is to say, to the abolition of any real army.

I have never concealed from the country my opinion of what to my mind are its most sacred interests; but it is for the nation to consent to what is necessary; our institutions do not authorise us to impose it on it.

Accept, dear Minister, my sincere wishes for the restoration of your health.

I hope also that you will obtain the patriotic co-operation of the Chambers for the displacement of the *enceinte* and the completion of the fortification of Antwerp. These measures, which have preoccupied your attention for a long time, are indispensable to the harbour and navigation works of our great commercial city, and necessary to make of it the most accessible, the best furnished, and the best defended port in the world.

Believe me,
Dear Minister,
Your very affectionate,

October 10th, 1904. LEOPOLD.

It is significant that this letter, which was not written primarily for publication, was published by the Cabinet which passed the law of 1902 with regard to voluntary enlistment. The Cabinet naturally feels itself bound to defend its recent measure by declaring that it has not yet been proved that the attempt to create a volunteer army is a failure, and the violent parties in the Chamber have sought to raise a whirlwind about it in which the wishes and the aims of the country and the King are equally distorted and misrepresented; but nevertheless it is clear that King Leopold has again voiced the opinion of the country, and there can be little doubt but that the wishes expressed in his letter to the Minister for War will be gratified by the nation before any long period has elapsed.

There is nothing new in these wishes; they are the wishes which have animated the Kings and people of Belgium from the first moment of the establishment of Belgian independence. Belgium's attitude when her national defence is placed on its firmest footing will

BELGIUM AND THE FOREIGN POWERS.

remain that which was imposed on her from the first by the Great Powers : the guardian of her own independence and the warden of the peace of Europe, and it might appear as if the Great Powers had no further interest in the matter beyond seeing that Belgium was really able to defend herself, since at its greatest strength the army of Belgium remains a small one.

The real interest of the Powers is, however, something very different and much more personal. It does not lie alone in the fact that if Belgium chose to throw the strength of her small but efficient army into one side or the other during a general war, her aid would not be despised or left out of count. Belgium's strength does not lie solely in her army. Within late years she has thrown up fortifications which strengthen her immensely ; and within late years the strategetic value of her territories, always great, has grown more than many statesmen of countries near to her, preoccupied as they have been with the affairs of distant lands, seem to have realised. To these an awakening might come from the perusal of the passage in King Leopold's letter to the Belgian Minister for War in which he speaks of the work which is to make Antwerp " the most accessible, the best furnished, and the best defended port in the world." These words contain no idle boast. It is well known that the Belgian army has for a generation brought forth some of the greatest military engineers of modern times. It is well known amongst military men that immense works have been carried out, and it is equally a fact that the plans have been laid for the completion of still greater works which will go far to render the boast of the King of the Belgians, vaunting though it is, absolutely true. Not only is Belgium fortified from the Scheldt to the Meuse, but great railway lines, which at any moment might become of the highest strategetic importance, run from the sea to every point, and connect the heart of France with the heart of Germany.

Where, then, will Belgium stand should a great war break out in Europe? She can defend herself beyond doubt, and give belligerents against whom she shows a firm front reason to pause before they attack her or infringe her neutrality; but what will happen should Belgium herself consider her neutrality threatened, or her existence menaced in the course of such a war? or should she, from any cause, cease to oppose the advance on Belgium of one of the combatants?

When Belgium won her freedom the Great Powers sought to make her a new protector instead of a new disturber of the peace, by proclaiming her territories neutral; but it must be remembered that, except in so far as it rests on self-interest, the neutrality of Belgium is without a real guarantee, and must remain so as long as Belgium remains an independent State. It cannot be forgotten that, from the moment the Great Powers guaranteed the neutrality of Belgium, they all of them —with the exception of England—began to plot with one another in secret for her occupation, her overthrow, or her partition amongst themselves. Neither must it be forgotten that for forty years, from 1830 until the close of the Franco-Prussian war, Prussia in every calculation of a possible war which she made counted upon Belgium and the forts of Belgium as being in the hands of her foes.

Prussia was wrong, as the event proved. In the great Continental war the King and the people of Belgium showed that they were determined to stand in the noblest manner by their pledges to Europe. Should another war break out, the King and people of Belgium will again, beyond doubt, give the same proofs of steadfast loyalty to their engagements, and the same perception of their real interests—unless they are tempted, or pushed too far, or taunted too much.

How Belgium acted during the war on her frontiers is known to every statesman. Probably every statesman

BELGIUM AND THE FOREIGN POWERS.

knows what the policy of Belgium is, and has been, with regard to European wars. It is very clearly outlined in a letter of Baron Stockmar's, published in his memoirs. Stockmar, as is well known, was the confidential adviser of both the English and Belgian courts. His note on the policy of Belgium at the moment of a European crisis was written as long ago as 1850, but Belgium is a country which never changed its policy from the moment of its first king's accession, and the policy outlined by Stockmar remains as true to-day as it was fifty years ago. These are what he lays down as the maxims of the policy of a Belgian premier at the moment of a crisis:

"(1) To uphold the stipulated neutrality of Belgium in the full sense of the word.

"(2) To claim for myself the right to interpret this neutrality in the face of Europe.

"(3) In order properly to carry through this act of Belgian autonomy, I would set on foot the largest possible military force, firmly persuaded that, under such circumstances, no European Power would think of tampering with the neutrality of a State that could, according to its own choice, join one or other of the contending forces with 100,000 men."

It is shown here that the possibility of Belgium throwing in her lot with one or other combatant can never be overlooked. At first sight it may seem as if she would do so only at the direst extremity. As far as can be seen, Belgium has nothing to hope for, but much to dread, from a war. She wants no territories in Europe. A slice of Holland would be a trouble to her; she has refused Luxembourg; she could not be so insane as to covet French soil. At the same time, it must be remembered that nations have before now been goaded into wars against which their self-interest must have warned them; and while no Power need—as yet, at least—follow the example of Prussia before 1870 and count Belgium amongst her foes, it would be well for every Power to pause before goading Belgium on, and well for some to consider in what direction their goading drives Belgium to turn.

That Belgium is being goaded at the present time —goaded almost to the point at which endurance becomes neither virtuous nor possible, and that by the Power she looked upon as her greatest friend, and to which, from the first moment of her history, she gave continuous proofs of her fidelity and her affection— is, unhappily, too true. Whencever they arose, the attacks of England on Belgium have long since passed the bounds of reason and of justice, and they have long since passed the bounds of English interest. These attacks were first made in connection with the administration by the King of the Belgians of his Congo State. Some account of that administration is given in later chapters of this work, from which it can be seen on what foundation the attacks on the Congo State were based. But although the attacks in the commencement were against the Congo, they have long since developed into indictments of the whole Belgian race and nation. Men in England often speak lightly, as men do in every land; but the words of England are never lightly heard. What, then, must be the feeling of a proud and independent race like the Belgians which finds itself branded, day after day, by England as a race of murderers, torturers, and robbers!

English statesmen who live in an atmosphere above that of newspaper abuse and platform denunciation may say that no such abuse of Belgium comes from England; but for the people of foreign countries the newspapers of England remain the exponents of English opinion, more especially when they seem to be an echo of Parliament itself; and for a long time past the Belgians, finding the vilest abuse poured out on them by the English Press, have come to believe that the attacks on them come with authority from England, and reflect the English mind.

So unbridled are these attacks, and so fiercely does Belgium resent them, that the situation has already become a grave one; and the seeming ignorance of it in which English statesmen remain contrasts strangely with the eagerness with which it is grasped and the profit which is made of it by others, outside Belgium, who are not friendly to England. The events of recent years have turned the eyes of Englishmen away from Europe, and turned them upon distant lands—a state of things by which certain Continental statesmen have not been slow to profit; and this neglectfulness of European affairs has been increased rather than lessened by the *entente* with France, which, amongst its many good effects, has had one which is not good—that of lulling England into security. It may, then, come with surprise to Englishmen to learn that an opportunity has been seized on in certain quarters on the Continent of fanning the flame of discord with England's abuse of Belgium.

There is not a single word spoken in England to the detriment of Belgium which is not reproduced and spread abroad by a certain portion of the Continental Press which is favourable neither to England nor to France.

The first feeling of the Belgians at finding the torrent of abuse poured out on them from England was one of bewilderment. Can England, our close ally, with whom we have had for centuries such constant and friendly intercourse, whose institutions we have copied, whose economic theories we have accepted, who has given us our Kings and protected our independence, believe such things of us? they asked. And their astonishment grew each time the answer, "Yes, England does believe them," was pressed home on them. In this respect the English Press has aided the Continental enemies of England well. So regularly is the report of every bitter and adverse word spoken in England spread over Belgium and the countries bordering on Belgium, that it is impossible not to believe that a deep-laid scheme is on foot to embitter England with these countries—a scheme which the attitude of Belgium shows neither to be originated nor worked from Belgium. As a matter of fact, two adverse currents have long flowed over Belgium : one originating in Belgium itself, and springing from that country's distrust of France and hatred of the anti-religious policy of the French Government, estranging Belgium from France ; the other, which has not had its origin in Belgium, drawing the country into close bonds of friendship with Germany.

Germany, in fact, has wooed Belgium for thirty years. In her policy, ever since the downfall of Napoleon II. and the creation of the German Empire, Belgium has held a place, one all the more important because the policy with regard to it was pursued noiselessly and with quasi-secrecy. Germany is too astute to desire to annex any portion of Belgian territory, or to arouse Belgian animosity by allowing it to appear that she desires to do so. Nevertheless, the steady invasion of Belgium from the side of Aix-la-Chapelle, entirely peaceful as it is, is not without significance. The development of the pride of race amongst the Flemish population of Belgium, and the spread of the Flemish language and literature in opposition to French, has done much within recent years to aid the furtherance of the designs of Germany ; while, on the other hand, the existence of a similar movement amongst the Walloon element has done little to hinder it, since from the moment that Walloon labour began to organise itself German ideals rather than French appealed to the Walloon population. In Germany itself, the rise of the Catholic party, and the marked friendship of the Emperor for the Holy See, aided materially in making possible a close union between Belgium and Germany by disarming the suspicions of the Belgian Catholics; yet notwithstanding all these adventitious aids, Germany has not yet succeeded in attaching the friendship of Belgium solely to herself, and in filling the Belgians with distrust and hatred of their ancient friends.

That Belgium still holds aloof from the camp in which the open foes of England are gathered is due partly to the respect which the Catholics and Liberals of the old school still retain for the institutions of England, and for the memory which they retain of England's friendship in earlier times. It is chiefly due to the influence and the exertions of the King of the Belgians himself. King Leopold, confident at all times in his aim for his country's good, is, most fortunately, a ruler who pursues his course unswayed by praise or blame. He has inherited and continued the political traditions, policy, and instincts of his father, who came to Belgium not as a German, but an English prince.

No one who has read the secret history of the times can forget the close bonds which existed in politics as well as in all other affairs between the courts of England and Belgium during the reigns of Queen Victoria and King Leopold I., or be oblivious of the fact that the Queen, and England through her, owed much to the sage and at all times loyal advice of the Belgian monarch. It is known now that when King Leopold II. succeeded to his father nothing was changed in the closeness of the relations between the two courts. Queen Victoria, it is true, had no longer an uncle to seek advice from; but she had, instead, a first cousin to consult with and, in her turn, advise. How the present King of the Belgians turned to the English court when danger threatened his country, and how England then gave him the support he needed, has been told in this chapter. The situation of Belgium and England then, and long after, is well described in the picturesque words of a Belgian: "England was the great patrician house; Belgium was her loyal client." For reasons which no sane man can think to be sufficient, a section of the English public and the English Press has joined with the enemies of England in trying to alter this situation. The friendship of King Leopold for the country of which his father was a citizen, and which a prince of his house reigns over, has up to the present prevented an open rupture in these relations from taking place; but every day Englishmen themselves make the King's task more difficult.

The writer of this book was present, as a spectator, at a meeting of officers on the retired list of the Belgian army, held in 1903, to prepare an address to King Leopold in protest against the attacks which were directed against the administration of the Congo. He saw how the anger of the meeting rose and swelled as an aged general read out the list of accusations made in the name of England by English politicians against Belgian soldiers serving in the Congo; and he saw how at every moment men wanted to break forth into indignant protest; but he saw also the restraining influences at work, and he heard the word of command passed round, "If you want to show loyalty to your King, you must not display hostility to England." Since then, as full light has been thrown on the affairs of the Congo, whatever excuses there were for attacks on the Congo administration have lessened every hour; but since then these attacks, instead of ceasing, have increased in virulence, until it becomes a question of how long, by the memory of ancient friendship, King Leopold can restrain the Belgian people from open enmity. Before that question is answered by Belgium throwing herself into the widespread arms of England's opponents, it would be well for Englishmen to pause, and ask themselves whither they are driving Belgium, and why.

BELGIUM AND THE FOREIGN POWERS. 87

Through good report and through evil, King Leopold has stood by England. It is now England's turn, while, with regard to Belgium, she has still the chance, to stand by herself. English politicians of the school whence the attacks on Belgium spring may laugh at the idea of England needing Belgium as an ally; but wise Englishmen will not ignore the significance of the meaning which underlies the simile of the patrician house and its client. It is not in war alone that the need of Belgium may be felt. Belgium, as a client or an ally, is one that the greatest Power may be proud of, one that the greatest Power may need. Belgium, with her four universities and her thousands of colleges and schools, is the centre of great mental and literary activity; she, in proportion to her size, is the greatest of all industrial countries. She has been called, and she deserves the name of, the Laboratory of Europe. Belgian influence extends far over Europe; Belgian opinion is one to be conciliated, if only for its justness and its clearness.

The story of the Independent State of the Congo, and the growth and development of its administration, is told in the succeeding chapters of this book. No attempt shall be made here to prejudice the reader one way or the other with regard to it. The fact, however, must be recalled that the attacks now being made in England are not attacks on that country or on its administration, but on the Belgian people itself; and, having recalled this, this chapter may be ended with a note of warning. Lord Salisbury, in one of his best-remembered sayings, urged that people should use large maps. To this the advice must now be added that those who take it on themselves to speak for England should not only regard those distant countries which are marked as English territories, or which are adjacent to them, but that they should also take heed of the place of Europe and of the situation of European countries on the map of the world.

CHAPTER IV.

BELGIAN EXPANSION.

WHEN King Leopold II. ascended the throne of Belgium, to provide for the expansion of that country had already become the first necessity of Belgian statesmanship. Belgium was then, and has been ever since, rich, prosperous, and contented. Her population growing continually, as only grow the populations of self-governed and contented lands, made the country the most densely inhabited one on the face of the globe; the energy of its people made it the most industrious. It was already clear to those who saw the country's trend that Belgium could not remain a petty State. And here I must pause for a moment to remove a misconception.

Belgium has been called a geographical expression, a buffer State existing by her greater neighbours' tolerance. This is true of Belgium as far as it is true of Switzerland. Belgium exists on tolerance as much as Switzerland; as much, and no more. In other words, the statement is entirely false. Belgian independence sprang from the bravery of Belgian people, as the Switzers' did from theirs, and the limits of Belgian territory are marked by the Belgian race, and by no arbitrary geographical line. The Belgians, while they resemble the Swiss in their independence, differ from the Swiss in so far, however, that they cannot remain a little race within a restricted territory as the Swiss have done.

The Belgian is perhaps the finest race of men on the whole of Continental Europe. Sprung from Latin and Germanic peoples, the Belgians unite French quickness with German solidity; their energy is boundless, while their prudence is notorious. For such a people

BELGIAN EXPANSION.

expansion is an absolute necessity. Belgium was expanding already when King Leopold came to the throne, but in the wrong direction. The Belgians who found their own country overcrowded were hastening across the frontier into France; and there were Belgian patriots who said, half humorously, half boastfully, that Belgium's colony was France, since hundreds of thousands of Belgians had gone to settle there, carrying their Belgian energy and hundreds of thousands of Belgian money with them. The contrary was, of course, the fact; the more numerous people threatened to absorb much of the best of the smaller race.

The greatest danger which threatened Belgium from the moment of its independence was the too ardent development of its French sympathies. It was fortunate for Belgium that the King to whose initiative the diversion of the flood of Belgian settlers from France is due was one whose own French descent and whose love for France placed his actions, with regard to that great but jealous country, beyond suspicion. The problem with which King Leopold found himself confronted was a double one. First, how to check the drain of the best Belgian blood to France; and then, how to provide, outside of France, for the necessary expansion of Belgian energy and intellect. He might well look in vain around him at the bounds of triple-guarded Europe. America offered him no field it pleased him to take advantage of, for to send out colonists to the American continent was to lose them to Europe; and, above all, it was to strengthen the adventurers' ties with their mother country Belgium, and not to loosen them, the King of the Belgians sought.

In this dilemma King Leopold turned his attention towards Central Africa, the unknown and neglected land, which before his time no European statesman, however daring, had dreamt of colonising. In those distant days all equatorial Africa was an unknown land, which men's imagination peopled with horrors and death rather than with riches.

"Impassable deserts and impenetrable forests, inaccessible mountains, towering cataracts, a climate of fire, Stygian swamps, such," in the words of one of the most recent writers on Africa, "were the obstacles to be surmounted before the unknown land could be explored." The traveller who ventured into this land returned from it sickened and disheartened, telling of horrors he had seen amongst the black races of interior Africa, and shuddering at the memory of things unspeakably foul.

It is no wonder that little thought of European settlements in that land entered into men's minds either at the distant date I write of; long afterwards, at the time of the sitting of the Geographical Congress in Brussels; or until the date of the Berlin Congress, when experience and advanced scientific knowledge united to prove such settlements possible.

Great as were the deterrents of climate and savagery, they were not the only or the greatest causes which held men back from venturing into Central Africa. The greatest of all was the supposed absence of quickly gatherable wealth from the greater portion of the continent. Races whom a hint of gold mines would have roused to enterprise of feverish recklessness remained cold to the instincts of humanity. Therefore, by all the Great Powers, Central Africa was left alone, and few troubled about its sterile wastes or its brutalised inhabitants. That King Leopold II. saw the future possibilities of equatorial Africa I do not for one moment doubt. A man of deep thought, trained to foresight, his mind bridged the gulf the edge of which others had scarcely discovered, and which science and discovery are even yet still cautiously bridging over. If King Leopold foresaw the vast future possibilities of Africa, he, a statesman even in his visions and eminently practical in all things, saw also the immediate advantages to be reaped from African enterprise for Belgium.

These advantages were not those of increased wealth ; they were those to be gained by a binding together of Belgian interests, a raising up and direction of Belgian sentiment towards national ends, a stirring of patriotic pride ; in a word, they were those of making Belgium know itself a Nation.

Belgium did not want wealth, nor did the country need or desire a colony for its cast-out sons and surplus population to settle in. The Belgians are a race of traders and mechanics. Wealth could be found by them in the counting-houses of France and the workshops of America more easily, and by means more accustomed, than in the richest wilds. The Belgians had no cast-out sons. They are not a race of colonists in the sense in which colonisation is understood, for example, in Australia ; they love their homes too much to leave them willingly for ever. But they are also of an enterprising and adventurous spirit ; they will venture with stout hearts anywhere, explore the Polar regions, or open up untrodden continents in search of wealth or glory, but always with the hope of ultimately returning to their native land to end their days in untroubled rest.

Their rest once earned, they turn homewards to enjoy it in their own land. A Flemish proverb, often quoted, tells their feeling : " Oost, west, 't huis Best."

It is this feeling in the Belgians which made them a nation. Other races have the same feeling as strongly as Belgium, have as great energy, as great industry, as noble aims, and as fixed a purpose as the Belgians. Pitiless misgovernment stamping ruin on their lands has forced them to fly their homes before starvation, and become tributaries to the greatness of freer lands, whose prosperity they have built up, while their own unforgotten lands lay waste behind them—places of ruined homesteads and empty harbours, living only in the bitter memories of exiles which all the desolate wastes of ocean were powerless to blot out. The fate of these races whose misfortunes grow by the emigration from their native land of their strongest and brightest children might even yet overcome Belgium. The men whose modest fortunes are made, having found a resting-place at home, are content to step aside from the struggle, and rear their children in peace ; their wisdom is beyond question in doing so, but it endows their land with an ever-increasing population of eager youths wanting neither in intellect nor education, nor in moderate means ; wanting only an opportunity to turn their brains or their strength to account in some enterprise which will enable them to end their days as their fathers are doing—in peaceful comfort in Belgium.

That enterprise, the King foresaw, should be of a kind to turn the adventurers' and the toilers' minds always backwards to Belgium as to home, if Belgium's greatness was to last and spread—not of a kind to weaken the ties of home in the hearts of the young Belgians; and that he found in Africa. It is to his credit and Belgium's glory that his call to African enterprise was made and responded to in Belgium not in the cause of greed, but of humanity.

CHAPTER V.

THE OPENING OF THE GEOGRAPHICAL CONFERENCE OF 1876.

For the furtherance of the great ends he held in view, King Leopold looked at first not to the Belgians only, but to the peoples of the whole civilised world. The friend of explorers and a traveller himself in many distant lands, he sought especially the aid of those engaged in geographical enterprise; but from his earliest utterances on the subject he made it clear that it was to other and greater aims he looked than those of exploration merely. His was not the spirit of the hunter who seeks skins or tusks, nor even that of the adventurer who sails towards an undiscovered pole.

His first great move towards the settlement of Africa was the convention of a Geographical Conference at Brussels for September, 1876. This convention was summoned by the King personally, and its sittings were presided over by him. It was attended by the representatives of six Great Powers—England, France, Germany, Austria, Italy, and Russia—and by a numerous body of explorers and geographers who had already achieved renown.

King Leopold, in his opening address, laid his object in summoning it before the congress and the world in the clearest terms. These were his words:—

"Gentlemen,—Permit me to thank you warmly for the amiable readiness with which you have accepted my invitation. Besides the satisfaction to which I look forward in listening here to the discussion of the problems in the solution of which we are interested, I feel the most vivid pleasure in meeting the distinguished men whose labours and valorous efforts in favour of civilisation I have seen for years.

"The subject which unites us to-day is one of those which deserve in the highest degree to occupy the friends of humanity. To open to civilisation the only part of our globe where it has not yet penetrated, to pierce the darkness which envelops entire populations, is, I dare to say, a crusade worthy of this century of progress; and I am happy to see how much public sentiment is favourable to its accomplishment—the current is with us. Amongst those who have studied Africa most, many have come to think that it would be an advantage for the common end they pursue to be able to meet and confer, with a view to regulating the movement, to combine the efforts, to share in all the resources, and to avoid useless repetition.

"It has appeared to me that Belgium, a central and neutral State, would be a well-chosen ground for such a meeting, and it is that which has encouraged me to summon you all here at my home in the little Conference which I have the great satisfaction in opening to-day.

"Need I tell you that in summoning you to Brussels I have not been guided by egoistical views? No, gentlemen; if Belgium is small, she is happy and satisfied with her lot, and I have no other ambition than to serve her well. But I cannot go so far as to affirm that I should be insensible to the honour which would result for my country that an important movement in a question which will mark our epoch should date from Brussels. I would be happy to have Brussels become in some sort the headquarters of this civilising movement.

"I have ventured to think, therefore, that it would be convenient for you to come to discuss and determine in common the means to follow, and the means to employ to plant, definitely, the standard of civilisation in the soil of Central Africa, to decide on what must be done to interest the public in your noble enterprise, and lead it to the contribution of its obolus. For, gentlemen, in works of this kind it is the assistance of great numbers which makes success, and it is the sympathy of the masses which it is necessary to solicit, and to know how to obtain.

"What resources would there not be, indeed, if everyone to whom a franc was nothing, or a very small thing, would consent to pay one into the fund destined for the suppression of the slave trade in the interior of Africa!

"Great progress has already been made; the unknown has been stormed from many sides, and if those here present who have enriched science by so many important discoveries wished to recall the principal points again for us, their accounts would be powerful encouragement to everyone.

"Amongst the questions which are yet to be examined or referred to are the following :—

"(1) The precise designation of the basis of operation to be acquired, amongst others, on the coast of Zanzibar, and near the mouth of the Congo, either by conventions with the chiefs, or by purchase or hire from the holders.

"(2) The designation of routes to follow successively towards the interior, and of stations—hospital, scientific, and pacificatory—to be organised as a means of abolishing slavery, of establishing concord amongst the chiefs, of procuring for them just and disinterested arbitrators, etc.

"(3) The creation, the work being well defined, of an international and central committee, and of national committees, to carry out its execution, each in that which concerns itself, and to make known its aims to the public everywhere, and make the appeal to charitable sentiment which no good cause has ever made in vain.

"Such, gentlemen, are some points which seem to merit your attention. If there are others, they will suggest themselves from your discussions, and you will not fail to elucidate them.

"My desire is to serve, in whatever way you indicate to me, the great cause for which you have done so much already. For this end I put myself at your disposal, and I wish you a hearty welcome."

These words were addressed, it must be remembered, to sage diplomatists, men skilled in weighing phrases, the representatives of all the Great Powers of Europe, as well as to travellers and writers. Plainer words could not be spoken. The King called on the world to aid him in planting the standard of civilisation in Africa, and in suppressing the slave trade there, and in opening up the only part of our globe the darkness of which had not yet been penetrated. It cannot have been otherwise than that King Leopold thought first of Belgium when he spoke of opening up Africa to civilisation; and the diplomatists who heard him would have been culpably negligent if they had failed to connect his speech to them with the views he had so often previously expressed on the necessity and the desirability of Belgian colonial expansion—for instance, with that made in 1861, when he said the advice its best friend, if consulted, could give to Belgium would be: "Extend beyond the sea whenever an opportunity is offered; you will find there precious outlets for your products, food for your commerce, an occupation for all the hands which you cannot employ at the moment, a useful way of disposing of the surplus of your population, a new source of revenue for the treasury, a certain increase of power, and a still better position among the great European family."

Diplomatists do not forget; and none of those who heard King Leopold unfold his plans for the peaceful invasion of Africa were for a moment blind to the fact

THE KING'S PALACE, BRUSSELS.

THE GEOGRAPHICAL CONGRESS OF 1876.

that he dreamt of carrying out that invasion with Belgian forces, and of planting the standard of civilisation on African soil with Belgian hands. They fully realised all this ; but they were in no way disturbed by their knowledge, for they considered King Leopold little better than a senseless fanatic when he spoke of planting civilisation at the Equator, and opening up Central Africa to commerce. In view of their many solemn engagements in the past from the time of the Congress of Vienna in 1815, and that of Verona in 1822, no Power for shame's sake dared refuse its aid to any movement started for the suppression of the slave trade ; but in private the diplomatists shrugged their shoulders at the King of the Belgians' words, and, damning his visions as Utopian, serenely left him and his geographical guests to plan out on paper what schemes they would for the regeneration of mankind.

CHAPTER VI.

SLAVE HUNTING IN THE CONGO—THE RESOLUTIONS OF THE CONFERENCE.

WITH himself, King Leopold associated thirteen of the most distinguished Belgians as representative of that country at the conference. They were all able men, were headed by Baron Lambermont, a singularly able diplomatist, and could have impressed their views on the conference, where all was amiability and harmony. Instead of seeking to do so, however, they scrupulously held aloof from putting forward any views of their own, acting in obedience to the King's intimation that " the initiative would be left to the representatives of the States whose authority in this matter is founded on long experience and brilliant services."

Two projects were laid before the conference, but neither was adopted ; and it is clear from the manner in which the official Belgian historian of the conference records the matter that the cautious resolution finally arrived at was far from satisfying the Belgian representatives. It is not strange that this was so. King Leopold had determined on suppressing the slave trade. He had appealed to those he thought most certain to aid in that great enterprise ; and it must have been a bitter disillusionment to him—the first of many such—to find that the daring travellers whose assistance he sought were after all nothing more than travellers, whose most enlightened dream was of discovery alone, and who looked to no farther ends than the careful records of their discoveries.

The horrors of the slave trade were very real things to King Leopold. He might know little of the riches or the resources of Central Africa, but he knew

NATIVE BRIDGE OVER THE LUFU.

NATIVE CANOE ON THE ARUWIMI.

SLAVE HUNTING IN THE CONGO.

much of the evils which made it a hell; and when he selected that land as a field for Belgian expansion, the enterprise he planned was that of good against evil. Fortunately, we are able to find from contemporary documents what was in the King's mind at this time, and on what data he founded his opinions. Immediately after the conference its history, and the history of all that led up to it, was published by one of the chiefs of the Belgian Civil Service, M. Emile Banning, Director of the Ministry of Foreign Affairs, himself a member and secretary of the conference. Pages of his book are filled with details of the slave trade and the loathsome horrors which attended it. That I may bring home to the reader's mind the knowledge which spurred King Leopold to action, I shall quote the last passages, relating to the slave trade in the Congo district, in M. Banning's book:

"Livingstone," he said, "whose noble and heroic figure appears at all the points of this immense field of carnage as the representative of justice and the avenger of the rights of humanity, denounced similar scenes (to those related on the previous pages, which I forbear to quote) at every step, the disgust and the horror of which poisoned the last days of his life. 'When I have attempted,' he wrote a short time before his death, 'to render an account of the slave trade in the East of Africa, I have had to stop far short of the truth for fear of being taxed with exaggeration; but, to speak frankly, the subject does not allow of exaggeration. To heighten the calamities is a pure impossibility. The spectacle which I have under my eyes, incidents common to this traffic, is so revolting that I try ceaselessly to efface it from my memory. With time I arrive at forgetting the most painful souvenirs; but the scenes of the slave trade repeat themselves in spite of me, and make me start up from sleep, struck with horror by their vividness.'

"Let no one think that these things are the tales of a past time; testimonies of yesterday, those of the missionary, Horace Waller, and of Lieutenant Young, of the English Royal Marines, for example, confirm them in every point. The slave trade continues in these countries, particularly favoured by nature, with exceptional fury; the famine and epidemics which act as its *cortège* complete its work. Slaves, a part raised by force, the others bought—the value of an adult is here 2 francs 50 centimes in Indian money—go in troops numerous as armies, some to the south amongst the Kaffirs, others to the north towards Zanzibar, and others again to the east to Mozambique, not without covering the route with their bones. The Consul Elton learned that the mortality in the slave caravans which go from Quiloa to the north is 25 per cent. Lieutenant Young declares that he has seen the ground covered with thousands of skeletons. He saw himself one poor woman carrying a child and a burthen; as she was not fit for the double task the child was taken from her and killed by being dashed against a tree.

"The lot of slaves in the hands of Arab merchants, and even of the Portuguese planters—who, it must not be forgotten, said Horace Waller, are for the most part convicts condemned to deportation—is extremely hard. It is true the Portuguese Government has just taken energetic measures with regard to the latter, and that the period fixed for the emancipation of the blacks in the colonies of that country will expire next year. In the meantime, legions of natives continue to furnish the slave trade; Consul General Rigby calculated at nineteen thousand the number of negroes who are exported every year from the region of Nyassa towards the north. Lieutenant Young said that twenty thousand slaves traversed the lake in 1875, going towards the east; the missionary Mullens added that six thousand slaves at least are transported across the Mozambique canal towards Madagascar. Need it be astonishing after that that depopulation makes fearful progress in those fair lands which, with the aid of Europe, a little security and peace would soon cover with flourishing villages, perhaps with opulent cities?

"It was thought until recently that the slave trade in Central Africa did not pass beyond the immediate borders of the Lakes Tanganyika and Nyassa; the recent journey of Captain Cameron has proved that this was an error. There exists in the very heart of Central Africa a third centre of the infamous traffic, where its ravages are hardly less considerable than on the coast itself. The great States of Kassongo and Muata Yamvo are the theatre of infernal hunts, the products of which flow towards the south in exchange for ivory, arriving sometimes as far as the vicinity of the Atlantic. Arabs and adventurers, who surely usurp Portuguese nationality as they do the name of Christian, of which they are equally unworthy, are the organisers of these hunts. They apply to the native chiefs, who for some guns lend them soldiers to destroy as many villages and capture as many slaves as they please.

"Cameron, who was a witness of the hideous exploits of two of these brigands named Alvez and Colmbra, could not find an expression sufficiently strong to stigmatise their atrocious brutality. He saw the latter depart with a troop of one hundred and fifty men and come back to the camp leading fifty-two women tied together by groups of seventeen and twenty. Some carried their babies, others were far advanced in pregnancy, and were laden with cloth and stolen goods. Exhausted with fatigue, their feet bleeding, the unfortunate creatures were covered with wounds and welts, signs of the cruelty of the monsters who called themselves their masters. One should be a witness of this heartbreaking spectacle to form an idea of the ruin and the destruction of human existence caused by the capture of these women.

"Ten villages, representing a population of fifteen thousand men, were destroyed. Supposing that some of them escaped to the neighbouring villages, the greatest number incontestably perished in the flames of their burnt dwellings, others were killed by the fusillades in trying to save the women and children, or were gone to die of hunger in the jungle, unless the wild beasts put a quicker end to their sufferings.

"It can be judged from these words what it costs in life to furnish one of these caravans. That of Alvez comprised fifteen thousand head, and took two hours to pass. Women and children, overladen, their feet in ribbons, were struck without cause by their torturers. Arrived at the camp they found no repose there. They had to seek water, build the cabins, and prepare the food of their masters; there hardly remained a moment for them to improvise a shelter. During all these labours the slaves were kept chained in groups; to get a jug of water from the river, to cover a roof with leaves, twenty slaves had to move. Had one of them need of stopping, all the troop halted. If one of them fell, five or six tumbled too.

"Add the duties and the outrages to these miseries. Cameron spoke with profound indignation of the acts of the wretches whom he had to accompany during long weeks. 'One could not imagine such beastly cruelty,' he said, 'without seeing it.' These things happened on the frontiers of the Portuguese Colony at Bihé, at less than four hundred kilometres from the Atlantic. Even beyond that point the road was marked by tombs and skeletons. Fetters and forks, still attached to the whitened bones, covered the soil; while instruments of torture, newly hung on the trees by the road, proved that the slave trade still flourished in these countries."

SLAVE HUNTING IN THE CONGO.

"Africa," adds Cameron, "bleeds its best blood by every pore. A rich country, which needs only labour to become one of the best productive markets of the world, sees its population, already very insufficient for its wants, decimated daily by the slave trade and internal wars. . . . The superior of the Catholic Mission of Central Africa estimates at as much as a million of men the figure of the loss which the slave traffic inflicts annually on the African population."

Such was the state of things in Central Africa when King Leopold summoned the Geographical Conference at Brussels. The ending of such a state of things is what King Leopold's rule in the Congo has effected. Had not that rule brought with it the introduction of all the blessings of civilisation, as it has done, the stoppage of the slave raids it has effected would in itself alone be a glorious and all-sufficing result for the King's administration. Possessed of a quick spirit and of boundless energy, it is no wonder that the King of the Belgians, with such tales of horror as I have recited ringing freshly in his ears, should have appealed to the world for the relief of Africa. Seeing the great need there was of acting there he cried for aid from all sides, and, confident that it would come, spoke of the obolus of the poor. He had still to learn that the great States of Europe would move only for self-interest, and that they would leave Central Africa alone, ignoring its horrors and its needs, until his successes there showed them there was wealth to be drawn from it.

His undeceiving began at the conference itself. The Great Powers, notwithstanding their solemn and ancient treaties for the suppression of slavery, smiled openly at his zeal. The plenipotentiaries at the conference praised him, and praised again; but they did nothing but praise. The geographers thought only of geography. The King had expected a great and richly endowed central organisation to be the outcome of the congress.

To this organisation he looked for the rapid spread of civilisation over Central Africa. In his opening speech he indicated the formation of stations—hospital, scientific, and pacificatory—as one of the means to be employed for abolishing slavery; but he cannot be supposed to have heeded the opinion that pacification of the moral suasion order would have any effect in checking the raids of the brutal Arabs and their debased European competitors. To the erection of wholly pacific stations he was, however, pinned down by the diplomatists from the first. Possibly there was a tacit understanding that the armed action which was manifestly necessary was to be entrusted to the national committees, the formation of which the King also suggested; but, if so, great care was taken that it should remain a tacit understanding only, and no words were spoken save those which enjoined peace at any price.

Sir Bartle Frere laid down the principles on which the stations were to be established, principles which would have seemed idiotic to an assembly of Quakers were such an assembly to undertake seriously to grapple with a problem similar to that before the conference. "The stations," according to the representative of England, "were to operate in every circumstance by mildness, by persuasion, by the natural ascendancy which the superiority of civilised man creates. Further, the staff need not be considerable. A chief—who should be at once a man of action and a man of science, either theoretical or technical, a medical-naturalist, or, perhaps, an astronomer-physician—five or six skilful artisans, versed in different trades, would be sufficient in most cases."

King Leopold II. of Belgium is one of the most remarkable men of his age. If he were not, he most inevitably would have abandoned the great undertaking he set himself to when, in answer to his invitation to

NATIVES PREPARING RUBBER.

NATIVE WOMEN MAKING FLOUR.

SLAVE HUNTING IN THE CONGO. 105

Europe to aid him in the suppression of the greatest curse on God's earth, in the fulfilment of the largest undertaking of his time, the civilisation of the dark continent, Europe replied, by the mouth of the plenipotentiary of a great philanthropic Power, that she would aid him with an astronomer-physician, warranted peaceful at any price, and six jacks-of-all-trades.

Bad as this was, worse was to follow. There was some hope still that the stations, if properly organised, and if supported by the national committees, might prove of assistance to these committees ; and a plan was proposed to the congress by Sir Henry Rawlinson, Vice-Admiral de la Roncière le Nowry and Commander Negri which had, it was admitted, high political and economic value. This plan suggested the establishment of a line of communication between the eastern and western coasts of Africa from Bagamoyo to St. Paul de Loanda, from which three branch lines were to run towards the Congo, the Nile, and the Zambesi. Along this line of communication stations and agencies should be permanently maintained ; while the land routes were to be connected by steamboats on the Nyassa, the Tanganyika, and the Victoria Nyanza.

This plan was rejected. A plan of infinitely less scope, in which nothing but purely geographical interests were provided for, was presented by M. de Semenow, the representative of Russia. By this plan the exploration of Central Africa by isolated travellers was to be organised, and some disconnected posts were to be formed. Even this plan seemed too daring to the cautious conference, from the deliberations of which it will be remembered the Belgian representatives refrained, through an exalted idea of their duty as hosts, to leave their guests uninfluenced. Instead of either plan, establishment of stations on the coasts of the Indian and Atlantic Oceans was decided on, with smaller ports at Ujiji, Nyangwe, and another station at a place undetermined in Central Africa, in the territories of a chief named Muata-Yamvo ; and, finally, the congress expressed a pious hope that a line of communication, such as was suggested in the rejected plan of a settled advance, would be made between the various stations " as far as possible continuous."

If this had been the sole result of its deliberations, the summoning and the sitting of the conference would have been worse than useless, for in place of encouragement it would have brought disillusionment. It justified its existence, however, by one wise act : the formation, with the sanction of the representatives of all the Great Powers, of an International Commission under the presidency of King Leopold, to whom it entrusted the widest powers. The formation of autonomous national committees was also authorised.

CHAPTER VII.

THE INTERNATIONAL ASSOCIATION—KING LEOPOLD'S FIRST AFRICAN ENTERPRISE.

ALTHOUGH the Great Powers of Europe were represented at the Geographical Conference by plenipotentiaries, none of these diplomatists were officially accredited to it by their Governments. Europe still viewed King Leopold's aims with nothing more than contemptuous tolerance, though once any State had moved in the matter of the suppression of the slave trade none of those which had bound themselves at the already ancient congresses of Venice and Verona to assist in every undertaking for that end dared venture to treat the King of the Belgians' enterprise with open indifference.

It is evident, however, that at the time of the conference, and up to the publication of the results of Stanley's explorations on the Congo, which changed the whole aspect of the African problem, every Power, both great and small, was privately determined to waste no energy and throw away no money on what seemed to it the philanthropic follies of the Belgian monarch. The Powers, therefore, carefully guarded themselves from being bound in any way farther than that of the most general approval and permission of the King's private adventure in what they believed to be a dark and unpromising land. To avoid the taunt of neglecting the interests of humanity, they expressed loud-voiced praise of every noble sentiment uttered by King Leopold, but they took good care that their approval should be recorded in the resolutions of a meeting of scientific men, not in the protocols of assembled nations.

Nevertheless, these resolutions, voted by the

diplomatists of every country summoned to the meeting, and authoritatively accepted by their Governments, embodied the consent of Europe to King Leopold's advancing in Africa with a perfectly free hand to do as he chose there, provided that every other king and State remained at liberty to do likewise, should other kings and countries be bitten with a like generous mania for civilising negroes, or should the Belgian King's success prove his generous mania to be profitable. The great continent of Africa seemed, at that time, large enough for all comers, and King Leopold was well content. All he wanted was the consent of the Powers to his advance, and this they gave him.

It was probably more to gratify verbally the desires of King Leopold than with the intention of giving it their real aid that the countries represented at the Geographical Conference agreed that the association, which was formed as the outcome of the conference, should have an international appearance, and bear the name of the International Association for the Suppression of the Slave Trade and the Opening of Central Africa.

King Leopold was named president of this association, and of the International Commission which was constituted as the parliament of the association. The King of the Belgians, as president, was also left supreme power in the formation of this commission, to which a resolution of the Geographical Congress gave him the right to name as many members of his own selection as he thought fit. This parliament of the association, as formed by the congress, was to consist of the presidents of the principal geographical societies represented at the congress, or adhering to its programme; of two members delegated by each of the national committees (bodies also to be formed as the outcome of the congress); and of as many members, active and honorary, as the president chose to add to it.

Nothing was done by the Geographical Congress

THE INTERNATIONAL ASSOCIATION. 109

towards the formation of the various national committees. The conference contented itself with securing them representation in the explorers' parliament; but at the same time that it framed the constitution of the parliament and chose its president, it nominated its cabinet. This cabinet—or executive committee, to give it a more modest designation—consisted at first of Sir Bartle Frere, an English statesman, then Vice-President of the Council for India; Doctor Nachtigal, the celebrated German explorer; and M. de Quatrefages, a learned naturalist, a member of the Institute, and vice-president of the Geographical Society of Paris. This executive committee was designed to carry out the work of the International Commission, which could meet but seldom. That work was defined in the words of the resolution of the Geographical Conference by which it was formed as "the direction of the enterprises and works tending to the attainment of the ends of the association, and the management of the funds furnished by the Governments, by the national committees, and by private individuals."

King Leopold was not mistaken in his belief that the formation of national committees would at once follow the publication of the proceedings of the Geographical Conference. Within a year, national committees to co-operate with the International Commission were formed in Germany, France, Austria, Italy, Spain, Switzerland, Russia, Holland, and Portugal. The Spanish committee was placed under the presidency of the reigning monarch; in the other monarchical countries the presidents were members of the reigning houses. M. de Lesseps was elected president of the French committee, and M. Bouthchier de Beaumont president of the Swiss committee. Few of these committees, however, proved willing to work in any real or whole-hearted manner under the flag of the International Commission. National jealousy showed itself from the first, even before Stanley's news of the rich harvests to be garnered in Central Africa came to stir up national greed.

England was the first to seek a pretence for abandoning the association. Her retreat from it was decorously managed. The statutes of the Royal Geographical Society were invoked, though somewhat late in the day, as a reason for holding aloof from an enterprise not of exploration purely : instead of a national committee in connection with the International Association, those whom the proceedings of the Conference of Brussels had stirred to encourage the opening up of Africa were invited to subscribe to a purely English African exploration fund, and Sir Bartle Frere resigned his membership of the association, as well as his place on its executive committee, on being appointed Governor of Cape Colony, no further delegates being appointed to that association from England. It was, however, officially declared that England would maintain friendly relations with the International Association, and a sum of £250 was subscribed to it as an active proof of English sympathy.

At the same time it was admitted that England's withdrawal was due to a fear of being trammelled with engagements of an international nature. Her withdrawal was not followed by that of any of the other Powers, although before long the committees of France and Germany developed into the purely national enterprises under the flags of their respective countries, to which the foundation of the present French and German territories in Central Africa may be traced ; and against the defection of England there was placed the adherence of the United States of America—thenceforward the firmest supporter of the International Association and of the Congo State, which sprang from it. The place vacated by Sir Bartle Frere on the executive committee was filled by the appointment of a more eminent diplomatist, General Sanford, sometime Minister for the United States at Brussels.

If King Leopold saw, from the manner in which the advances of the International Association were met by foreign Cabinets, that, whatever semblance of cooperation the various national committees lent to him, he would in reality have to rely on himself alone for the success of his gigantic enterprise—and one so clearsighted must have seen that soon—he did not allow the fact to dismay him or damp his ardour in the least. No sooner was the sitting of the conference over than he turned his energies to the formation of the national committee for Belgium. As a first step towards its foundation he summoned a meeting for a date six weeks after the close of the conference—November 6th, 1876—of all who were willing to join in it.

The King was present at this meeting and addressed it in a vigorous speech, which deserves to be studied for the deliberate statements it made on the horrors of the slave trade on the one hand, and on the beauties and riches of Africa on the other. This speech, which went brusquely and forcibly to the point, is one of the most characteristic of King Leopold's pronouncements. The King's whole future policy towards Africa was indicated in it in the most unmistakeable manner. This was the speech :—

" Gentlemen,—The slave trade, which still exists over a large part of the African continent, is a plague-spot that every friend of civilisation would wish to see disappear.

" The horrors of that traffic, the thousands of victims massacred each year through the slave trade, the still greater number of perfectly innocent beings who, brutally reduced to captivity, are condemned *en masse* to forced labour in perpetuity, have deeply moved all those who have even partially studied this deplorable situation ; and they have conceived the idea of uniting together and concerting, in a word, for the founding of an International Association to put an end to an odious traffic which makes our epoch blush, and to tear aside the veil of darkness which still enshrouds Central Africa. The discoveries due to daring explorers permit us to say that it is one of the most beautiful and the richest countries created by God.

" The Conference of Brussels has nominated an executive committee to carry into execution its declarations and resolutions.

" The conference has wished, in order to place itself in closer relationship with the public, whose sympathy will constitute our force, to found in each State national committees. These committees, after delegating two members from each of them to form part of the International Committee, will popularise in their respective countries the adopted programme.

" The work has already obtained in France and Belgium important donations, to the subscribers of which we owe a debt of gratitude. These acts of charity, so honourable to those who have performed them, stimulate our zeal in the mission we have undertaken. Our first task should be to touch the hearts of the masses, to gather our adherents into a fraternal union, little onerous for each member, but powerful and fruitful by the accumulation of individual efforts and their results.

" The International Association does not pretend to reserve for itself all the good that could or ought to be done in Africa. It ought, especially at the outset, to forbid itself a too extensive programme. Sustained by public sympathy, we hold the conviction that if we accomplish the opening of the routes, if we succeed in establishing stations along the routes followed by the slave merchants, this odious traffic will be wiped out ; and that the routes and stations, while serving as *points d'appui* for travellers, will powerfully contribute towards the evangelisation of the blacks, and towards the introduction amongst them of commerce and modern industry.

"We boldly affirm that all those who desire the enfranchisement of the black races are interested in our success.

"The Belgian committee, emanating from the International Committee, and its representative in Belgium will exert every means to procure for the work the greatest number of adherents. It will assist my countrymen to prove once more that Belgium is not only a hospitable soil, but that she is also a generous nation, amongst whom the cause of humanity finds as many champions as she has citizens.

"I discharge a very agreeable duty in thanking this assembly, and in warmly congratulating it for having imposed on itself a task the accomplishment of which will gain for our country another brilliant page in the annals of charity and progress."

In response to the King's appeal subscriptions flowed in from all sides of Belgium; and whilst the subscriptions to the national committees of other countries amounted to little more than a few thousand francs, those in Belgium reached a total of 287,000 francs in donations, and 44,000 in annual subscriptions during the first year of its committee's existence. By 1877 it amounted to 410,000 francs, when, including annual subscriptions, the Belgian national committee—which was under the presidency of the Count of Flanders, the King's brother—estimated its income at 75,000 francs, and felt itself strong enough to proceed to active measures for the attainment of its ends.

It was not money only that was readily forthcoming in Belgium. When the novelty of the enterprise wore off, while the attainment of its ends seemed to remain as distant as at first, the subscriptions inevitably declined; but there was never any falling off of eager volunteers in Belgium to fulfil the King's behests, and undertake the labours and brave the perils of pioneering in Africa, not even at a time when every success that was gained was gained at the cost of death or of disease.

When he called to his people for volunteers for the work, there, at least, King Leopold was never disappointed ; and the response made to his every appeal cannot but have been of the most gratifying nature to the King, since in the majority of cases it came from soldiers of the Belgian army, prompted by their loyal affection for their sovereign's person to venture their lives in obedience to his call. These men of action who fear to face the present, appeal ofttimes, and with excellent oratorical effect, to the judgment of posterity, although posterity forgets most of men's deeds, and distorts all it remembers. Far nobler are those who, having commanded, dare to submit themselves to the open judgment of their servants. King Leopold of Belgium faced the people's judgment unhesitatingly, when, expedition after expedition having been decimated by death, he still called for further volunteers. The answer to his call may stand in judgment for him, for it proves that in the army, amongst those who serve him and who know him best, there is for him that sentiment of absolute devotion which only stern and strong men raise in the hearts of those who know them true and reverence them for their justice.

The money and volunteers being forthcoming for the commencement of the work of the Belgian committee, King Leopold summoned a meeting of the International Commission at the Palace of Brussels. In reply to his summons, delegates arrived from all the countries excepting England and Russia, which had been represented at the conference of the previous year ; and a sitting was held which lasted for two days —June 20th and 21st, 1877. The absence of the Russian delegates was explained and excused ; that of

THE INTERNATIONAL ASSOCIATION. 115

delegates from England was not referred to. The meeting was an echo of the Geographical Conference. Various details of business were settled, and approval was given to the Belgians' intention of commencing operations without delay, by means of an expedition despatched by way of Zanzibar towards Lake Tanganyika, with the object of establishing stations, either on the lake itself or at certain points beyond it, and of sending out explorers who would make the stations their bases of operations.

One of the most interesting discussions at this meeting was that on the selection of a flag for the Association. Don Francesco Coello, one of the Spanish delegates, suggested that the flag of the Association should bear the Belgian Lion ; but King Leopold declined this compliment to his country on the grounds that the Association, being international, its flag should not recall that of any kingdom. A suggestion made by the Archbishop of Kalosca, one of the Austrian delegates, that the Sphinx should be taken as the emblem of the Association, was also rejected : the Association setting out to decide the Central African question, did not think the sign of the unsolved riddle a happy omen. Finally, a choice was made of the azure flag charged with a golden star which now waves over every station in the immense expanse of the Congo State.

At this same meeting, King Leopold was re-elected president of the Association, not without some suggestion on his part that his work in founding the Association being accomplished, another president should be chosen.

The story of the expeditions sent out to the East Coast of Africa in the name of the International Association is the story of Belgians' pluck and of King Leopold's determination. When the first of these expeditions was decided on there was no knowledge of the Congo waterway ; but almost immediately after the plans of the expedition had been made, the publication of Stanley's map of his discoveries disclosed the fact that in that mighty river there lay, ready for man's service, a way to the centre of the continent. King Leopold was the first to grasp the full significance of Stanley's great discovery, and the only one to profit by it; but because he found an opening greater than he had hoped for in the west, he was not one to abandon of himself on that account the other opening he had determined on making in the east.

Soon the name of the International Association became more than ever a misnomer, for all the interest in it, all its organising energy, and all its funds came from King Leopold alone. Undeterred by inauspicious beginnings, undeterred by loss of money, as his pioneers were undeterred by loss of life, King Leopold flung expedition after expedition, during five years, into the heart of Africa from the Coast of Zanzibar.

In all six expeditions were sent, and they were nearly all decimated by death. Still, neither the King nor his lieutenants lost courage. The station on Lake Tanganyika, which the expeditions were sent out to found, was successfully established. The sovereignty over this station, and the district controlled from it, was subsequently transferred by diplomatic means from King Leopold to Germany, but not before it had proved successful in its greatest ends, and repaid the sacrifices of their lives which so many intrepid Belgians had made for its foundation.

A king strong-willed as King Leopold may be judged by the actions of his chosen servants in the carrying out of his work. It is fortunate, therefore, that the clearest proof exists of the manner in which the chiefs of these, the earliest expeditions sent out by the King, discharged the greatest duty imposed on them—that of bringing peace and spreading civilisation. A bare account of two incidents will suffice to show what these men did, and how the natives regarded them.

The first is that of the death of the chief Mpala, in whose district Captain Storms, head of the last of the expeditions sent out from Belgium by Zanzibar, established a flourishing post. The account of the chief's death was given by M. Storms himself on his return, in an address delivered before the Geographical Society in 1886. Mpala had become the blood-brother of the Belgian leader. After the death of the chief's brother by smallpox, said M. Storms, " his affection for me became still greater. He never passed a day without paying me a visit ; and he often said to me : ' My brother, what would I do if you went away ? I would have no relation then.'

" A month before my departure my friend Mpala was struck down by the inexorable malady which had already carried off his brother. He felt himself dying, and thereupon he called to his bedside the elders of the village, and said to them :

" ' My friends, I feel that I am dying. The white man, my brother, will give you another chief. Whoever replaces me must follow my traditions and obey the white man, as I would have done myself. He has often chided me ; but if he called me in the middle of the night to cut off my head, I would have gone where he directed without hesitation. All he has done was for our good. If my successor does not follow my example, you will all quit this village and go to my sister's.' "

Mpala died the night he made this speech, and M. Storms installed his successor, who, with all the neighbouring chieftains, continued to obey the white man, as the dying chieftain had ordered, bringing him, as long as he remained amongst them, all their quarrels and disputes for his arbitration.

The second incident, which throws a flood of the clearest light on the relations between the white men who came out from Belgium and the native Africans, happened not in Africa, but in Belgium, in Brussels itself, in the Rue des Rentiers, in the house of Captain Ramaeckers, chief of the fourth Belgian expedition, one of those who died in harness in Africa, struck down by fever, but, at the time of this occurrence, home on leave. Captain Ramaeckers, while he was in charge of a scientific mission in the Fezzan, had in his service a negro named Bamboula, whom on his return he left at Tripoli. One day, long afterwards, there was a knock at Captain Ramaeckers's door in Brussels, and the explorer, looking up, saw to his astonishment Bamboula standing before him, draped in a burnous. "I could not live without you, master," said the poor negro; "that is why I have come to rejoin you."

Spurred on by his affection to seek out his master at any cost, Bamboula had embarked as a sailor for Marseilles, and landed at the French port without money, and with nothing but a vague indication of the white man's address in Brussels. At Marseilles he had toiled patiently at many callings, until he gathered together the money to take him to Brussels, where at length, his devotion overcoming every obstacle, the black man found himself again under the protection of his white chief.

Such were the explorers first sent to Africa by King Leopold II., and in such a light did the natives regard them.

CHAPTER VIII.

DIPLOMATIC VICTORIES.

ANY man who stands before a map of the world and marks on it the huge extent of Equatorial Africa, cannot fail to be astonished at the immensity of the task which King Leopold set for himself when he said : " I will pierce the darkness of barbarism ; I will secure to Central Africa the blessings of a civilised government, and I will, if necessary, undertake this giant task alone."

No mightier task was ever set by man unto himself. It is not because Belgium is so small—a mere speck of colour on the maps on which the Congo State fills a great space—that the undertaking seems so stupendous. England on these maps is also small, and Rome on them is barely distinguishable ; the square miles which surround the cradle of a conquering race count clearly for nothing. It is because so great a task, if dreamt of, was never before planned by man. Other colonies and empires grew from seemingly chance developments, from lucky hazards blindly followed ; or they were wrenched at the sword's point from those whose toil had made them covetable in past times. Warriors had conquered kingdoms and sighed for worlds to conquer, but the worlds they sighed for were the worlds of men. No one, king, statesman, or adventurer, had been found before King Leopold came, sufficiently daring and sufficiently reliant to say, " I will conquer men and nature, and found an empire in the savage wilds."

This is what the King said—this is what he did ; and no man more than he knew the gigantic nature of the task he set himself. Probably no man but himself knows a tittle of the difficulties he faced and overcame, and probably no man but himself could have faced or overcome them. Those who believe in a guiding power which is not chance must note how the King was fitted for his task. Independent, strong-willed, and well instructed, King Leopold's position in Belgium— a free but neutral country—gave him at once the prestige and the freedom from hampering alliances necessary. His extended travels gave him, more than any other reigning prince, the inclination to listen to explorers' tales; while his wide geographical studies furnished him with the knowledge of how to profit by them. Above all, his skill in kingcraft and in statesmanship taught him how to found his empire, and to maintain it in the face of envious potentates.

When King Leopold first planted his flag in Africa Europe was asleep; long afterwards she simulated sleep. But her sleep was a dangerous one for the new State; it was a sleep from which at the first favourable moment she was ready to spring, to pounce upon what seemed her easy prey. One false step would have been fatal; a moment of hesitancy, an instant's check, the slightest failing, and Europe, in the shape of one or other of the Powers (or of several Powers united, that they might afterwards partition it out in private amongst themselves), would have snatched the Congo morsel out of King Leopold's hold, protesting, of course, the while that they only did so to fulfil the noble work which the King of the Belgians, though so laudably enterprising, had proved himself too weak to accomplish.

Fortunately for the success of his undertaking, King Leopold was awake to the danger which threatened him, and able to avoid it. He permitted nothing to check his work; he prevented failure in it, seeing that all that was necessary to be done was undertaken with sufficient force and proper calculation; he took no false step, and allowed his servants in Africa to take none; but at every move, and in unsuspected directions, he strengthened his position, until when the day which he saw

DIPLOMATIC VICTORIES.

from the first to be inevitable arrived, and the Powers assembled to decide over a council board the fate of Central Africa, his Congo State came before their congress, not as a philanthropic body weakly whining for recognition on the ground of good intentions, but as a sovereign State moving amongst other Powers with equal rights, and amidst the inevitable barter of diplomacy dictating terms from its unassailable positions, and making concessions from its coveted riches.

Apart from the King of the Belgians, even the wisest statesmen in Europe remained blind, when the Congo State was founded, to the possibilities, and totally ignorant of the great richness of Central Africa. Otherwise, philanthropic though European statesmen may be, he would never have been allowed to plant his standard in Central Africa. Even up to the eve of the Berlin Congress those who guided affairs in the various chancelleries of Europe believed that the heart of Africa was a place hopeless to turn to profitable use for colonisation or for trade. They were content that King Leopold should have it for a plaything, to waste his private fortune and his people's lives on if he wished ; but they were sufficiently enlightened to think otherwise of the seaward portions of the continent. What riches there were in Africa should flow to the coast. This was a self-evident proposition. Therefore the Powers resolved that the coast should belong to them. King Leopold might gather riches, if he could, beneath the baking sun of the Equator ; but those riches should pass through the border territories of France or Germany, of England or of Portugal. Such, at least, was the secret intention of these Powers ; and the student of history must be a singularly heedless person if he needs to be told that it was also the further intention of each Power to make these riches pay tribute to itself, if it could not absorb the whole of them.

The geographical formation of Central Africa aided

the colonising Powers of Europe in their designs. King Leopold's African enterprise had been undertaken without special thought of the Congo or its basin; and his first, and more than one of his later, expeditions into Africa were sent out to open up the country to civilisation and form connections with the coast in places which no geographical sophism could construct into portions of the Congo basin. But by the action of the rival Powers of Europe, the Belgian sphere of influence was gradually crushed into the Congo basin, and the work of the International African Association was identified in the end with the foundation of a Congo State; whilst " on the sea coast of the two seas there extended the German, English, French, Spanish, and Portuguese possessions, which enveloped and sustained the central depression like so many counterforts."

Of all the Powers, the pretensions of Portugal to property in African soil were the most ancient and the most shadowy. These pretensions—so far, at least, as the district around the mouth of the Congo was concerned—rested solely on the fact that Portuguese mariners had discovered the entrance to the Congo River in the fifteenth century. To support her claims in this district Portugal had neither an African colony to show nor treaties to produce. She could point only to a time-worn and long-neglected pillar, brought centuries since from Portugal by adventurous navigators in the hold of some forgotten vessel, and set up by them on the wind-swept headland of Pillar Point, at the entrance of the great African river. More than once in the centuries which followed the erection of this pillar, Portugal had put forward claims of sovereignty over the district in which it stood; but in every instance these claims had been repudiated. France at the end of the eighteenth century, and England throughout the nineteenth, had deliberately refused them recognition.

Ignoring the claims of Portugal, the Powers agreed by

DIPLOMATIC VICTORIES. 123

tacit accord to consider the district of the Lower Congo as subject to no civilised State ; and European traffic was carried on in it under a *régime* of absolute liberty ; one in which vile abuses, though known to exist, were allowed to continue unchecked. Portugal's claims, however, remained, if shadowy, still menacing for any other authority which sought to establish itself on the Congo. Any great Power inimical to the growth of King Leopold's colony by allying itself with Portugal, and advancing the Portuguese claims in the name of international justice, might interfere with some show of right in African affairs to crush the enterprise of the Belgian King.

King Leopold was not blind to this danger. He knew the moment Europe awakened to a knowledge of the richness and the importance of Central Africa, there would be a general scramble for its soil ; and he felt that moment to be at hand. Portugal itself, the most lethargic of colonising Powers, might rouse up at any instant ; and it was doubtful if he, through the International Association, and in spite of all the work it had accomplished and of the binding treaties it had made, could alone cope with the Power of Portugal and resist its claims. For this reason, if for no other, King Leopold welcomed the appearance of French explorers in the heart of Africa. They came to plant the tricolour upon the banks of the Congo, but King Leopold wisely welcomed their coming as that of generous allies instead of dreading it as the appearance of grasping foes.

The first French expedition to the Congo was, in fact, as well as form, a private undertaking. It was led by Count Savorgnan de Brazza, a naval lieutenant, to whose initiative and courageous enterprise France owes her great Congo possessions. M. de Brazza arrived at Stanley Pool while Stanley, acting as the representative of King Leopold's association, was occupied on the weary task of constructing a road past the cataracts from Kiri to Isangila, which occupied him from March, 1880, to February, 1881. On October 1st, 1880, when as yet only thirty of the fifty-two miles of Stanley's caravan road were made, M. de Brazza concluded a treaty with the King of the Batekes, by which he obtained ground for a settlement on Stanley Pool, and by which the native chief put himself under the protection of France. When Stanley arrived at Stanley Pool in 1881 M. de Brazza had months previously departed, leaving as sole representative of his occupancy a black servant, who carried a French flag in his hand wherever he went and showed to all comers a paper which proved to be a copy of M. de Brazza's treaty.

There was much difference between this paper occupancy and the solid roads and lasting settlements which the Belgian pioneers made wherever they advanced, but no exception was taken to the Frenchman's action. Stanley contented himself with establishing a station in the name of the International Association on the bank of the lake opposite the spot which M. de Brazza claimed, and on which afterwards a regular French station—called Brazzaville, after the explorer—was built ; and from that time onwards the flags of the two friendly States waved in peace on the opposite shores of the great river.

At the end of 1882, when both Stanley and de Brazza returned to Europe, the secret of the Congo's riches and possibilities became known to all. Immediately the general scramble for the possession of Africa, which King Leopold had foreseen, took place ; but before the partition of the centre of the continent could commence the Belgian King was able to render his position impregnable by the loyal assistance he had hoped for so confidently from France.

To attain the end he desired, King Leopold addressed himself personally to France ; and on October 16th,

DIPLOMATIC VICTORIES. 125

1882, the French Premier, M. Duclerc, addressed a letter to him, in which French support was unequivocally promised to his colony. M. Duclerc wrote :—

> According to the desire your Majesty has been good enough to express to me, it is understood that no obstacle will be placed to the relations between the stations established, or to be established, by the International Association and the Committee of the Study of the Congo.
>
> The passage from one to the other of the said stations through the territory situated between Stanley Pool and the Impila and Djoué Rivers will not be submitted by us to any charge or hindrance, either as to the persons or as to the goods carried in transit.
>
> I am glad to be able to give, in the name of the Government of the Republic, an express assurance to your Majesty. I have the pleasure to hope that your Majesty will find in our ardour a new proof of our sentiments for your Majesty's person, and of the value which we place on facilitating, as far as lies with us, the generous enterprise placed under the high patronage of your Majesty.

To this letter King Leopold replied:

> I know that the Government of the French Republic does justice to the enterprise pursued in the widespread design of civilisation and progress by the Association, and by the Committee; and that it manifests the intention of facilitating, as far as depends on it, its definite success. I firmly hope that nothing will prevent us from maintaining as good relations in Africa as in Europe.

This was the first recognition given in Europe to King Leopold's colony; and it was the most valuable. In common with everything else which was done for the foundation of the Congo State, it came from the initiative of the King of the Belgians, and was gained by the King's wise and prudent statecraft. None but he, or one as wise, as prudent, as patient, and as far-seeing as he, could have built up the Congo State, and upheld it under all the attacks, open and secret, which were made on it from the moment Europe learned it was a land the possession of which would repay the trouble of assault.

For years Central Africa was the battle-ground of Europe; and though its battles were fought by diplomatists with maps and protocols, in the place of generals with castles and armies, the war, with its marchings and counter-marchings, its engagements and assaults, its plots and its single combats, its loyalties and its treacheries, its victories and its defeats, and its final triumph, is as moving as any tale of pitched battles and of tented fields. Throughout it all, from first to last, King Leopold moves, a commanding and victorious figure. Other great men, those whose names sounded greatest in the Europe of their day, mixed in the contest; but from the greatest to the least they moved as the puppets of the King of the Belgians, and the work they did, great as were its results for their countries, was but the work of shaping the Congo State to its founder's ends.

France, moved by the tales of M. de Brazza, aided his enterprise with money and authority. Portugal, stirred up when too late, appealed to France and was repulsed by the ally King Leopold had secured; appealed to Germany, and was again practically repulsed by the ally King Leopold was soon to gain; appealed to England, and first repulsed from there, was for a time sustained by a ministry whose foreign policy brought no credit to England, and whose wavering assistance was of no real aid when the great struggle came.

In 1882 the Belgian Comité d'Études de Haut Congo and the International Association were merged in each other, and it was in the name of the Association that the final treaties were concluded with the African chieftains. These treaties, the legality of which was beyond question in international law, vested the sovereignty of the whole of that great portion of Equatorial Africa, which is now known as the conventional basin of the Congo, and of great districts outside of it extending practically from sea to sea, in the International African Association. In addition to the districts of Central Africa, unknown no longer, since the officers of the Association had mapped its rivers and planted stations upon them, the Association had acquired rights over territories which France coveted on the coast of the Atlantic, and over territories which Germany desired on the Indian Ocean. These territories, which lay in the same degrees of latitude as the Central territories of the Association, seemed the natural outlets towards the sea on either side of the new State; and a less wise statesman than King Leopold would have strained every effort to retain them, or at least one or other of them, if he could not retain both. King Leopold, however, had a better use for them. By abandoning all claim to them in favour of the two Great Powers, and requiring no more than an outlet at the mouth of the Congo, he secured the friendship of these Powers and the stability of the Congo State. This arrangement was the crowning act of the great feat of statesmanship by which the new African Empire sprang from the monarch's brain.

When the diplomatists of Europe turned their attention to the affairs of Central Africa, the sovereignty of the International Association over that immense district had become an accomplished fact. Forty stations were then already founded by it; its administrative and police services were organised, and it had established a service of five steamers on the upper river beyond the cataracts which maintained a constant connection between the caravan route from the coast, and the Equator. France, on the one side, would certainly, and Germany, on the other, might possibly, have sooner or later put forward claims to the great territories they now hold on the sea-board, though it seems more than probable that the interests they suddenly showed in these districts were excited for diplomatic reasons from Brussels; but Europe as a whole would not have dreamed of interfering to regulate the affairs of Africa but for the persistent clamouring and preposterous demands of Portugal.

Besides her shadowy claims to the sovereignty of the district of the Lower Congo, Portugal had other claims to huge territories on both the west and east coast of Africa, and Portuguese statesmen had dreamed of building up a great African empire extending from coast to coast, across the whole extent of the continent—dreams which nothing but their own supineness had prevented them from realising in the past. It was only in 1882, when it had become too late to do so with success, that Portugal determined to act. In November, 1882, the Portuguese Government opened negotiations with the English Cabinet, and in December of the same year Lord Granville—then Foreign Secretary—proposed the basis of an agreement by which England, while stipulating that the navigation of the Congo and the Zambesi should be free, was to recognise the sovereignty of Portugal over the territories on the west of Africa, situated between the parallels of 8″ and 5′ 12″ south latitude; and that the rights and pretensions of all sorts held by Portugal over the territories on the west coast of Africa between 5° of east longitude and 5° of west longitude were to be transferred to England. The most remarkable point in this proposed arrangement was the recognition given by England under it to the sovereignty of Portugal over the Lower Congo.

Difficulties as to agreeing to clauses in the treaty regarding tariffs and other questions were raised by Portugal; while a strong opposition to the recognition of Portugal's claims on the Congo was manifested in the House of Commons. Before this opposition the English Government displayed weakness of purpose.

Photo: L. Fabronius, Brussels.

COUNT DE SMET DE NAEYER.

President of the Council of Ministers, Minister of Finance and Public Works.

Photo: Géruzet Frères, Brussels.

BARON DHANIS.

Vice-Governor-General of the Independent State.

Photo: F. C. Schaarwächter, Berlin.

BARON LAMBERMONT.

Minister of State.

DIPLOMATIC VICTORIES. 129

In a remarkable note, stuffed full of admirable platitudes, and published on March 15th, 1883, Lord Granville explained away, or sought to explain away, all he had done. In his note he spoke of Livingstone and of Stanley, of geography and of ethnology, of slavery and of civilisation, and of the development of legitimate traffic; and declared that, in the opinion of her Majesty's Government, " rivalry and competition which would be fatal to growing commerce" would be "largely prevented by an arrangement between Great Britain and Portugal, founded on the principles of liberty and of equal advantages for all countries." In this note Lord Granville said also that his proposal to extend the sovereignty of Portugal over the mouth of the Congo was a pure concession, not a recognition of historic right; and, moreover, an intimation was given by England to Portugal that England would not stand by her agreement unless other countries approved of the treaty.

At this Portugal saw the necessity of gaining the assistance of some firmer Government, and addressed herself to France, offering as a bribe for French support a recognition of France's right to all the territories claimed by M. de Brazza. Portugal had now to learn that in the game of diplomacy she had more than met her match. King Leopold had foreseen her action, and had laid his plans so that he was able to outbid her in every way. The King of the Belgians had spread his lines with great judgment, and placed his stations so that the realisation of France's African desires could only be attained through his concession or by ignoring his rights, to do which would be to invite like treatment of the similar rights under which M. de Brazza's posts were held.

Up to the very moment of the commencement of negotiations, King Leopold's agents were overrunning the district which France desired to hold, exploring its rivers, erecting stations in it, and entering into treaties with the native chieftains in the name of the International Association. Everywhere they had out-distanced Brazza; and at the very time that Portugal was vainly trying to bribe France with a promise to recognise the French flag on the Atlantic coast of Africa where planted by Brazza, the sailors of the French explorer were on the same coast, at the important post of Loango, saluting the flag of the Association which they found waving in sign of sovereignty over the station and the neighbouring Kinlu river, which they had arrived three days too late to annex. Portugal, possessed only of a shadowy claim, had clearly nothing to offer which could tempt France to desert the ally who, beside the unforgotten ties of blood and friendship, had valuable concessions to make. France waived aside the proposal of Portugal that she should acquiesce in the English arrangement, bringing forward in its place a proposition known to be distasteful to Portugal; and the baffled Portuguese statesmen turned again to England.

Here, at last, Portugal had some success. An imposing treaty, embracing fifteen articles, was drawn up and signed on behalf of Portugal and France in London on February 26th, 1884. This treaty recognised the claims of Portugal on the Congo, and left Portugal free to impose what dues she liked on shipping entering the river; while, by the agreement to appoint a mixed commission of English and Portuguese delegates to draw up the rules concerning the Congo and other waterways comprised in the treaty, it gave England power of dominating the politics of the district.

Such an attempt on the part of a great maritime Power and its lesser ally to seize for themselves the mouth of the Congo naturally aroused the indignation of the rest of Europe. Nowhere was the indignation more generally felt or more loudly expressed than in

Germany, which at once insisted on the decision by Europe of the Congo question.

The attitude of Germany in this matter was one frankly on the side of liberty of trade, which also happened to be that of the Congo State. That Germany's attitude may have been solely directed by high motives of human interest I do not for a moment deny; but I must point out a fact which is likely to be lost sight of in the consideration of the case: that at the very moment of these transactions Germany was engaged, with the consent, at least, of King Leopold, in annexing wide territories near the east coast of Africa, extending from Zanzibar to the Congo basin at Lake Tanganyika, in which territories the earliest founded stations of the International Association stood. These territories form the German East Africa of to-day. They were formed into a German protectorate on the very day after the signing of the final act of the Congress of Berlin; and it is certainly permissible to believe that Germany's action in summoning the Congress of Berlin to put down the unwarrantable pretensions of Portugal, and in upholding the State founded by King Leopold, was due to King Leopold's statesmanship in allowing the Germans to possess themselves unopposed of that great district from which he retired to give place to Germany.

CHAPTER IX.

THE RECOGNITION OF THE STATE.

IF King Leopold was forced to *finesse* against the diplomatists of Europe, and to be ready to pay dearly for every concession made by Europe in the name of humanity, he had, nevertheless, from the commencement of his undertaking, the unwavering support of the great Power of America, the United States, the pure philanthropy of whose action in regard to all that concerned the affairs of the Congo was beyond all question.

When the English representatives withdrew from the International African Association through a fear of trammelling themselves with engagements of an international nature, King Leopold had the great fortune to be able to fill the place they left vacant with American statesmen of the most distinguished reputation, who had at their head in America Judge Daly (of New York), Mr. Latrobe (of Baltimore, one of the founders of Liberia); and, in Europe, General Henry S. Sanford, of Florida, ex-United States Minister to Belgium, who succeeded to the place vacated by Sir Bartle Frere as representative of the English-speaking races on the executive committee of the Association. When the work of founding the Congo State was finished, and the moment for recognising its government had arrived, the United States were officially informed of the situation of affairs in Africa by a letter addressed by General Sanford to Senator Morgan, from which I may give the following extracts. In this letter, dated March 24th, 1884, General Sanford said :—

RECOGNITION OF THE STATE'S SUPREMACY. 133

Dear Sir,—

In reply to your request for specific information as to the origin and objects of the International African Association, I have the honour to state that it owes its origin to the King of the Belgians, who in 1876 convened a conference of distinguished African travellers of different nationalities at his palace in Brussels in September of that year, to devise the best means of opening up to civilisation Equatorial Africa. The result of this conference, which recommended the establishment of stations, provided for a permanent central organisation and branch organisations in other countries, was the convoking of a commission or congress, which met at the Palace at Brussels in June, 1877, and at which delegates from Austria, Belgium, France, Germany, the Netherlands, Spain, Switzerland, and the United States were present. An executive committee—consisting of three representatives of the English-speaking, Germanic, and Latin races, in the persons of Henry S. Sanford of Florida, Dr. Nachtigal (the African explorer) of Berlin, and M. de Quatrefages (of the Institute) of Paris, for these races respectively, under the presidency of the King—was confirmed, and the practical means of carrying out the objects of the Association were discussed and determined on. These were the organisation of a branch in each of the various states of Europe and in America, which should aid in attracting attention to this work and in founding "hospitable and scientific" stations, under the flag of the Association, which flag it was determined should be a blue flag with a golden star in the centre. It was also decided to commence the founding of these stations on the east coast, at Zanzibar, stretching over to the lakes. . . .

The result of this movement has been the opening up of a highway, so to say, from Zanzibar to Lake Tanganyika, mostly with capital furnished by the Belgians, the last of the stations being at Karema, on the lake, two of the intermediary stations being founded respectively by the French and German branches of the Association.

After Stanley discovered the Upper Congo in 1877, a branch of the International Association was formed the year following for special work on the Congo, under the name of the Comité d'Études of the Upper Congo, but under the flag of the

Association; and special contributions for it were made by philanthropic friends of the Association. This work, which the King of the Belgians has taken under his especial personal and financial protection, has developed to extraordinary proportions, and has had for a practical result the opening up to civilising influences and to the world's traffic this vast, populous, and fertile region, and securing certain destruction to the slave trade wherever its flag floats. The only practical difficulty in this wonderful progress proves to be an unrecognised flag which is liable to be misunderstood or abused, and the people under it subjected to impediments in their philanthropic work on the part of those engaged in the slave trade, or for other selfish ends.

I have the honour to be,
Very respectfully yours,
H. S. SANFORD,
Member of the Executive Committee of the International African Association.

Senator Morgan presented a report on this letter to the Senate of the United States, which report was accompanied by emphatic statements of the rights of the International Association according to the law of nations, made by the great international lawyers, Sir Travers Twiss and Mr. Arntz. On April 10th, 1884, the Senate, having considered this report, passed a resolution requiring the President of the United States to recognise the Association as the governing Power of the Congo; and on the 22nd of the same month the necessary documents were signed and the formal recognition by the United States of the International Association as a sovereign and friendly Power became an accomplished fact.

The United States of America having thus recognised the flag of the International Association, and the sovereign rights of the Association being undeniable by the law of nations, its recognition by the Powers of Europe followed within a year. Portugal was still struggling to gain diplomatic recognition for the African empire

ARMS OF KING LEOPOLD II.

ARMS OF THE INDEPENDENT STATE.

RECOGNITION OF THE STATE'S SUPREMACY. 135

she had neglected to build up; and Portuguese statesmen hoped that, in the self-interest of France, they might even yet find the support they sought. Here, however, King Leopold again baffled them. Instead of putting forward claims as Portugal did, and demanding congresses and arbitrations, at the moment when his infant colony most wanted strengthening he riveted his ancient alliance with France by fresh treaties, which provided that the two countries united so closely in Europe should become equally, if not still more closely, united in their African colonies.

King Leopold might have advanced claims on what is now the French Congo; his agents, as I have shown, had concluded treaties with the natives and erected the flag of the International Association all over that district, from its inland boundary on the Congo outward to the coast of the Atlantic Ocean itself. The treaties were there, as was the right of prior possession; but King Leopold waived them all, and without haggling he conceded all France cared to claim. Not only did he put forward no claims to the district France desired to hold under her own flag, but he secured the all-powerful protection of France for his colony by a convention with the French Republic, entered into on April 23rd, 1884, the day following that on which the formal recognition of the sovereignty of the International Association was notified by the Government of the United States, by which convention France recognised the rights of the International Association, and by which the Association bound itself not to cede its possessions to another Power without a prior understanding with France; and agreed that if it were compelled to alienate any of its territories, France should have the right of pre-emption over them.

From the moment this convention was signed the stability of King Leopold's colony was secured. Those who sought to encroach on it in future would find themselves confronted not only by the unarmed king of a small neutral State, but by the armies of a great military Power; those who planned its overthrow could contemplate only the passing over of the sovereignty of the whole of the immense area of the Congo to the great Republic, the growth of whose power their self-interest, if not their hatred, must teach them to dread. Writers who are not of the Latin race have before now taunted the Belgians with the love their King bears for France and France's capital, and called King Leopold the Franco-Belgian monarch. It is well for Belgium and for France that those mockers have truth in what they say, though the truth is far other than they think.

King Leopold's love for France has never led him to advance French rather than Flemish interests in Belgium; but it, and the reciprocating love that France gives him, has enabled him to work good in innumerable ways for either country. This consolidating of French and Belgian interests in Africa—which in 1884 was a practical cry of "Hands off" to the rest of Europe already advancing, greedy and rapacious—was but one, if the greatest, of the many peaceful achievements of King Leopold's diplomacy in France which in his own time have benefited and enriched humanity, and done more to preserve and strengthen peace than congresses or arbitration boards.

King Leopold was now secure in the possession of the colony he had founded, and secure in the knowledge that, let diplomacy bestir itself and bespeech itself as it might, a proper outlet to the sea would be assured to him by France's insistence. The exact boundaries of the French and Belgian colonies remained to be delineated, and there were other points to be agreed upon; but all that was vital was now agreed on, and agreement on details was certain.

The Government of the French Republic had not waited for the formal completion of its convention with

RECOGNITION OF THE STATE'S SUPREMACY. 137

the International Association to declare its hostility to the Anglo-Portuguese Treaty. In March, 1884, it intimated to the Portuguese Government that France would not admit to her subjects the application of the clauses of that treaty. Holland, the United States, and Germany followed the example of France. The protest of Germany was addressed in identical terms to the Cabinets of London and Lisbon in the middle of April. German commercial interests were by this time fully aroused to the danger threatened to the freedom of trade by the treaty; and the Imperial Chancellor, Prince Bismarck, addressed an invitation to the French Government to join with Germany in the prevention of the recognition of it.

France having announced her willingness to do so, the English Cabinet saw it was useless to make a longer stand, and abandoned the untenable position it had taken up by refusing to ratify the treaty with Portugal. Lord Granville announced the abandoning of the treaty to Parliament on June 26th, 1884, and with his announcement there closed a most discreditable chapter of British diplomacy.

England could not now refuse to acquiesce in the summoning of an international congress to consider the question of the freedom of trade on the Congo. An effort made by the English Cabinet to enter into a prior agreement with Germany as to " the attitude to be taken and the course to be followed with regard to Portugal as well as to the Belgian International Society " was waived aside by Germany, and the recognition of the territorial and sovereign rights of the International Association was left to be brought about by direct negotiations between Brussels and the various courts of Europe. In the despatches exchanged between France and Germany preliminary to the summoning of the Congress it was insisted upon that all such questions as those relating to territory and sovereignty should be excluded from the purview of the congress. These questions were, in fact, practically decided on before the congress was summoned, although the negotiations regarding the fixing of boundaries and those required to bring Portugal to reason, in some cases, protracted their final settlement until the sittings of the Congress of Berlin had begun.

The formal recognition of the sovereignty of the International Association was given by Germany in a treaty signed on November 8th, 1884, eight days before the opening of the congress. Within the following three months similar treaties were concluded between the International Association and each of the following countries: England, Italy, Austria, Holland, Spain, France, Russia, Sweden and Norway, Portugal, and Belgium; with all of the Powers, in fact, except Turkey, the signing of a treaty with which followed within a short time; and on February 23rd, 1885, King Leopold was able to inform the representatives of the Powers assembled at the congress that solemn and practically universal recognition was accorded to the sovereignty of his African State. This information was conveyed in a letter addressed to Prince Bismarck as president of the congress by Colonel Strauch, president of the Association, who announced that he brought the fact under the notice of the congress "in conformity with the intentions of his Majesty the King of the Belgians, acting in the quality of the founder of this Association."

Colonel Strauch's letter was read to the congress by Herr Busch, who presided at its sitting in the absence of Prince Bismarck, and who spoke in high praise in the name of the congress of the work to which King Leopold had set his name. Following his speech came speeches of graceful congratulation to the King of the Belgians from the plenipotentiaries of the various Powers. Mr. Sanford, the representative of the United States, recalled with pride the fact that his Government

RECOGNITION OF THE STATE'S SUPREMACY. 139

was the first to render public homage to the great work of civilisation of King Leopold II. in recognising the flag of the International Association of the Congo as that of a friendly Government.

In their speeches, the representatives of the Powers vied with each other in eulogising the work of the King of the Belgians, whom, without extravagance or exaggeration, the French Ambassador described as a "Prince surrounded by the respect of Europe." More than one diplomatist who sat at that council board must have been already sickened with jealousy at the thought of the vast and fertile kingdom which King Leopold's genius had snatched for the Belgians from before the unseeing eyes of his more powerful and ever greedy neighbours; but at the moment every other feeling was hidden beneath the display of generous enthusiasm at the success of the King's gigantic enterprise. Only the English Ambassador spoke half regretfully of the blindness of Europe in the days when it had stood aloof and unconcerned, predicting failure, and watching King Leopold's efforts in what then seemed a sterile land with contemptuous pity.

cannot end this chapter on the recognition of the Congo State by the Powers better than by quoting Sir Edward Malet's speech at the congress on King Leopold's achievement. He said :

"The part which the Queen's Government has taken in the recognition of the flag of the Association as that of a friendly Government warrants me in expressing the satisfaction with which we regard the constitution of this new State, due to the initiative of his Majesty the King of the Belgians. During long years the King, dominated by a purely philanthropic idea, has spared nothing, neither personal effort nor pecuniary sacrifice, which could contribute to the realisation of his object. Nevertheless, the world in general regarded these efforts with an almost indifferent eye. Here and there his Majesty aroused sympathy, but it was in some degree rather a sympathy of condolence than of encouragement. It was thought that the undertaking was beyond his power; that it was too great to succeed. We now see the King was right, and that the idea which he pursued was not Utopian. He has brought it to a good end, not without difficulties; but these very difficulties have made success all the more brilliant. In rendering this homage to his Majesty of recognising all the obstacles he has overcome, we greet the new-born State with the greatest cordiality, and we express a sincere desire to see it flourish and increase beneath his ægis."

CHAPTER X.

THE CONGRESS OF BERLIN.

THE Conference of Berlin was summoned by Germany, acting in accord with France, not because of the philanthropy, but because of the jealousies of Europe.

There never was a conference yet which, judged by its protocols, was not one half of its time a mutual admiration society, and the other half an assembly of devout worshippers seeking the justice of Almighty God; and the Congress of Berlin formed no exception to the unbroken rule. High-flown phrases are the small change of diplomacy. Boasting speeches, vaunting virtues, and invocation of the Deity, serve, however, but little to disguise facts; and though, not only at the time of its sitting, but at every period since in which its memory has been invoked, nations have pleased themselves to talk of this congress as something sacrosanct, bald facts remain to prove it of the earth earthy in the narrow self-interests which actuated all its prime movers from its inception to its close. The congress was summoned because the fears of the German traders urged them, through their chambers of commerce, to call upon Prince Bismarck to insist that neither the Power of England nor Portugal, nor of any other foreign country, in obtaining possession of the passes to Central Africa would be allowed to assume authority to set upon them prohibitive tariffs, or what is known as the most-favoured-nation clause, against Germany.

Then, and, as it were, until yesterday, Free Trade was looked upon as a doctrine of perfection, which could not be questioned in theory, to the abstract beauties of which all States should be prepared to pay the homage of lip-service at home, and on behalf of which they should be willing, at any cost to their neighbours, to carry on a propaganda in foreign lands. It was in sustenance of this beautiful theory of the right of free import into your neighbours' lands that each high-souled diplomatist so nobly fought at the congress; this and the equally beautiful and eternally true theory that all foreigners who chose to trade on their neighbours' land should have the right to do so, not only on equal terms with each other, but also with the natives and rulers of the country. This theory, so sadly blown upon at the present moment, was the theory on which the Powers relied at the congress. All questions touching on sovereignty were carefully excluded from the consideration of the congress. It does not enter into the programme of the congress, said the French Ambassador at one of the first sittings, " to trace a complete fiscal and economic programme for the territories which it is considering. It avers clearly its desire to exclude all differential taxes, but it cannot make itself a judge of the raising of future imports or of the details of administration; there must not be a renewal of the colonial experience made in the sixteenth century, when colonies were brought to ruin by those who claimed to fix their financial and administrative mode of existence from Europe, regulating it entirely from the point of view of the metropolis."

It must be remembered that the congress, in dealing with commerce within the area delineated by itself as the conventional basin of the Congo, was dealing with the territories of other Powers besides those of King Leopold's State; with those, indeed, of France, of Germany, of Portugal, and of England, every one of which countries was determined to allow of no meddling with its sovereign right regarding any matters except those of trade and slavery. Even these matters the congress approached in the most cautious and conciliatory manner; and though every Power was agreed

THE CONGRESS OF BERLIN.

as to what to do on them at the moment, care was taken over and over again in the speeches and protocols of the diplomatists, as well as in the final act of the congress itself, to state that the laying down of rules regarding them implied no abrogation of sovereignty, and that the rules laid down themselves extended no farther than the mapped-out limits of the Congo.

"England," exclaimed the French Ambassador with something like horror at the sixth session of the congress, "would make the Act suppressing the slave trade applicable to the entire world"; and, to quote from the protocol of the proceedings, "the representative of Great Britain having replied that such was really, in effect, his desire, the Baron de Courcel observed that the question took, therefore, an unforeseen extension, on which it seemed the plenipotentiaries could not resolve without reference to their Governments." Here, at least, England spoke with the bold voice which her subjects expect from her in every case; but even on this question of slavery the more cautious counsels prevailed, and the clauses referring to slavery called for no more than its suppression in the Congo basin.

It must in truth be admitted that the combined action of the Powers at the convention compares in the least favourable manner concerning their treatment of the question of slavery and the welfare of the blacks with the noble words and projects of King Leopold, who, in his every address and his every act regarding the Congo, placed the duty of suppressing slavery in the forefront. It was not in the forefront, but in a very insignificant spot in the background, that the congress placed this question. It was a trade congress, it is true, and not a philanthropic one, whatever writers of sickly sentiment may claim for it; and it gave its first and serious thoughts to the regulation of trade questions. This is, perhaps, not a thing to be wondered at, at an assembly guided by the Iron Chancellor. Nevertheless, it is to be regretted that the diplomatists sitting at Berlin did not exercise some of their wits in devising means to put down the greatest pest of mankind instead of devising highly ingenuous and entirely unworkable regulations for the formation of an international commission on the Congo to regulate shipping matters, and prevent them from tricking each other out of undue advantages in navigation.

It is to the congress as a whole this blame attaches. Individual countries and individual diplomatists are altogether free from it. King Leopold's wishes were made clear again and again to the congress both by the official representative of Belgium and by General Sanford, who, although officially a representative of the United States, was none the less, though unofficially, a representative and spokesman of the founder of the Congo State, to whose International Committee, it will be remembered, he belonged. The representatives of the United States and of England both strove hard for the interests of the native Africans, Sir Edward Malet in especial displaying firmness and ability in every discussion, and showing that whatever the policy of the Government at home might be, in him his country was worthily and nobly represented abroad ; but these representatives of three Powers effected little against the real indifference of many of their colleagues. The congress could not separate without some act regarding slavery, and one of the clauses of its convention bound each of the Powers " to employ all the means at its disposal for putting an end to this trade "—the slave trade—" and for punishing those who engage in it."

It is beyond question that domestic slavery could not be abolished in Africa by a stroke of the pen ; but it is also beyond question that it was neither beyond the wit of man nor of the means of the Powers of Europe, united as they were at this congress, to devise efficacious measures for the speedy suppression of slave raids.

THE CONGRESS OF BERLIN.

Such measures could not have been adopted, however, without inconvenience or even without causing disturbance to the policy of various States. This was pointed out, and the congress restrained its ardour for the welfare of African humanity within the inefficacious boundaries of the vague, if pious, wish I have quoted.

Its action regarding the sale of drink was still more significant. The Government of Siam had a short time previously taught Europe that legislation on the entire suppression of drink was a possible thing, and the congress showed itself willing to imitate Siam on the Niger, where, the population being Mussulmans, no alcoholic drink was used; but not on the Congo, where drink vendors found avid customers.

One of the representatives of Belgium—the Count van der Straaten—made an appeal to the congress to consider its responsibilities on the drink question. He " recounted with emotion," records the protocol, " how, having lived in the midst of Indian populations with missionaries who exerted themselves to imprint the seal of civilisation on them, he had witnessed the despair of these Christian priests, who saw the Indian race succumb to the excess of strong liquors; how he observed in the plantations of South America the same ravages effected by alcohol on the black races, those precisely which inhabited Central Africa."

The Belgian plenipotentiary said the native races should be sober, or soon they would no longer exist; that there was, besides, a difference between the effects produced by alcoholism on the Indian race on the one hand, and on the African race on the other: the negro did not succumb physically to drunkenness, he succumbed morally. If the Powers did not save him from this vice, they would make a monster of him who would devour the work of the congress. In his appeal the Belgian diplomatist was supported by the representative of the United States and by Sir Edward Malet, and his humanity was praised on all sides ; but it was pointed out that to prevent the sale of strong drink to savages would be to interfere with the paramount interests of Free Trade. The plenipotentiary of the Netherlands declared, moreover, that the sale of drink was notably established in commercial usage, according to which spirits represented money in a way, and were the principal instruments of exchange in the Congo basin, and before such a consideration the mere cause of the duty of humanity towards savages could not be expected to prevail.

The congress applauded the Belgians' desires and passed another vote commending them ; but the pious wish this vote contained was one the majority of the congress did not think proper to embody in any of the numerous clauses of their Act, and the Act will be sought in vain for any reference to the subject.

Having thus provided that nothing, neither the rights of man nor the duties of civilisation, should interfere with the sacred cause of trade, the congress turned itself to the completion of its Act regarding the freedom of trade on the Congo. Some surprise might, perhaps, arise that a congress so very tenacious of the rights of sovereignty should attempt in any way to bind a sovereign's power. Self-interest was undoubtedly the moving power which made it do so. Each Power aimed, if in secret, at drawing profit, without cost to itself, out of King Leopold's State ; but there were plausible precedents for advancing the interests of outside States in the Congo basin. If the protocols and the Act of Berlin are studied carefully, it will be found that that Act was, in the thoughts of those who framed it, more of a navigation Act than any other thing. From their first meeting to their last there is nothing whatever in the reports of the sittings of the congress to show that the diplomatists of Europe even then looked forward

THE CONGRESS OF BERLIN. 147

with any clear outlook or with any firm belief to the foundation of European settlements in Central Africa other than those of trading stations on its navigable waters. There is nothing in their deliberations to prove that any of them considered the establishment of a settled State amidst the equatorial forests and miasma-covered swamps as probable. Their idea, although not expressed in so many plain words, was, beyond yea or nay, that the Congo navigation being supplemented by railways and caravan roads where rapids rendered the river unnavigable, its course would be turned into a traffic way along which traders would spread civilisation by means of cloth and beads, or rum in lieu of money, in exchange for African produce fetched in unending continuance by the natives from their impenetrable forests.

There were in the history of Europe and of America several respectable precedents for the united action of the Powers in regulating the sovereignty of great waterways running through the territories of various States, as the Congo does. The Congresses of Vienna in 1815 and of Paris in 1856, which dealt with similar cases, were specially invoked, and it was on the lines of their treaties that much of the Act of Berlin was formed. The stipulation with regard to freedom of trade—that stipulation which has been aptly described as one for " freedom, equality, and moderate taxation "—was in some respects a new one ; but it was little more than an enlargement of the theory embodied in these earlier treaties.

The congress freed trade from all import duties. It did not act wisely in doing so, under any circumstances ; but its action with regard to taxation must appear to have been nothing other than imbecile, if it is to be supposed it envisaged anything else on the part of the Congo State than the creation and maintenance of a trade route, to the stations of which the Africans were coming to be civilised while trading.

One clause in the Act provides, it is true—that regarding the coasts of the African continent—that the signatory Powers bind themselves to recognise the obligation to ensure the establishment of authority in the regions occupied by them; but no recognition of any such obligation was called for in the equatorial regions of the centre of the continent. The Powers, careful of their taxpayers' money, and anxious only for certain gain, did not dream that King Leopold's philanthropy would prove great enough, as it did, to lead him to lavish millions of his own private funds on African enterprise.

It must be granted they had no wish to be stingy; and in taking means to deprive the Congo State, as they thought, of all resources—excepting those barely sufficient to keep open and construct trade routes, steamer services, and short railways—they were simply allowing him all they conceived to be necessary for his purposes in his "vast demesne" on the Congo. To think otherwise, to believe that the diplomatists who drew up the financial clause regarding taxation in the Act of Berlin foresaw the springing up of the great State of the Congo, with its inevitable money needs in its first stages, would be to believe that these representatives of the Powers of Europe who praised King Leopold's glorious enterprise so glibly were nothing more than disguised assassins, determined to murder the new State at its birth, by depriving it of the needful monetary means of sustenance.

Apart from its perfunctory resolution regarding slavery, and its resolutions of a like nature referring to missionaries, travellers, and religious liberty, the congress considered nothing in its deliberations on the Congo excepting commerce; and the commerce it foresaw and provided for was of the rudest nature—that of barter with savages for the products they gathered. The protocols of the congress bear abundant proof of this.

Baron Lambermont, in a report adopted at the fourth sitting of the congress, said, referring to the first clause of the Act—"'The commerce of all nations shall enjoy complete freedom.' No doubt whatever exists as to the strict and literal sense which should be assigned to the term in *commercial matters*. It refers exclusively to traffic, to the unlimited power of everyone to sell and to buy, to import and to export products and manufactured articles. No privileged situation can be created under this head; the way remains open without any restrictions to free competition in the domain of commerce, but the obligations of local government do not go beyond that point."

This was the statement of Baron Lambermont, as reporter of the conclusions arrived at by the commission charged to examine the draft of the declaration of the congress; and as such it was signed by the French Ambassador, chairman of the commission. It did not represent the Belgian diplomatist's opinion solely.

At the same sitting of the congress as that at which this report was read, Baron Lambermont, still speaking in his capacity of spokesman or reporter, said: "In these countries, where the organisation is still rudimentary, commerce is carried on exclusively by means of truck. The German delegate has shown consequently how the introduction of import dues suits the actual necessities of commerce." Baron Lambermont went on to explain that in twenty years' time, in the opinion of the German expert, things might be different in the Congo; but twenty years seemed an interminable period to the sages at Berlin, and the congress of 1884 troubled itself in no way about what might happen in 1904.

"Applied to the rising colonies," said M. Descamps in his work on "New Africa," "the measure ignored the fact that similar colonies had practically no other sources of revenue but those which it forbade.

"Adapted to countries whose economic *régime* was in course of formation, and might undergo material changes, the measure does not seem to have been the subject of wise foresight."

In fact, the congress saw in the Congo State neither a rising colony nor a country whose economic *régime* would undergo any material change from the barbarous system of truck dealings which it laid down for it for twenty years. It foresaw no other needs for the State than those of opening up a traffic route by steamers and a short railway on the Congo. For this it made, as it thought, ample provision in the clauses that "wares of whatever origin, imported into these regions under whatsoever flag, by sea or river, or overland, shall be subject to no other tax than such as may be levied as fair compensation for expenditure in the interest of trade, and which, for this reason, must be equally borne by the subjects themselves and by foreigners of all nationalities. All differential duties on vessels, as well as on merchandise, are forbidden."

Every other clause of the Act of Berlin was conceived in the same spirit. These are the regulations which it made for the Congo basin:

Article I.—The trade of all nations shall enjoy complete freedom.

Article II.—All flags, without distinction of nationality, shall have free access.

Article III.—All differential dues on vessels as well as on merchandise are forbidden.

Article IV.—No Power which exercises, or shall exercise, sovereign rights in the above-mentioned regions shall be allowed to grant therein a monopoly or favour of any kind in matters of trade.

The Congress also adopted a provision regarding the neutrality of territories comprised in the conventional basin of the Congo—an admirable provision, but one which recalls the remark of the French Ambassador,

THE CONGRESS OF BERLIN.

the Baron de Courcel, made during the debates on it that "when a nation is at war it uses all its resources." The advance of mankind in twenty years has done nothing to lessen the force of this remark, or, when nations go to war, to cause men to place more reliance on the solemn treaties made in peace than they would on idle, wind-swept scraps of torn paper.

CHAPTER XI.

THE SUPPRESSION OF THE SLAVE TRADE.

THE slave trade, the suppression of which King Leopold set to himself as his first duty on assuming the sovereignty of the Congo, was something much more formidable than any trafficking amongst savage tribes could be. The brutal slave traders whom the King had solemnly pledged himself in the name of humanity to destroy were not ignorant negroes, defenceless against civilised men ; they were Arab traders, skilled in warfare, armed and organised, rich in money and in men, maddened by fanaticism, and flushed by victory over the greatest Powers of Europe. It was not slave traders only ; it was Mahomedanism itself, its powers united in a whelming mass, which King Leopold faced and overthrew in Central Africa.

It was not only as a suppressor of slavery or a spreader of civilisation that King Leopold advanced his standard into Africa. It was as the champion of Christianity that he stood forward, alone amongst nations, to fling back the onrush of conquering Islam. Absolutely alone, he came forward at the moment that the Cross had fallen before the Crescent, and while it was being trampled in the dust with England's honour. It was on January 26th, 1885, that Gordon was murdered at Khartoum by the Mahdists, and it was on the 19th of the following July that Sir Francis de Winton proclaimed the Constitution of the Independent State of the Congo at Banana. It was while Wolseley was retreating, broken and defeated, before the Arabs of the Soudan that King Leopold was laying his plans and forming his forces for the overthrow of the Arabs in the Congo.

THE SUPPRESSION OF THE SLAVE TRADE. 153

King Leopold has never been without loyal and brave men in his service, men who were able administrators and daring soldiers; but fate has willed it so that he never had in his service an able statesman to aid him, the ablest of living statesmen, in his task of erecting a Christian empire in a barbaric land. Once only was he able to call into his counsels a statesman with a mind as clear and as far-seeing as his own. Some years before those disastrous days for England that I write of, he was able to take counsel with Gordon, to receive his advice, and even to obtain the promise of his service for the carrying out of his work in the Congo.

Unfortunately, Gordon had to withdraw his promise to serve King Leopold, who would have upheld him to the sacrifice of the last penny of his private means, in order, at her need, to serve his country, whose rulers deserted him rather than sacrifice the pennies of some taxpayers. But Gordon did not withdraw without reluctance from his promise to serve King Leopold, whose scheme he had searched to the bottom, not without leaving on record his estimation of the King and of his work. Even after this lapse of time the opinion of Charles George Gordon is not one to be overlooked; and looking back on what the King has achieved it is well to remember that he entered on his great undertaking cheered on by the generous enthusiasm and clear-sighted encouragement of that noble and far-seeing Christian soldier. In January, 1884, while he still hoped to serve King Leopold in the Congo, General Gordon wrote to Stanley, " We will, God helping, kill the slave traders in their haunts "; and he added in the same letter : " No such efficacious means of cutting at the root of the slave trade ever was presented as that which God has, I trust, opened out to us through the kind disinterestedness of his Majesty."

Excepting Gordon, there was perhaps no one who at that time formed a correct estimate of the difficulty and the necessity of the work undertaken by King Leopold. If the Governments of Europe had realised the danger which threatened, and from which they were only saved by King Leopold's action in Africa, it is hardly conceivable that they would have left him to face it—as they did from first to last—without the smallest aid from them, and with no other resource than that of his own private fortune. The Arab slave traders who overran the Congo were of the same race as those who triumphantly overran the Soudan, and their aims were the same. They were not raiders merely ; they were the advance guard of Islam, and their intentions were to plant their standard and found a Mahomedan empire in the district which it had pleased the plenipotentiaries at Berlin to map out as the free trade area of the Congo basin. Such an empire had been founded by the Khalifa in the Soudan ; and it is no exaggeration to say that had not King Leopold blocked the way in the Congo and broken the Arab power there, instead of the empire of the Khalifa having at last fallen after such a long struggle with England's forces, it might be still flourishing to-day in all its baneful force, not only in the Soudan, but all over Central Africa, and from Zanzibar in the east to Nigeria on the west.

The work of King Leopold in saving Central Africa from Islam and its slave raiders was one which might well have taxed the powers and added to the lustre of the strongest and most glorious empire. That he achieved it of himself, alone, with his own private means, is a thing forever to be wondered at and forever told of with praise.

Eight years passed before the King was able to strike the decisive blow planned with Gordon in 1884 ; but they were not idle years, nor were they uselessly spent. In them the boundaries of the State were fixed, its territories explored, its government set up, its roadways

TIVE STREET, BASOKO.

NSTRUCTION OF A NATIVE STOREHOUSE, TURUMBU.

THE SUPPRESSION OF THE SLAVE TRADE. 155

extended, its railways planned, and its river navigation arranged. For all that was done there was a constant drain on the treasury of the State, which treasury was nothing else than the King's private purse, and during all these years all the needs of the State were supplied by the King's generous donations.

The posts of the State were gradually extended and strengthened in order to close the country as far as possible against the Arab raiders from without. By the directions of the King strong detachments were sent to form entrenched camps on the great affluents of the Congo for the same purpose. There was still constant danger, however, of incursions by the Soudanese Arabs from the Bahr-el-Gazal country, and the Arabs of Zanzibar were still so powerful in the land that within the wide Kasongo or Manyema districts the Government of the State had no control except such as it obtained by precarious and often illusory alliances with their chieftains, who were in constant communication with Zanzibar.

It is of these Arab chieftains of the Manyema district that Stanley wrote in 1887, when he said, " Half a dozen resolute men, aided by their hundreds of bandits, have divided about three-fourths of the great Upper Congo forest for the sole purpose of murder and of becoming heirs to a few hundred tusks of ivory. They have levelled into black ashes every settlement, every canoe on the river has been split into pieces, every island has been searched ; and into the darkest recesses, wherever a single track could be traced, they have penetrated with only one dominating passion, which was to kill as many of the men and capture as many of the women and children as craft and cruelty would enable them to do." Similar tales of horror were reported from the other African States, which were nominally under English, French, and German rule ; and while King Leopold was still gathering his forces and making his preparations for the final overthrow of the slave raiders in his territories, the world around him woke once again to the realisation of the horrors of the human traffic, and once again resolved to hold a congress to vote that they should be suppressed.

The first move towards a new crusade came from the Church. On May 5th, 1888, Pope Leo XIII. addressed an encyclical to the bishops of Brazil, in which, after dwelling with joy on the fact that a whole empire of the new world had been cleared of slavery, he turned to the consideration of the lamentable condition of Africa, and called upon "those who wield power, those who sway empires, those who desire that the rights of nature and humanity be respected, and those who desire the progress of religion, to unite everywhere for the abolition of this most shameful and most criminal traffic." At the same time the Pope commissioned Cardinal Lavigerie to preach a new crusade against African slavery.

The cardinal journeyed from capital to capital, preaching his great mission; and everywhere he went he met with success. In every country of Europe societies were formed to aid in the work he advocated. The Belgian Anti-Slavery Society was the first of these to be formed, and the one which did the most valuable service. This society sent out two expeditions, which took a noble and a useful part in the war which crushed the Arab slave raiders. While Cardinal Lavigerie was preaching his crusade, the Governments of Europe were arranging for their congress. England and Germany were both sufferers in their territories at least as greatly as the Congo State from the slave raiders, and great public meetings were held in each country to call for the suppression of slave hunting. This time the suggestion for the summoning of a conference came from England. It was recognised as fitting that the formal initiative should come from King Leopold, the sovereign

THE SUPPRESSION OF THE SLAVE TRADE.

to whom all that was done for the civilisation of Central Africa was due; and he was accordingly invited by England to summon the congress. "The change which has occurred in the political condition of the African coast," said the English Minister at Brussels, addressing the Belgian Cabinet, "calls to-day for common action on the part of the Powers responsible for the control of that coast. That action should tend to close all foreign slave markets, and should also result in putting down slave hunting in the interior.

"The great work undertaken by the King of the Belgians in the constitution of the Congo State, and the lively interest taken by his Majesty in all questions affecting the welfare of the African races, lead her Majesty's Government to hope that Belgium will be disposed to take the initiative in inviting the Powers to meet in conference at Brussels in order to consider the best means of attaining the gradual suppression of the slave trade on the Continent of Africa, and the immediate closing of all the outside markets which the slave trade continues to supply."

Acting on this suggestion, King Leopold summoned the Congress, which met in Brussels on November 18th, 1889, to decide upon a course of action calculated to "put an end to the crimes and devastation wrought by the African slave trade, and to protect effectively the native populations of Africa."

The measures taken at this congress are summed up by Baron Descamps in his work on "New Africa" as follows: "The Brussels General Act attacks the slave trade in the stronghold of the man-hunters, follows it on the caravan routes, on the coast, by sea, where the action of the cruisers is called in, and finally to the countries of destination, the great Oriental slave markets. At each of these stages the Act prescribes repressive, protective, and liberating measures, in accordance with the end in view. The various Governments are appealed to with a view of effective and uniform penal laws being passed. The regulation or restriction of the trade in spirits and firearms is also provided for, permanent institutions are appointed in Europe and Africa to help in carrying out the provisions of the Act, and financial measures were agreed upon to facilitate the new task."

These were certainly a most admirable set of resolutions. They served at least the purpose of placing the fact undeniably before every Power that the means of remedying the evil which all the world deplored lay ready to its hand. They served also to strengthen the hand of the ruler who had hitherto been fighting alone against the slave raiders in the Congo by cancelling the unwise agreement against import dues entered into at the Congress of Berlin, which had had the effect of restricting King Leopold's measures for the advancement of the Congo State and its natives to those the expenses of which he was able to pay out of his private means. It is to the clause on this subject that M. Descamps refers when he alludes to the financial measures of the Congress of Brussels. He refers again, at greater length, to these financial measures in the same chapter of his work as that I have already quoted, defining the new agreement regarding import dues as " the permission to levy moderate import duties, exclusive of any differential *régime*. These duties were to be uniform throughout the Congo, and could not exceed a maximum of ten per cent. of the value of the imported goods."

The passing of these measures gave the diplomatists assembled at the congress a fresh opportunity of bearing testimony in the names of their respective Governments to the admirable results of King Leopold's labour. Of them Lord Vivian, the English Minister, spoke in these words :

" As to the question whether this modification is opportune, the fact must not be lost sight of that the

THE SUPPRESSION OF THE SLAVE TRADE. 159

Berlin Conference never intended to fix unalterably the economic system of the Free State which, as was already then foreseen, would undergo radical modifications under the influence of progress, nor of establishing for an indefinite period regulations which may hinder, check, and even arrest its development. Provision was wisely made for the probability of future changes, which would require a certain latitude in economic matters in order to secure their easy realisation. . . .

"The moment has now come when the marvellous progress made by the infant State is creating fresh needs, when it would be only in accordance with wisdom and foresight to revise an economic system primarily adapted to a creative and transitional period.

"Can we blame the infant State for a progress which by its rapidity has surpassed the most optimistic forecasts? Can we hinder and arrest this progress in refusing her the means necessary for her development? Can we condemn the sovereign who has already made such great sacrifices to support for an indefinite period a burthen which daily becomes heavier, and at the same time impose upon him new and heavy expenses necessitated by the suppression of the slave trade?

"We are convinced there will be but one answer to these questions."

This speech of the English Minister was followed by a chorus of similar praise from his colleagues. The matter to which it referred, the agreement to consent to the imposing of import dues in the Congo State, was of much importance at the moment, as it gave a guarantee that there would be a means of recovering some of the expenses of the war with the Arabs, which all knew to be coming, from the foreign traders, who could not but profit materially by the improvement of the country, and thus enabled the Belgian Government to agree readily to a loan to the Congo State of twenty-five million francs. Five million francs of this loan, being advanced at once, formed, when added to the sums given to the State by the King, a sufficient fund to carry the war to a successful conclusion.

In the meantime, while the diplomatists were drawing up their admirable sets of rules in Europe for the restraint of the Arabs in Africa, the Arabs themselves were massing their forces on the Congo to raise again the standard of Islam and sweep the detested infidels off the face of the earth. They had not really the least intention of submitting to the dominion of any Christian ruler, much less of abandoning their slave raiding at the dictates of any body of men gathered together in some distant land oversea. Their chiefs had accepted service under the sovereign of the Congo only to gain time, and with the intention of breaking their trust at the first favourable moment. They accordingly took care to select a time for their rising while the forces of the State were still unprepared for war. They had opposed the advance and the entrenchments of the forces of the State at every possible point; but until the moment they deemed the most opportune arrived there were always Arab chiefs who protested their fidelity to the Government, and their general rising, when it came, was commenced by the treacherous murder of M. Hodister and the members of his trading expedition who had trusted them.

This was in May, 1892. The Arabs' next move was to murder Emin Pasha, " who was at that time," says Dr. Hinde in his account of " The Fall of the Congo Arabs," " a harmless traveller through their country, and under the protection of a powerful Arab chief." Lastly, they organised a large army and attacked the expedition to which Dr. Hinde was attached, and which was led by Commandant Dhanis, whose military genius, added to his own and his officers' bravery, enabled him to bring the war to a speedy conclusion.

" Realising," says Dr. Hinde, " what was at stake,

OF ARAB MOSQUE, ISANGI.

NATIVE DWELLING, BAFUMU.

IMPROVED NATIVE DWELLING, BAFUMU.

and fully recognising the gravity of the position, the Mahomedans fought to the bitter end, returning again and again to the attack, even when there was no hope of success. An almost incredibly large loss of life was the result. To the casual reader, unfamiliar with African history, this might on the surface appear to have been a curious little war, with a dozen white officers and four hundred regular black troops on the one side, and a couple of hundred Arab chiefs supported by a few hundred half-bred Arabs, and commanding large numbers of irregular soldiery, on the other. But it must be borne in mind that, unlike the Soudan struggle, this war took place in a thickly-populated country, whose whole population, used to savage warfare, took part in the fighting, and that large bodies of men were constantly changing sides as the prestige of one or other party increased or diminished. As the Arabs were driven back towards Tanganyika, they succeeded in enrolling all the fighting men of fresh tribes under their banners. This was the easier since for thirty years they had been the sole power; Europeans were also unknown, and the credulous natives readily believed the tales spread among them by the Arabs of European cruelties to their subordinates. Though large, our losses and those of our allies, the Arab loss was immensely greater; it is, in fact, estimated at seventy thousand men."

Even with such a great loss of life, and the large expenditure of money which it had entailed on the King during all the tedious years of preparation for it, this war was well worth all it cost, since it rescued Central Africa from Islam, suppressed the slave trade in the Congo for ever, and left King Leopold, one great task accomplished, free to face the other and still mightier one he had set himself—of civilising the negro.

CHAPTER XII.

THE CONGO LAW AND THE NATIVE'S FUTURE.

NOTHING is more clear to the student of the history of Africa than the definite purpose which animated all King Leopold's legislation from the commencement of his rule over the Congo through all the changing years to the present moment. That purpose has ever been to secure the prosperity of the wide realm of the Congo and of its inhabitants. It is clearly shown and clearly observed in every decree the sovereign of the Congo has made. All that has been done in the Congo rests on the King's sole authority. In accepting the sovereignty of the Independent State King Leopold faced the greatest problem and undertook the weightiest responsibility of our age, but he faced it unfettered. The diplomatists who sat at the Congress of Berlin seem to have looked to no more than the interests of foreign traders and, in a somewhat vague way, the protection against slavery of the native races of Africa. It is well for mankind that the sovereign of the Congo looked farther, and that his views were wise.

King Leopold undertook to protect the native races from the raids of slave traders, and he undertook to free them from slavery; he undertook to open up Equatorial Africa to trade, and to establish a settled government in it; but these undertakings, great though they were, were but the least part of his task. Besides them, he had to regulate his government so that trade and industry would flourish profitably in the land in the future, and he had to educate and to civilise the negroes. Politicians and pamphleteers who deal only with the present moment are apt to overlook these, the main, points of King Leopold's great undertaking;

CONGO LAW AND THE NATIVE'S FUTURE. 163

but it is with regard to them, and not to any passing need, that King Leopold's rule in Africa and his legislation for the Congo must be judged.

The regulations regarding equality of trading rights in the Act of Berlin do little more than show that the Governments responsible for the drawing up of that Act were aware of the tendencies of the time, and wished to prevent the dangers which threatened Africa in common with every other part of the world in which men lived and gained their sustenance. Men who thought themselves far-seeing statesmen still believed twenty years ago in the doctrines of Cobden and Bright. Free Trade was not the basis of these doctrines, though its theory was an outcome of them. Their basis was founded on the belief that the supremacy of the middle class would last, and that with it middle-class views regarding a fair average would prevail, that reason would restrain excess, and that moderation would everywhere regulate man's dealing with his fellow man.

To the diplomatists at Berlin in 1884 it seemed an easy thing to regulate the trade of Central Africa by some general rules; but since those days much has been learned, and the belief that mankind, pushing onward ever more feverishly, will be content to pause at any average, however just the reason which suggests it, has passed away. With it the last vestige of middle-class supremacy has passed, or is passing, for ever.

It is clear to every thinker that the struggle of the future lies—as far as the great industries are concerned—between individuals, overwhelmingly strong in purpose and financial resource, fighting singly or united in trusts, on the one hand, and the State on the other. Open markets are the merest fallacies unless every producer has exactly equal means of bringing his goods to them and every purchaser exactly equal means of conveying away his purchases. The example of the United States has proved this. Laws are made and strengthened, and trade unions become stronger every day; but every day's example shows more clearly that in great industries, such as those of coal mining and oil mining, neither trade unions by themselves, nor the law by half measures, can cope with the growing power of the trust organisers. It is toward trusts that unchecked industry is tending in every country. Industry was tending in the same direction twenty years ago, but its tendency was not then unmistakable; and at that time, to all but those with the clearest sight, monopoly seemed still a thing which could be fended off by a few partial laws and general regulations. Now, however, with the changes in industrial affairs marked as clearly as they are, those who talk about monopoly in great industries or in production as an evil to be checked by law do no more than exhibit their own blindness to facts, and their gross incompetence to act as judges, guides, or advisers.

The supremacy of the middle class—in which the middle class itself believed so strongly half way through the last century—was never fully established, and its disappearance marks no advent of socialism, as the wilder spirits amongst the people thought it would. It marks, however, as beyond all doubt the fact that men will in the future submit neither to half measures nor to exploitation.

The wild dreams of socialism are as far from realisation as the over-cautious ideas of the middle-class thinkers of the Manchester school. Commerce on its great lines and trade will remain free for the individual, and be made even more really free in the future than it has been in the past; but, that man's intercourse and commerce may be made free in reality, the State will take into its own hands, more and more absolutely, by land legislation, the control of the great producing industries and the means of conveyance. The well-being of the labouring classes demands that this must come to pass, and, perhaps, to-day, when the Trust peril looms so great, I may seem to labour the point unnecessarily; but I am writing of an epoch which began twenty years ago, when, to judge by the surest of guides—the statute books—the sovereign of the Congo was the only lawgiver who saw the tendencies and the needs of the world, and made wise laws to meet them. Moreover, I am treating of a country with regard to which disappointed financiers—themselves potential Rockefellers, Carnegies, and Morgans—try, by confusing trade with production and property, to make it appear that King Leopold has created trade monopolies in violation of his international engagements, whereas the prudent foresight of the King, by the wise laws he made, was the only thing which saved the Congo from becoming a monopoly-ridden land, and saved its rubber forests from the fate of the diamond mines of the Transvaal and the coalfields of America.

On August 1st, 1885, King Leopold addressed a letter to each of the Powers notifying the fact that, with the consent of the Belgian legislature, he had assumed the sovereignty of the Independent State of the Congo. An announcement to that effect was also published in the first number of the *Bulletin Officiel de l'État Indépendant du Congo*, the official gazette of the State, the regular publication of which has been continued uninterruptedly since then. Nothing can give a better idea of the earnestness and the wisdom which were brought to the building up of the Congo State than a study of King Leopold's decrees published in the successive numbers of this *Bulletin*. The main events in the history of the Congo are well known— the foundation of the chief posts of the Government; the explorations throughout the million square miles of its territory, by which the blanks on the map were filled in; the wars against the Arab slave raiders, as a result of which the cursed slave trade was suppressed—

but of the steady work of legislation and government which was carried on without intermission through all the years since 1885, burthened though they were by these other weighty deeds, little, indeed, is known outside of the Congo or of Belgium.

In his legislation regarding land in the Congo and its tenure by the natives King Leopold wisely followed the most successful example of English legislation for a similar colony. For his laws for white men he followed the main lines of the Code Napoléon, which is in force in Belgium; but he did not take his Congo laws cut and dried from any model in any instance. The code he has enacted for the Congo was made for the Congo; it has grown with the advance of years as necessities were foreseen or made themselves felt. As it stands, it forms a noble body of laws, backward in no one particular, and in several of their provisions far advanced before the laws of European States. Had the laws been all enacted on a single day, and due to the commissioned pen of some amiable legal Utopian, this would not have been wonderful; but then the Congo laws would have been unworkable without a doubt. As it is, each decree bearing King Leopold's signature is the direct emanation of the King's brain. It is noteworthy that in them there is nothing base. Man's freedom, whatever his colour—freedom of life, of speech, of religion—is guaranteed by them; the Congo law permits no slavery. The rights of property are respected by them, as are those of native customs. The law of the Congo is good where it is liberal, good where it is repressive (as in its clauses against the introduction of drink and firearms); and it is not least good in the clauses in which it reserves for the State the property in unoccupied lands, and safeguards the country from money grubbers.

King Leopold's policy would be a much easier one than it is towards the natives if it had been a policy for their protection only. Had he been content to let them lie in idleness and ignorance he would have saved himself a world of trouble ; but it can hardly be supposed that King Leopold planted his flag in Central Africa in order to save himself trouble. His aim in Africa has ever been what he avowed it to be—to civilise the land and its native races, and to colonise it with the aid of Belgians. To civilise the negroes it is necessary to educate them, and their education can only be effected by leading them into the paths of profitable labour. It was to this end—to civilise, not to oppress them— that laws entailing the necessity of labour upon the native races were introduced into the Congo State at the same time as slavery was forbidden by law in that State.

The enactment of such laws is not a thing which needs defence. That the coming of the white man, if it had not brought labour in its train, would have led the negro into unspeakable depravity instead of to civilisation, into crimes and debauchery so foul that the brutalities of savages would seem virtues beside them, is a thing which the example of history has made certain beyond the possibility of doubt.* King Leopold

* The United States, where the negro has lived for long generations in civilisation, finds the problem of the blacks more menacing every day, and realises every day more clearly that its only solution is to be found in education and labour. In an address delivered by President Charles W. Eliot in New York on February 12th, 1904, he expressed the whole public opinion of the States when he said : " There is no larger or graver problem before civilised man at this moment than the prompt formation of a sound public opinion about the right treatment of backward races ; and Hampton possesses the key-words of that great problem—education and productive labour. . . . Moreover, the Northern people are having at home abundant illustration of the way crimes increase when portions of the population have emancipated themselves from accustomed restraints, but have not yet been provided with any new effective restraints either from within or from without. In this respect they are prepared to sympathise warmly with their Southern brethren, whose situation is even more difficult than their own. Both parts of the country are feeling acutely the same need—the need of a stronger arm for the law, of a permanent, large, and pervasive police force, organised in military

did no more, then, than discharge a manifest and urgent duty in laying down laws which made labour necessary to the blacks.

In common with all the Congo laws, these laws have been wisely and humanely made, and instead of being over-burthensome upon the negroes or restrictive of their individual liberty, the only fault which can be found with them by those whose sympathies are with the negro races, and who seek their most speedy civilisation, is that they are not sufficiently stringent, that they give too much choice to the various negro communities of who shall labour and who shall not, and leave the negroes too free to fix themselves the extent and mode of each labourer's task, instead of forcing each one to fulfil a certain State-allotted task. Labour for the State is the duty of every civilised man—a duty which every man performs perforce in civilised States, but one from which no sane man dreams of escaping. Taxes, whether they be paid in cash or in kind, represent forced labour for the State. Army service, which the most free States exact from their citizens, is forced labour, pure and simple; but soldiers are not slaves, nor are the natives, who, possessing no unearned increment in any savage land, toil laboriously with picks that they may earn the money to pay hut-taxes in cash, or cut trees that they may pay rubber-taxes in kind. The arguments which liken to slavery the labour of men, black or white, for the State, are arguments which those take note of only who study the chatterings of imbecility.

What is slavery is written too clearly on the page

fashion and provided with all the best means for instantaneous communication between stations. The presence of a competent public force would tend to prevent those sudden gregarious panics which cause lawless barbarities. . . Finally, let us all remember that the task of making competent freemen out of slaves is not the work of a day or of a decade, but of many generations. How many Anglo-Saxon generations have gone to dust on the long road from serfdom to freedom!"

CONGO LAW AND THE NATIVE'S FUTURE. 169

of history; its dreadful horror is too real in the mind of every thinking man to make it possible to confuse by any means that which is slavery with that which is not slavery. It would be as possible to confuse night with day because the day is sometimes dark. Wise men use no misnomers, and weak men use them only when they seek by desperate means to disguise the weakness of the cause they plead. If the native labour for the State in the Congo was a brutal thing, it would have been enough for those who denounced it to have said so. Its denunciators, in giving it a claptrap title, brand themselves in the minds of intelligent men as agitators trading on false sympathy, and by their exaggeration itself they induce the belief which investigation proves to be true—that the Congo laws of labour, which cannot be slave laws, are not brutal or even harsh in the slightest degree.

Under the name of labour laws there may be joined the laws regarding civil labour and those of army service. Service in the army, where much besides drill is taught, is, perhaps, the quickest means of instilling the rudiments of civilisation into savages. It is proved by many examples in the Congo that one time-served soldier returning to his native village, introduces into every home in it something lasting of the benefits of civilisation. Even amongst civilised men those who most detest militarism recognise the benefits which spring from the military habits of obedience, promptness, discipline, and cleanliness. Such benefits are incalculable to savages; and it is a matter of regret that the army is as yet so very small in comparison with the number of the population—a matter of regret, that is, to all those who think intelligently and have the welfare of the native races at heart. At present the number of recruits levied for the Congo army every year amounts only to one out of each ten thousand of the population. Small, however, as this number is, it would fall away to nothing if all the volunteers who presented themselves to join the army were enrolled, and if the King, true to his policy that the influence of his civilising government should be extended as widely as possible, did not decree that recruiting should be continued over the most widespread area, and men levied from as many different tribes as possible. At the same time preference is given to native volunteers when they come from many different districts and their enlistment does not threaten to confine army service to the natives of any single or restricted locality. Service in the army becomes more popular, naturally, as the natives become better acquainted with the advantages which appertain to it, and the number of volunteers increased steadily: in 1902, 4,917 offered themselves for service; in 1903, 5,278; in 1904, 5,860; the recruits raised by levies on native tribes numbering 9,684 in the last year.

Until 1887 the Congo army was mainly composed of foreign soldiers. In 1887 the formation of the national army began. At first it was largely composed of natives freed from slavery, the rescued victims of slave raiders, who could not be repatriated because they did not know the situation of the distant homes from which the raiders had dragged them, or who did not wish to return to their homes. After some years of organisation the definite formation of the army was fixed, and on July 30th, 1891, the decree regulating the recruiting of the Public Force was published, which holds good to-day. By this law the Governor-General is required to regulate the annual levies, to fix the districts where the levies will take place, the proportion to be furnished by each district, and the localities in each district from which the men are to be drawn.

The decree fixes the term of each soldier's service as seven years with the colours, at the termination of which time the soldier is placed in the reserve for a further term of five years, unless he prefers to re-enlist in the active service for a new term of three years, at the end of which further term he is relieved from the obligation of any service in the reserve and fully discharged. The length of the service of the volunteers is determined by the contracts they make on enlistment, as is the special amount of their pay. The soldiers other than volunteers receive as pay twenty-one centimes a day, a sum increased on re-enlistment to twenty-five centimes a day for those re-enlisting for their second term, and to fifty centimes a day for those re-enlisting for their third term. In addition to this pay all soldiers, volunteers and others, receive a monthly allowance of one franc twenty-five centimes deferred pay, the total amount of which is paid to him on discharge, but which can be withheld from him as punishment for a grave offence.

Freedom of religion is one of the fundamental clauses of the Congo law, and no one has ever pretended that the law which permits it has ever been violated there; but the sovereign of the Congo does not forget that he is a Christian prince, and he, alone of all the European rulers in Africa, permits his Government there to have no truckling with Mahomedanism.

No Belgian writer calling himself a Christian has ever dared to contend that the laws of Christianity should not apply to the negro races of Africa, and no "Director of Mahomedan Education" has ever been appointed in the territories over which King Leopold rules. The civilisation taught in the Congo is Christian civilisation, and the soldiers of the Congo State, taught by Christian missionaries, are encouraged to obey the Christian law. Marriage is encouraged everywhere throughout the Congo by the officials of the State, and special privileges are given to married soldiers. Married soldiers are lodged apart; their legitimate wives receive salaries from the State, and daily rations are given to them and to their children. The soldiers

—who are all young men, it must be remembered—receive technical as well as moral education; and it is through them and the children educated in the infant colonies of the State that the lessons of civilisation are beginning to spread over the wide region of the Congo territories and to take root in the dark forests of Equatorial Africa.

The labour of civilising more than twenty millions of savages scattered over more than a million of square miles is not one which can be accomplished in the lifetime of any man; but it stands eternally to King Leopold's credit that he has commenced it, that he forwards it on the right lines, and that he has enacted laws, the continued observance of which will ensure the glorious achievement of the great work he has commenced.

The laws regarding labour are another step towards the civilisation of the negroes. Amongst all the senseless statements which are repeated about Africa there is none more senseless, and none more often repeated, than that which says the blacks are idle. Blacks are human beings—surely it is late in the day to have to say so—and black nature is the same as white nature. It is not in the nature of man to rest idle; but men in a low state of development, living in an abundant land where little labour produces great results, find vent, inevitably, for their unrestrained energies in the fierce excitement of battling with their kind. Long ages, or strong hands, are needed to turn races to the paths of peace; the missionary succeeds, but he succeeds only where he understands and fulfils his mission, and, Heaven inspired, teaches the savage to labour and to pray.

In the Congo the administrator is working side by side with the missionary, and each prepares the field for the other. King Leopold's duty as a civiliser in the Congo was, in the first place, to provide work for the natives other than that of cutting each other's throats from the mere joy of fighting or the foul desires of cannibalism. That work he provided in part in the army service, and it must be noted that work in the ranks of a disciplined army, commanded by civilised men, curbs and quells the brutal instincts of the savage, to which it panders in no way.

For the great mass of the population King Leopold found work by providing that the natives should pay their taxes in kind by the collection of rubber for the State. The day, it may be believed with reason, is not distant when the Government, continuing its civilising work, will have educated the races living under its rule sufficiently to employ them at higher tasks; but at present the native races are fitted for none higher, and the lesson of regular work, apart from mutual strife, is the first great lesson the savage must learn. When he has learned it he is no longer wholly a savage; and he is learning it in the Congo. The means used for teaching him are of secondary importance; but there is some reason for rejoicing in the fact that the conditions of the Congo State are such that he can be made to work beneath the sky, gathering rubber, a useful product, and not delving in hateful mines for useless gold.

Whatever the conditions of the labour, the native as yet uncivilised cannot be expected to embrace the necessity of continued work with joy unalloyed, and beyond doubt there must be natives who hide themselves or fly to live more savage and congenial lives; but a study of the laws laid down by King Leopold reveals the fact that all that can be done by wisdom to make them content to labour has been done. The labour of rubber collecting is exacted as a tax, but at the same time it is paid for. The King's decrees are explicit on this point. A report of the Government, dated July 15th, 1900, which treats of this subject, is of sufficient importance to be quoted. It says:

"The object the Government aims at is to succeed in turning the private domain of the State to profit, exclusively by means of voluntary contributions from the natives, in inducing them to work by the sole allurement of a just and adequate remuneration. The rate for this must be necessarily sufficiently high to stimulate a desire in the natives to obtain the remuneration and consequently to lead them to gather the products of the domain. It is this kind of collecting for profit which is in force at the present moment in many districts.

"Where the attraction of commercial gain is not sufficient to assure the working of the private domain it is indispensable to the tax in kind ; but it must be noted that even in this case the work is remunerated in the same manner as the voluntary contributions. The instructions of the Government are positive on this point. The tax in kind, such as established, is not, then, properly speaking, a tax, since the local value of the products brought in by the natives is given to them in exchange.

"The Government has never lost an opportunity of reminding its agents entrusted with the collection of the taxes in kind that their *rôle* is that of an educator, their mission that of inculcating the taste for work into the natives, and that the means employed would fail in their aim if constraint became violence."

The taxes in kind are collected by the State officials. It is, of course, impossible to fix any hard and fast rule for so immense a country of the exact amount of produce which each taxpayer must bring in ; and in the early days, when the State officials were in part paid in proportion to the taxes they gathered, natives must have suffered beneath their exacting pressure. Such pressure was, however, at all times contrary to the law and—the higher responsible officials protest in their reports—to their instructions ; and it is declared

CONGO LAW AND THE NATIVE'S FUTURE. 175

that in no instance was there a case of extortion or cruelty told of which was not sifted to the bottom, or one in which wrongdoing was proved where fit punishment was not meted out to the offender.

The danger of cruelty in the collection of the tax by the officials passed when the Government abolished the system of payment by results, as it did several years ago, and none, except those who prefer idle to industrious natives, can take exception to the instructions of the Government issued for the guidance of its officials, which Baron Descamps, a Ministre d'État of the Congo, states in his work on " New Africa " to be that " the quantity of products to be delivered up ought not to exceed that which may be produced by one-third of the male adult population, and even then this result must be arrived at progressively." Indeed, if the further statement with regard to the tax, made in " The Native Problem " by Alexander Davis, is correct—that " the tax is so organised that when properly imposed no native need devote more than forty hours a month to this duty, and in some districts twelve hours is found sufficient for the purpose "—those who hope for the speedy civilisation of the natives by labour will be more inclined to complain of laxity than to cry out at cruelty.

The taxes in kind are imposed throughout the private domains of the State, and the consideration of the law regarding these domains must be taken in connection with the question of the law regarding the native races.

King Leopold, from the commencement of his African enterprise, regarded Africa as a land for the Africans. His earliest project was to form in the district of the Congo a federation of native states. That appeared at the time to be impossible, but King Leopold is not a ruler whose aims are bounded by the possibilities of the moment, and there is much in his African policy to show that it is intended to lead in time to the fulfilment of this noble project. Men forget now that twenty years ago they called King Leopold a dreamer; yet they were right in calling him one then, and they would be right in calling him one now, for a dreamer he has ever been. Moreover, his dreams are always wise ones—dreams of far-seeing statesmanship, which may come true if only the wise plans he builds from them are not destroyed by meaner men.

The first step towards preserving Central Africa for its natives was taken in the same month as that in which King Leopold assumed the sovereignty of the Congo, when an ordinance was issued by the Governor-General of the Independent State—Sir Francis de Winton—the second article of which prescribed that "no one has a right to occupy without title any vacant land or to dispossess the natives of the lands which they occupy; the vacant land must be considered as belonging to the State." This ordinance was published in the second number of the *Bulletin Officiel*, issued in the same year. It was not only the right, but also the duty, of the sovereign to make such a regulation. No man needs to be told what would have become of the land of the Congo and of the native races who inhabited it when the discovery was made that possessions in the Congo were valuable if such a provision had not existed. The savage tribes who inhabited these lands held no possession of them, either as property was considered by the natives or understood by civilised men. These tribes made no real attempts at the reclamation of the land from its virgin wildness or at settled habitation.

This history of the Congo tribes, as far as it can be traced, is a history of a long series of migrations—wanderings into the unknown, undertaken because food was scanty or strangers to fight with were sought. Their idea of tribal boundaries was of the vaguest, their respect of them absolutely wanting, and such a thing as the right to property in land was non-existent amongst

CONGO LAW AND THE NATIVE'S FUTURE. 177

them. The most they possessed were certain rights of bonitary occupation and customary cultivation, which rights the sovereign secured to them in his decrees and orders.

The unoccupied lands which formed the greater part of King Leopold's savage African realm having been preserved to the State by the ordinance I have quoted, the King's next measure with regard to it was to secure its fruits to the State. The African savages who toil to collect rubber in the private domain of the State cannot be expected to realise in the present stage of their development that they are labouring for their country's gain alone, for that of themselves and of their descendants; but such is the fact.

From the commencement of the work in Africa until long after the formation of the independent State, King Leopold continued to intervene regularly in the expenses of the administration, and the budgets from 1890 to 1900 show that he paid annually a subsidy of one million to the State. The whole of this great sum has been presented to the State of the Congo by King Leopold. The King has distinctly renounced every claim on the State which the advance of money to it in his private capacity gave him, and as a private person he neither retains, nor has acquired, the least interest, either directly or indirectly, in the monetary affairs of the Congo State or those of any company, commercial enterprise, or undertaking whatever which is in any way connected with the Congo. On the other hand, King Leopold, by his legislation and his policy, has secured to the State, both in the present and for the future, the full products of the greatest and the richest industry within its territories—the rubber industry.

In waiving his personal claims for the repayment of the millions advanced by him to the State, King Leopold gave proof of unexampled benevolence; in his legislation regarding the private domain he did more—he practised in it a wise statesmanship far in advance of his time, and as a result founded in the Congo the system to which the Government of every civilised land must adhere eventually in the defence of its people from the exploitation of capitalists; but to which it must be feared the Governments of other lands, less sagely and less strongly ruled than the Congo, can only come after long periods of strife and suffering amongst their unhappy peoples. The law and the practice of the Independent State of the Congo regarding land and its products is the first great move of any State towards the system of the State control of the great producing industries of which I have written earlier in this chapter; it is the herald and the promise-bearer of the more prosperous and the saner times to come, and the credit for it is due in its entirety to King Leopold, the sovereign ruler of the State.

In legislating thus for the future, King Leopold took care to protect every immediate right of the native races. The decree which was signed on October 30th, 1892, for the exploitation of the rubber on the lands of the private domain by the State was not made until it had been proved by a careful legal inquiry that the natives had never collected rubber themselves, and therefore had no shadow of a prescriptive right to its uncontrolled collection. The rights of occupancy on the part of the natives, on whatever lands they were located, were upheld in the order of July, 1885, which laid down that "no one has the right to dispossess the natives of the lands which they occupy." This was followed in September, 1886, by a no less important decree, which stated that "the lands occupied by native populations under the authority of their chiefs shall continue to be governed by local customs and uses." This decree of September, 1886, made further provisions for the continuance of the natives on their lands without disturbance. It enacted that there "are forbidden all acts or conventions which would tend to expel the natives from the lands that they occupy, or to deprive them directly or indirectly of their liberty or of their means of existence"; and on April 9th, 1893, it was still further decreed " when native villages are surrounded by alienated or leased lands, the natives shall be able, as soon as the official measurement has been effected, to extend their cultivation without the consent of the proprietor or the lessee over the vacant lands which surround their villages."

There seems to be no law which the wit of man could devise to bring the savages of Africa within the influence and the control of civilisation, and to protect their lives, their liberties, their means of livelihood, and their native customs which King Leopold has not decreed for the Independent State. I have shown how the King provided laws for the protection of the natives and for bringing them under the bounds of labour, the only true instructor of civilisation, and how he provided laws for the preservation of the land and the products of the land by the State. I have now to show how King Leopold has made provision for the inclusion of the negroes in the government of the State.

To make civilised administrators of barbarous savages must be a slow work and a difficult one which few would care to undertake. It is another proof of the King's unaltered purpose of making his African State a land in which all the inhabitants, black and white, shall ultimately be civilised and equal, that he has even now commenced to place governing power in the hands of the most intelligent native chiefs, and provided for the admission of all civilised natives to citizenship and the exercise of all civil rights on a perfect equality with their white fellows. The authority entrusted to the native chiefs is naturally that over their kinsmen and fellow tribesmen. The constitution of officially recognised native chieftaincies was decreed in October,

1891. This decree provides that "In certain given regions, determined by the Governor-General, the native chieftaincies will be acknowledged as such, provided the chiefs have been confirmed in the authority attributed to them by custom by the Governor-General, or in his name."

The chiefs so recognised are solemnly invested and given certificates and insignia of their office. They are placed under the authority of the district commissioners, and it is decreed that they shall exercise their authority according to usage and custom, provided it is not contrary to public order and is in accordance with the laws of the State. These chiefs are held responsible for their tribes' supply of public labour, as notified to them annually. There are at present two hundred and fifty-eight of these native chiefs exercising the power delegated to them by the State.

The admission of all civilised natives to the full rights of citizenship was an equally important and significant measure. This admission is granted in virtue of the Sixth Article of the Civil Code, which is as follows : "Shall enjoy all civil rights: (1) Individuals who have obtained naturalisation ; (2) Natives, whose birth or acknowledgment has been duly registered in the books of the État Civil, who have recourse to the officers of the État Civil for the registration of their marriages, and those who have obtained their matriculation by public authority on the registers of the civilised population." Truly a wider or more wisely thought-out scheme for the protection and the civilisation of Africa could not be devised than that built up in King Leopold's code of laws.

CHAPTER XIII.

THE CONGO MISSIONS.

THE crowning part of all King Leopold's work in Africa must be sought for, and will be found, in the history of the Congo Missions. There never was a promise more fully or more conscientiously performed than that which King Leopold made to spread Christianity in the Congo State. This was no promise exacted from him by a congress. At the Congress of Berlin, where political considerations outweighed all others, the representative of the Sultan of Turkey insisted forcibly on the rights of Islam, and the equal protection for the "religious enterprises" of every cult and nationality which he demanded was made binding on each Power exercising sovereign rights over the Congo area by the Sixth Article of the Act of Berlin—the article relating to the protection of missionaries and religious liberty.

To the word "protection," as used in this clause, the plenipotentiaries at Berlin attached the most definite and the most narrow meaning, it being laid down in the protocol of their second sitting that "the principle of the separation of Church and State, applied by certain Governments, well allows them to profess themselves ready *to protect*, but not *to aid*, the religious enterprises which are of the province of the Church only." The various conferences and public meetings which were held in Belgium and in the other countries of Europe in the early days of the Congo movement were equally silent on the point of religion. Few men amongst those of mediocre abilities who aspired to seem philosophic dared in the latter half of the last century to parade their religious beliefs; and at the congresses, conferences, and meetings philanthropy, vaguely indicated, as a general object, with the suppression of the slave trade as a particular aim, was the most the speakers and the resolutions treated of.

The sovereign of the Congo, then, in establishing his rule over that country, would have acted entirely within his right if he had ignored all considerations of religion and trusted the civilisation of the negroes to the working of the civil Government alone. It might be too much to say that those who posed in Europe then—as they do now—as the chief friends of the natives, hoped that this was what King Leopold would do; but it is certain that it is what they believed he would do. At the most what was looked for from him was toleration of the unofficial efforts of missionaries— "protection, but not assistance," as laid down at the Congress of Berlin—and an insistence on the clause of the Act of Berlin which provided for "the freedom of conscience."

It cannot be supposed that there were any so densely blinded by their desire that the native Africans should enjoy freedom of conscience as to expect that they would be allowed to remain sunk in the barbarous beliefs and practices of Fetishism; but there was an openly expressed desire that they should be led towards the Mahomedan religion, as more adaptable to the wants of the African nature, than to Christianity. Nearly every English writer who wrote on the subject with knowledge and authority expressed this desire more or less openly, or said much which caused its being held, from "the eminent Dr. Blyden," who asserted that "Islam is the form Christianity takes in Africa," to Miss Kingsley, who wrote that Christianity would not give the solution of the African question, and declared, as her last words, that she failed to believe that "Christianity will bring peace between the two races."

Viewing the failure of missionary work in South Africa, where, as is pointed out by Alexander Davis in his work on the native problem, "After a century of mission work, assisted throughout by the support of the various Governments and facilitated by the religious tendency so marked in the early Dutch, Huguenot, and British settlers, it may not be said that even in the earliest inhabited portion of South Africa the natives in the mass have been converted," Englishmen may perhaps be pardoned for looking on the conversion of the black races as a practically hopeless task, one to be abandoned to amiable faddists and isolated missionaries, and, for the same reason, the English Government may perhaps be held justified for its official encouragement to Mahomedan education in West Africa and Sierra Leone; but Christians of no country can deny to King Leopold the praise which is his due for resolving, undaunted by others' failures, that by him there should be introduced the Christian religion into his African State, and that through his means the natives of the Congo should be converted to Christianity.

That King Leopold made such a resolve, and that he has acted on it and is acting on it, is a matter proved beyond possibility of doubt by the testimony of the missionaries of each Christian sect in the Congo. Nothing could be more emphatic on this point than the words of Monsignor van Ronslé, the Vicar Apostolic of the Belgian Congo, and President of the Commission for the Protection of the Natives: "It is thanks to the initiative of the King that the Catholic missionaries established themselves in the Congo State at its foundation; and it is thanks also, in a great part, to the protection and the aid of his Majesty that they have obtained the success of which they have reason to be greatly satisfied"; or the words of the British Baptist Missionary Society in the address that society presented in 1903 in acknowledgment of the King's "gracious and helpful sympathy," and of the "signal and helpful proofs" they had received of King Leopold's "approval and support."

It was proper that the English missionaries should lay weight, as they did by twice repeating the word, on King Leopold's "helpfulness" to them and to all the missionaries who put forward wisely considered efforts for the enlightenment and uplifting of his Majesty's native subjects living within the territories of the Congo, for in this action of King Leopold lies the key to all his government in Africa, and in it, as has been said, is to be found the crowning glory of his statesmanship.

Those seeking proof after the event will find that King Leopold, when addressing the Geographical Conference at its opening meeting in Brussels in 1876, declared that "to pierce the darkness shrouding entire populations in Africa would be a crusade worthy of this century of progress," and it is at least probable that King Leopold, a clear speaker, who never utters a word in public which he has not weighed, when he spoke of a crusade meant exactly what he said, and did not intend his words to be regarded as an idle metaphor. No special significance, however, was attached to these words at the time, and none need be paid to them now, since we have the King's acts, more convincing than any words could be, to judge by.

When King Leopold assumed the sovereignty of the Congo, the condition of the whole of Africa—with the exception of the ancient Christian empire of Abyssinia—was both deplorable and discouraging from a Christian point of view. The Christian missionaries who had wandered over the land for centuries had made no lasting impression on it. No traces of Christian civilisation were to be found beyond the settlements where white men upheld their rule by the force of arms. It was remarkable that where Christians had failed Mahomedans had succeeded. The tenets of Mahomedanism, flattering the baser instincts of man, fitted easily into

TAILORING PUPILS, BAMANIA.

NATIVE TEACHER AND HIS CLASS.

THE CONGO MISSIONS.

the lives of the half-savage natives; and even those in Europe who were most forward in calling for the suppression of slavery—that promising sapling of Mahomedanism—called also for the acceptance of every other custom of Mahomedanism, nominally in the interests of the black races, but really, it cannot but be supposed, in the interests of European traders, whose desire was to have the blacks transformed into docile servants and reliable workmen, who, in truth, cared not one jot how that transformation was effected, and who, if not incapable of doing so, were at least unwilling to look into the future and consider the danger which would arise from the strengthening by European agencies of the forces of Islam.

To those loose thinkers who did not look to the future, the quick and surface civilisation which the propaganda of Mahomedan doctrines in Africa promised, seemed most tempting. Money-seekers have ever specious arguments at their command, and with a plausible appearance of truth it was urged that the conversion of the negroes to Christianity would be the more easy, and even the more certain, when these negroes had been subject for a time to the half-civilised customs of the Arab Mahomedans. Writers pretending to respect a prudery childishly out of place in serious works, glossed over the real causes which led to the extinction of the families of the blacks who hung around the mission stations or dwelt in civilised settlements, and, dropping their prudery when it suited them to do so, produced statistics and medical opinions, based upon the flimsiest data, to prove that Christianity was impossible for the negroes. Fortunately King Leopold not only saw through the flimsiness of these contentions, but, his statesmanship being never for the moment alone, he was not tempted to sacrifice the natives' future, and with it much of the safety and welfare of humanity, to the temptation of a surface civilisation. It was, then, at the very commencement of his Congo rule that he resolved his Government would march hand in hand with the missionaries of Christianity; that the only religion it would aid or countenance would be that of Christ, and that he, the sovereign of the Congo, would himself send out and sustain the Christian missionaries.

This resolve doubled the difficulties of King Leopold's task at the very commencement; but, as the King saw, it was the only resolve adherence to which would in the end secure the success for which he had taken up the heavy labour of settling the Congo. It must not be forgotten, in considering the history of the Congo, that the protection and civilisation of the natives was a part of the King's aim, equally with that of the spreading of Belgian power and the increase of Belgian wealth.

It was no part of King Leopold's programme to protect the negroes into extinction, or to civilise them off the face of the earth. His plans for their protection under the civil law were wisely made; but he, a student of history and of men, knew that without the protection of the Christian creed the extirpation of the blacks at the advent of the superior race was a certainty. Without Christianity, the negroes might linger for generations, if not as slaves, at least as hewers of wood and drawers of water for their white masters; and in such a condition their decline, however slow, would be inevitable. Christianity alone could lift them to the real level of their fellow freemen; and Christianity the King resolved to bring to them, heedless of the difficulties of the task.

The first difficulty with which the King was confronted in the fulfilment of his undertaking was that of finding missionaries for the Congo. It was no small difficulty. The forests and swamps of the Equator offered no inducements: the long records of missionary failures in Africa caused much discouragement. This body and that body, this worker and that worker, to whom the King addressed himself found excuse after excuse for refusing the task.

It was not that there was not missionary zeal in the world; but missionaries, even when Christian, are human; and the missionaries, and those who would be missionaries, must not be condemned if they saw work lying ready to their hand in lands more pleasant and amongst heathens less hardened. It needed all King Leopold's personal influence to gain the first volunteers for the regular evangelisation of the Congo State. It was as the result of a visit which he specially paid to the missionary fathers of Scheut, near Brussels, and of long pleadings with the heads of that house, in which the King put forward every inducement which a king could offer, that the missionaries of Scheut—whose work had hitherto lain in China—consented to undertake the charge of the Congo Mission. Missionaries now at Scheut, who were there when the King paid this visit to their house to plead for the negroes of the Congo, bear witness to the zeal for the cause of Christianity which King Leopold then displayed—a zeal which they declare has never diminished; and examination into the history of the Congo, added to the statements of high civil and military officials, confirms the statements of the missionaries, repeated by every one of them, and summed up in the deliberate words of Monsignor van Ronslé, the head of the missions in the Congo: that it is the King personally who encourages and sustains the Christian missionaries in the Congo.

The clause in the Act of Berlin which provides for freedom of religious worship in the area of the Congo is respected by the Government of the Congo State; but King Leopold regards the obligations of a king with a higher view than that of the diplomatists who drew up the Act, and he does not content himself with protecting missionaries and not aiding them. Aid and support come to missionaries and the Church directly from the King. For this, if for no other reason, it is well that King Leopold is unhampered in his sovereignty over the Congo. Government officials, civil as well as military, are seldom people to be found entirely in accord with the aims or the workings of missionaries. They are too often tempted to look on missionaries as meddlesome and impracticable individuals who interfere with the real business of life and government.

Lawyers are apt to look almost exclusively to good laws, and soldiers to regular drill, as the best means of civilisation ; and both are inclined to hold that if the natives are properly protected, obliged to work for their living, and to fulfil their duties as subjects to the State in the army or in civil life, the necessity of seeking to convert them to Christianity, either for their civilisation or their salvation, is non-existent. This attitude of the official mind is known to all who have any experience in such colonies. It may be taken as doing much to account for the small progress which the spread of Christianity has made in the colonies of some of the most Christian countries. It would, without doubt, be much more apparent in the Congo were it not that the sovereign of that State upholds the Church with no uncertain hand.

Thoroughness being innate in every act of King Leopold, it is not surprising to find that, having determined to spread the Gospel throughout his Congo dominions, he resolved that the missionary field should be as clearly and as fully mapped out and regulated as the fields of his military and civil administration. The clauses of the Act of Berlin to which he adhered bound him to throw open the Independent State to the travellings and preachings of the missionaries and propagandists of every creed and sect—Turk, Jew, and atheist, as well as Christian, or at least to the free

THE CONGO MISSIONS.   189

exercise of every form of belief; and his own liberal disposition, apart from any treaty, led him to make the field perfectly free for the missionaries of every Christian creed.

But it was apparent to him that a work so mighty, and necessarily so slow, as the conversion of the Central African savages could not be left, if it were to be successful, in the hands of roaming and unorganised preachers. It was also apparent to him that if, under the guise of religion, the subjects of other Powers were permitted to set up authority independent of his own in the Congo, not only would the peace of his State be endangered, but the cause of Christianity itself within it would be jeopardised.

Therefore, whilst he was successfully exerting his influence in Belgium to obtain missionary volunteers for the Congo, he addressed himself to the Papal See for the double purpose of having the missionary districts of the Congo defined, the religious authorities at the heads of the missions regulated, and of having the protectorates which any foreign Powers might claim to exercise over the missions in the territories of the Congo State definitely removed. In each effort he was successful; but in that regarding the withdrawal of claims of protectorates over missions and Christians his success was not attained without difficulty. While the Congo was as yet a land unknown to geographers and explorers, Catholic missionaries had penetrated into it; and though their efforts, up to the time of the foundation of King Leopold's African State, had not been attended by any far-reaching results, nevertheless, the Portuguese had some Christian establishments within their territories, the priests of which claimed religious jurisdiction over the Lower Congo and a large portion of what is now known as the East Kwango district, while the French claimed a like jurisdiction over what then, as now, was known as the Katanga district, in which an active community of French missionaries was established.

The French missionaries offered no opposition to the recognition of the laudable desires of the Belgian missionaries to direct the missionary work of the country the King of the Belgians had undertaken to civilise; and an arrangement was come to by which the missionary work of the Katanga district was handed over to a Belgian branch of the order to which the existing French priests belonged.

The Portuguese, however, who had abandoned the sovereignty of the Congo under the compulsion of Europe, clung to the shadow of their ancient power, and long and tedious negotiations were necessary before they were prevailed upon, in their turn, to withdraw their pretensions with regard to the missions. Finally, Portugal did withdraw her pretensions, and the whole organisation of the Catholic Church in the Congo State and of its missions was placed in the hands of Belgian missionaries; and thus, by the wise prevision of the King, the peaceful progress of Christianity in the Congo was secured, free, as far as the Catholic Church was concerned, from the disgraceful schemes and squabbles of the political partisans of alien Powers, using the cloak of religion to disguise their perfidious designs.

The Christian missionaries who were the longest established in the Congo, and whose efforts had been the most successful when King Leopold's State was founded, were the Pères blancs d'Afrique, members of a congregation founded in 1868 by the great missionary who preached the anti-slavery crusade, Cardinal Lavigerie. These missionaries laboured in the Arab-plagued district of Tanganyika, and followed the paths of the earliest Belgian expeditions sent out by King Leopold long before the formation of the Congo State, when the course of the great river was as yet untraced on the map.

The first detachment of the missionaries of this order

THE CONGO MISSIONS. 191

to penetrate into the regions which the members of King Leopold's first Belgian expeditions were opening up in the Tanganyika district consisted of five priests, sent out by Cardinal Lavigerie in April, 1878. Thanks to the protection afforded them by the Belgian pioneers, the missioners were enabled to arrive safely in the midst of the Arabs' territories; but it was clear that the Arab slavers would not allow them to establish themselves in their lands without armed opposition; and in the following year—1879—when sending another band of five missionaries to Africa to join those first sent out, Cardinal Lavigerie found it prudent to send with them a body of soldiers for their protection. Tnese soldiers were recruited from men who had served in the ranks of the Papal Zouaves, and they were almost all of Belgian nationality. In order to impress on them the Christian nature of their mission, Cardinal Lavigerie held a ceremony in the church of Notre Dame of Africa, at Algiers, on the eve of their departure, at which he handed to each of the volunteers a naked sword, called upon him to "use this sword for the defence of the works of God, never for unjust motives," and giving him the accolade, enjoined him to "be a soldier, pacific and courageous, faithful and pious." Calumny had not yet begun to attack the Belgians who fought for their God and for the welfare of humanity in Central Africa, and the praise this small band of soldiers' bravery deserved was not, at the time, denied to it. With the missioners they guarded, these soldiers sought for peace; but they did not find it until the end of the ten years' warfare which were needed to break the Arabs' power and clear the Congo from the pest of the slave raids.

The history of the Arab war need not be referred to here; but it is not unfitting to mention at this point that amongst the first martyrs in this new crusade was one of these Belgian volunteers, a soldier named Dhoop, who, with two of the missionaries—the

Fathers Déniaud and Augier—was killed in an Arab-incited rising at Ouroundi, one of the stations founded by the Pères Blancs for the education of children redeemed from slavery.

The Apostolic Vicariate of the Belgian Congo, the creation of which was decided upon in 1886, at the instance of King Leopold, was not actually formed until 1888, and during the earlier years of the existence of the Congo State the missionary labour in the whole of the district extending from Lake Tanganyika to Leopoldville was confided to the Pères Blancs. In May, 1888, a Papal Brief was issued by which the territories of the Congo State were divided into two ecclesiastical districts: one, that of West Tanganyika, called the Apostolic Vicariate of the Upper Congo, being confided to the ministrations of the Pères Blancs, and the other, which comprised the greater part of the territories of the State, and was named the Apostolic Vicariate of the Independent State of the Congo, being confided to the Pères de Scheut.

The personal exertions of King Leopold in connection with the spreading of Christianity in the Congo did not cease with the formation of these ecclesiastical districts, and the organisation of the labours of the missions of Scheut and Algiers. In turn the King addressed himself to each of the great missionary orders of the Catholic Church for aid in the work, and it is admitted by the heads of these orders that the fact of their giving that aid and establishing their homes in the midst of the African savages is due to the insistence of King Leopold. Indeed, the heads of the missionary orders do not deny that had not the persistent demands of King Leopold forced them to turn their attention to the Congo, it is more than probable they would have left it unentered by their orders to this day. Each missionary order was already involved in great labours amongst heathen peoples, for the conversion of whom, each order could say, its resources were already strained to the utmost; but to such a plea the King had a ready and a perfect answer. He did not call on the missionary orders to cease or curtail their labours in China, in India, or in Algeria, or to withdraw one worker from these immense fields of action. To the statements that every missionary priest was already occupied, and that the missionary path of every student in the colleges of the orders was already mapped out for him, the King replied that volunteers would spring up from amongst the Belgians for the new work, and this answer was sufficient. " Da mihi Belges " was the prayer of a great missionary of a former age ; with the promise of Belgian recruits, and the certitude of the royal support, the orders saw the means assured for the work which was urged upon them, and each order in turn acceded to the King's demands, and sent forth its members into Central Africa.

The district under the ecclesiastical control of the Pères Blancs remains as it was established in 1888. The missionary orders newly arrived in the Congo territories since that year have each been assigned districts which then formed part of the Vicariate of the Pères de Scheut ; but this Vicariate still remains the largest in the Congo, its district being as large as the districts of all the other missionaries united. The missionary orders now labouring in the Congo State, in addition to those of the Pères Blancs and the Pères de Scheut, are the Trappists, established in the Congo in 1892 ; the Jesuits, established in 1893 ; the Priests of the Sacré-Cœur, established in 1897 ; the Premonstrants, established in 1898 ; and the Redemptorists, established in 1899.

Of these the Trappists' work in the Equator district, the Priests of the Sacré-Cœur in the Stanley Falls and Arouhimi districts, and the Redemptorists in the district of the Cataracts, each of which districts remains within the original Vicariate of the Pères de

Scheut, the Vicariate of the Independent State of the Congo; while new Vicariates have been created in the Kwango and Ouellé districts and placed under the charge respectively of the Jesuits and the Premonstrants, and a further new Vicariate has been formed of the Upper Kassai, which remains under the charge of the Pères de Scheut.

A full knowledge of the situation of these missions, and of the influence exercised by them on the inhabitants of the Independent State, is necessary in order to arrive at a just estimate of King Leopold's rule in the Congo, and to understand the present condition and the future prospects of the country. The idea that missioners do little to effect the material condition of the land in which they labour must be dismissed at the outset in considering the Catholic missions of the Congo. It has been said that the evolution taking place in Central Africa is the most rapid which history has registered. If this is true, it is due to the work of the missionaries.

The tribes which are scattered over the immense territories of the Congo State vary in their intelligence as they vary somewhat in their manners and customs, and in the degree of baseness to which they have sunk; but they remain sufficiently alike in their chief characteristics to have similar methods of training and education suitable for each of them. The chief impediment to the rapid spread of Christianity amongst the adult population of the Congo is found mainly in the fact that it is impossible to make an adult native of the Congo comprehend a new idea. With the prodigious memory of the illiterate, the native will learn and repeat, parrot-like, any string of words, however long, which he is taught; but they will remain, however often he repeats them, or hears them repeated, nothing more than a senseless string of different sounds to him. The natives love to mimic the white men: they are quite ready to repeat the white men's prayers, and to call themselves

TRAPPIST WITH THE CHILDREN OF A FARM CHAPEL.

NATIVE CATECHIST PREACHING, BAMANIA.

worshippers of the white men's God ; but there are few adult savages in the Congo whom it is possible to bring to an understanding of what the worship of the white men's God means, or what Christianity implies.

The Catholic missionaries in the Congo have their churches often crowded by thousands of natives at a time. Nothing would be easier for them than to teach great numbers of these natives verses of the Bible and chapters of catechism, baptise them, and proclaim them as converts to Christianity. Instead of doing so, however, the Catholic missionaries rigidly refuse baptism to all those adults who do not give proof of a comprehension of Christian truths and laws, and a determination to abide by them. They never seek to force the profession of Christianity upon the natives ; they will not even baptise dying natives unless they themselves demand baptism in the name of Christ. By acting in this manner they deprive themselves of the possibility of issuing magnificent reports of great conversions, and of the rapid spread of Christianity all over the land ; but they ensure that the Christianity they plant in the Congo is real and firmly rooted, such as will spread and bear fruit for ever in the land.

Since there is little possibility of penetrating the understanding of the adult savage by any instruction, however clearly or however patiently given, the chief efforts of the missionaries are directed towards the education and the instruction of the youths and children ; and the education which they give them is something very much more than the education of the schoolroom.

Instability is the curse of Central Africa ; and the work of the Catholic missionaries is to combat and overcome it. They seek to make Christians of the natives by making " men " of them. " Every sensible man understands our work," says one of the missionaries writing in the " Missions Belge " for December, 1902. " What do we want, in fact ? Simply to instruct and elevate the blacks, to make men and Christians of them." These missionaries realise the fact that the only means which civilised man has of elevating savages towards his own standard is that of making them work. "The school is useless, it would be even dangerous," wrote another missionary in the publication I have just quoted, "if there was not another tendency side by side with it —the tendency to work, the fight against indolence and idleness, a powerful propulsion towards useful labour, agriculture, the cultivation of produce, trades."

The method which the missionaries adopt for carrying out the twofold object of making Christians and workmen of the savages is practically the same in all the missions. Starting with central stations, around which are grouped schools, workshops, and manufactories, they send out continually from these stations Christian natives whom they have instructed, and who, under their superintendence, erect farm-chapels in suitable places. Both farm-chapels and stations are centres of industry and learning.

At the stations the native children are taught trades, such as those of carpenter, mason, brick maker, printer, brewer, cigar maker, gardener, agriculturist. At them they are instructed in reading and writing, and in the ordinary primary school courses, as well as in religious knowledge; and from them the most intelligent and best conducted youths are drawn to become the heads of the farm-chapel settlements—little settlements which reproduce the activities and work of the stations to which they belong, in miniature. The population of the farm-chapels is also a population at first of children.

The native chiefs are easily induced to send young children to be educated at these schools and farm-chapels, which are self-supporting. At the farm-chapels, in the intervals of agriculture and other industries, the native catechists who are at their head teach the children the words of the scripture lessons and of the

THE CONGO MISSIONS.

catechism, the meaning of which is expounded by the missionaries, who are continually travelling in their districts. As the original stations formed centres from which to send out catechists to found and teach in the farm-chapels, so the farm-chapels in their turn become new centres from which in like manner native catechists are sent forth to found new farm-chapels still farther afield.

No check has yet come to the spread of these modest centres of Christianity and civilisation, excepting that caused to every work in Africa by the fearful ravages of the sleeping sickness ; and the missionaries are not too sanguine when they look forward to seeing the whole of the territories of the Congo State covered by a close network of Christian farms and stations. There are at present in the State, according to the official returns, eighty-six Catholic missionary stations, and 528 farm-chapels. This is not an inconsiderable number ; but in reality there is a much larger number, for the State returns divide the different establishments under various headings such as Christian villages, primary schools, secondary schools, and the like, instead of classifying them under the headings of stations or farms.

In the Tanganyika district, in the Vicariate of the Upper Congo—the earliest established of the missions in the State, the history of the foundation of which has been told in this chapter—the Pères Blancs have at present seven large central missionary stations, twenty farm-chapels, three homes for the aged, seven hospitals, ten orphanages, fourteen dispensaries, and nineteen schools. During the year which ended June, 1902, the missionaries of this district baptised 1,348 natives and married 102 couples. They had at the end of that year 2,124 pupils in their schools, the attendance at which is continually increasing. In this district the constant terror of the Arab slave-raiders, in which the natives lived up to the time of the coming of the Belgians, had led them to neglect even the most elementary labour; and it was a task of more than ordinary difficulty for the missionaries to induce their converts to settle down to regular labour. They succeeded in it, however, and are able to say of their Vicariate that in it now "agriculture, formerly neglected, despised even, has become an occupation held much in honour."

There is not here a Christian who has not his morsel of land perfectly cultivated. "Already," says the report from which I quote, and which was published in the *Revue Générale* for September, 1903, "some of our neophytes, the more ardent workers, who have become landowners, employ a certain number of workmen, to whom they give a part of their crop. They export the rest of their produce along the two banks of the lake for the revictualment of the European stations. When the outskirts of a mission are cultivated within a circle of many kilometres, the young households, finding no longer land there to reclaim, swarm out and found a new village in another spot. Large roads, bordered by trees, connect all these centres with each other. The marshes are reclaimed, bridges are thrown over the rivers, and great drains assure the public health."

During the dry season the missionaries instruct the native Christians in trades. The school children at their school at Mpala print their own school books. The missionaries have made expert smiths and ironfounders of the natives, and have so well taught them the trades of carpenters, masons, and builders that the great churches they have built at Mpala and Baudouinville are amongst the wonders of new Africa. In their district in 1902 the missionaries counted 3,701 Christians, and 11,088 catechumens. They boast—and not without reason—that their education of the blacks does not "make them grotesque caricatures of white men," but

THE CONGO MISSIONS.

that the civilisation of the natives in the Tanganyika region is that of modern progress, based firmly on religion and on law.

Following the course of the great river as it flows to the ocean, the missionary district next to that of Tanganyika is that of Stanley Falls. This district, while remaining a portion of the Vicariate of the Pères de Scheut, was placed under the care of the Priests of the Sacré-Cœur in 1897. In August, 1904, it was erected into an Apostolic prefecture, the Reverend Gabriel Grison, chief of the mission of the Sacré-Cœur fathers, being appointed to the head of the prefecture. The Stanley Falls district is situated in the centre of the great equatorial forest. Its frequent and diluvian rains, its sky of bronze, the electric tension of the atmosphere, all combine to make the district full of danger to the lives of Europeans living in it, and several of the missionaries of the Sacré-Cœur have fallen victims to its inclemency and died at their work, while many more have been forced to return shattered in health to Europe. Nevertheless, the missionaries of the Falls have succeeded in pushing onward their evangelising and civilising work without pause. The first station they established was that at Saint Gabriel, a few kilometres above Stanleyville on the Congo. At this station, founded on Christmas Day, 1897, they have a large orphanage containing five hundred children—sons of the victims of the Arab slave raiders, of men killed in the inter-tribal wars once so common all over the Congo, but now crushed out by the Government of the State, or of natives swept away by the terrible sicknesses which scourge the State. The latest report of the Reverend Father Grison regarding this and the other stations of the Sacré-Cœur mission is worthy of being quoted at length :—

" It is with these children (the victims of the Arab slave raids) that we commenced. Dividing the time between catechism, class, and manual labour, we cleared the forest around us, and made constructions, at first provisionally in *pise*, and afterwards permanently in brick. We have formed catechists, brick makers, masons, carpenters, joiners, and men of culture. We built at St. Gabriel a large church and many houses, and transformed the environs; where five years ago a savage and impenetrable forest reigned, we have now magnificent fields, in which rice, manioc, coffee, and the beautiful fruit trees of the tropics flourish easily. We have commenced to send catechists into the neighbouring villages, and we have thus founded various posts—St. Leo, St. Jean, Ste. Adéle, St. Vincent, St. Edmond. In brief, here at St. Gabriel we have baptised 746 people since the commencement of the mission."

The next station of the mission to be founded was that at Stanleyville, the capital of the Province. The mission there was founded at the request of the natives of the locality themselves, who, coming Sunday after Sunday to the religious school at St. Gabriel, a distance of twelve kilometres to and fro, begged the superior of the mission to send a missionary to them to teach them, to quote their words, " the things of God." The mission of Stanleyville was founded in 1899. According to the report of Father Grison, at it " there have been already baptised 487 people, and there are now twelve or thirteen hundred catechumens either at Stanleyville or at its four secondary posts, amongst the Waggenias, amongst the Watikaleros, and at one of the posts of the State, Bania Lukula."

The third station founded by the missionaries of the Falls district was that of Romée, at a distance of one day's journey down the Congo by steamer from the Falls. This station was founded in 1902, and at the date of the report of Father Grison, from which I quote, there were already thirty Christians and some hundreds of catechumens gathered together at it and the three secondary posts, or farm-chapels, attached

THE CONGO MISSIONS.

to it. The fourth station of the priests of the Sacré-Cœur in the Stanley Falls district is one at Basoko, three days' steamer journey from the Falls. This station was founded at the same time as that at Romée. It is situated at the mouth of the Aruwimi River, and some time before the station was founded the missionaries, making a voyage of exploration to the Aruwimi, found that Christianity had preceded them there through the instrumentality of some of their native neophytes.

A few native Christians, whom the missionaries of the Sacré-Cœur had instructed and taught to read, had set themselves to teach the catechism in the district, and the missionaries, on arriving at Banalya, were received in triumph by the converts whom their native disciples had made. They found already established on the Aruwimi two flourishing Christian settlements. This determined them not to delay the foundation of further posts on that river; and making Basoko a centre, they founded five secondary posts along the river, in which at the close of 1902 there were sixty Christians and five hundred catechumens. In all, in 1902, in the missionary district of the Falls there were, besides the five hundred children in the orphan schools, fifteen hundred Christians and two thousand five hundred catechumens.

The district of the Ouellé, which extends northward above that of Stanley Falls, was assigned to the Premonstrant Canons of the Abbey of Tongerloo in 1898, in which year the district, which includes portions of the districts of the Bangalas and the Oubangi within its ecclesiastical superscription, was erected into an Apostolic prefecture. As had been the case with the Belgian missionaries who were already working in the Congo, the Premonstrants of Tongerloo were prevailed upon to undertake the labours of evangelisation in the Congo by King Leopold, whose strongly expressed desire that they should undertake the mission was followed by the formal invitation of Pope Leo XIII.

The first body of missionaries sent to the Congo by the Premonstrants left Belgium in June, 1898. Death was soon busy in their ranks; and from the date of their first arrival it has been found necessary to keep sending a continual stream of fresh recruits to their mission on the Uele to fill the gaps caused by death and sickness. In the first four years of their work, out of thirty-seven missionaries who went out from Belgium to this district eight died and seven returned to Europe broken in health, prematurely aged, and unable to continue their work. The work went on, however, with the aid of the fresh recruits; and the mission at the time of the latest report had successfully established four chief stations, eighteen Christian villages, sixteen farm-chapels, and four schools. Its roll of Christians then numbered fifteen hundred, and that of its catechumens three hundred and ninety, not including the children—over a thousand in number—in its schools.

The Premonstrants commenced their labours in the Congo, it must be remembered, at a date when the pest of the slave raids was only recently stamped out, and when the country was still suffering from its evils, and from the effects of the sanguinary war which had been necessary to crush the power of the Arab marauders. It was for the reception of the children rescued from slavery, or left orphans and found deserted after the war, that the orphan schools in the Uele district were established. Though war has ceased, orphan children are still to be found in numbers in the country where in recent years the sleeping sickness has proved almost as fatal as the murderous slave raids, and the missionary schools are still crowded with orphans, for whose support and education the Government of the Congo grants a subsidy to the missionaries. These children not only receive a technical and religious training, but also,

STATE STATION AT THE EQUATOR.

TRAVELLING THROUGH THE FOREST, KATANGA.

THE CONGO MISSIONS. 203

when they are of an age to leave school, each one is given a piece of land on which he can live, the cultivation of which is sufficient for the support of himself and his family.

The next district through which the Congo flows is that of the Equator. This district forms part of the Vicariate of the Independent State, of which Monsignor van Ronslé, the superior of the Congregation of the Pères de Scheut, is the ecclesiastical head. While the missionary work in the greater part of that wide Vicariate is carried on directly by the congregation of Scheut, their labour is shared in the Equator district by the Trappists, and in one of the districts on the Lower Congo—that of the Cataracts—by the Redemptorists.

The Trappists began their fine work in the Congo in 1892. In 1895 they built the Abbey of Bamania, their chief station in the Equator district, which is presided over by a mitred abbot. They have in the district three large and five accessory stations, four farm-chapels, two schools, and many churches and chapels. They have also a hospital for those suffering from the sleeping sickness. The number of Christians on the district of the Equator is twelve thousand. There are three thousand catechumens in the district, and one thousand and thirteen children were in the schools of the Trappist missionaries at the end of 1903.

The missionary order which shares with the Pères de Scheut in evangelising the Vicariate of the Independent State—that of the Redemptorists—was established in the district of the Cataracts on the Lower Congo for the special purpose of ministering to the spiritual needs of the labourers employed on the construction of the railway from Matadi to Leopoldville, on which, during the continuance of the work, there were occupied six thousand men. The missionaries of this order have now three chief stations, those at Matadi, Kinkanda, and Tumba, from which they serve the seven posts of the district. At Kinkanda the hospital is under their charge, and at Matadi they manage the library and the natives' savings bank. By the means of this institution—the savings bank—they have succeeded in introducing something of the saving habits of the Belgians into the lives of the native Congolese; the bank being organised in such a manner that a large proportion of the wages of the natives employed on the railway finds its way into it, instead of being spent the moment it is earned, much of it being afterwards used to establish the households of the workmen on their marriage.

As is related in the commencement of this chapter, the duty of teaching Christianity throughout the greater part of the immense territories of the Independent State was undertaken at the moment of the State's foundation, and on the insistence of King Leopold, by the Congregation of Belgian missionaries, known as the Pères de Scheut, from the name of the Brussels suburb in which their mother-house is situated. At present the districts confided to the care of these missionaries are divided into the two Vicariates: that of the Upper Kasai (which comprises the basin of the Kasai River and its affluents), and that of the Independent State (which comprises all the rest of the territories of the State, with the exception of the districts of Tanganyika, Aruwimi, Uele, and Kwango). The successes achieved by these missionaries can be summed up in a few words; the difficulties they overcame in their work, and the sorrows they suffered in seeing the country where they laboured made desolate by the ravages of a fearful disease, could only be told in many volumes. So sad, indeed, is the history of the ravages of the sleeping sickness amongst the native population of these districts, that the chief of the missionaries, their bishop, inured by years of residence to the horrors and the sorrows of a dark and savage land, faltered when he sought to speak of it; and the writer may well congratulate

THE CONGO MISSIONS.

himself that here he need do no more than touch upon the outskirts of the tale of the sufferings of those struck by the disease.

In the district of the Upper Kasai the Pères de Scheut have five chief posts, the first of which—that at Luluabourg St. Joseph—was founded by Père Cambier, now superior of the mission of the Kasai district. There were, at the close of the year 1902, a population of two thousand native Christians in this mission station, exclusive of the Christian families which had been sent out from it to found five other stations. Many of the people forming this large population were employed for years in erecting the various buildings needed at it, by the work at which their training as tradesmen was completed. These buildings being now finished, numbers of the native Christians are being sent out from Luluabourg to found farm-chapels in the district. The other chief stations in the district are those at Merode Salvator, founded in 1894; St. Trudon, founded in 1895; Hemptinno St. Benoit, founded in 1897; and Tielen St. Jacques, founded in 1898. An example of the difficulties which the missionaries of the Kasai district have to face is found in the history of the station at St. Trudon.

Twice the situation of this large station was changed; but still, in spite of every effort of the missionaries, the natives in it are swept away by the sleeping sickness. Formerly its population numbered thirteen hundred native Christians; in 1903 it was only eight hundred; and the missionaries, in the hope of preventing the further spread of the disease, dispersed its population, scattering it in small settlements of about twenty families, each within the distance of half a league from the station. Besides watching over the Christian settlements, the missionaries of the St. Trudon station teach twenty neighbouring native villages, in which they have about two hundred children attending their classes. They have, besides, a hospital for the sufferers from the sleeping sickness, where they not only tend their own people, but to which they bring the sufferers from all the savage tribes around. For these they search in the highways and byways, and for leave to minister to their long dying agonies they often pay heavily to the native chiefs. The description of the visit of one of the missionaries—Père Handekyn—to the village founded by Pania Mutomba, written by him from St. Trudon on November 2nd, 1903, and published in the *Missions en Chine et au Congo* for March, 1904, throws a light on the condition of the country and the actions of the missionaries.

"Before the possession was taken by the State," says Père Handekyn, "the old and cruel Pania Mutomba gave himself up for a long time to the brigandage which made him the terror of the whole country. By raids pushed into distant places he had increased his village by an immense crowd of captives taken from different tribes—Balubas, Batételas, Bazangas, Babindis, etc. But to do so he had introduced into his home the contagious scourge, the sleeping sickness, which now ravages the whole country, and has been transmitted even to our residence of St. Trudon, where the first victim was a slave liberated by us from the hands of Pania.

"In 1897 Pania thought himself sufficiently strong to fight against the State. Betrayed by one of his people, he died deprived of all power, and the State gave him for a successor his son, Mutshifula. This latter has neither the sanguinary character nor the conquering genius of his father. Leaving all the government to his ministers, he has no other occupation than luxury and drunkenness." On learning the purport of the missionaries' visit, Mutshifula was "enchanted" with the proposal, as well he might be, for it was, in effect, one not only to remove the dying people from his village, but also to pay him for permission to remove these unfortunate creatures, the contagious character of whose disease rendered them objects of dread even to the thoughtless natives. The chief granted full leave for the preaching of the Gospel in his village, and, says the missionary, " The ministers and all those present, a very numerous body, declared that they also wanted to become the children of the good God, of whom I preached. I profited by that to speak of the supernatural ends of every man. They listened to me for some time very attentively, when my harangue was cut short by the exclamation of an auditor who could not detach his eyes from my long red beard : ' That white man must be very old, and must have seen many rains ! '

"On this the whole assembly, music and dancers at its head, conducted me to the cabin destined for me. . . The next day I was able to ascertain the surprising number of the sick. At the price of a small compensation I was given nineteen, all natives of the village. But the possessions of the chief, constituted by other agglomerations less important, extended to more than five leagues in every direction. I went to them on the second day, and was able to baptise fifteen dying, and ransom fifteen unfortunate people affected with the contagion.

" The number which I started to lead to the mission was then thirty-five heads. By prolonging my sojourn I could have certainly tripled that figure; but I had to take into account the dimensions of our hospital, and I left very happy at the result. But what pains there remained for me to suffer in order to conduct my expedition to its end !

" In effect, from Pania to St. Trudon, the route, measuring twelve leagues, did not pass any village where provisions could be renewed. Besides my sick were at the end, without force, exhausted. Many had not eaten for several days when they were given to me.

It is true a good meal had been prepared for them before their departure, without counting the large ration which I had given them for the journey; but their weakness dated from too long. We had hardly set out for five minutes when, ascending a slight acclivity, I saw a woman stagger, stumble, and drop heavily to the ground. I instructed her, rapidly baptised her, and, leaving her to the care of my men from St. Trudon, I followed in the route of the other somnolents. Some paces further on I found the corpses of two sick people I had baptised the previous day, and whom I had sent in advance. The bodies were already in the most horrible condition.

"'Father,' cried someone to me a few minutes afterwards, 'this woman can do no more; come quickly and baptise her.' I went.

"'Master,' said the unfortunate woman, 'do not strike me. I wish I could walk on; my legs won't carry me. Baptise me, then, I beg of you!'

"'Do not strike!' This cry of terror cut me to the heart like a knife. Alas, the slave merchants acted in this manner with their victims, to push them on as long as a last breath allowed of a last step!

"Farther on there was another woman, carrying a little child in her arms. Both resembled real skeletons. The mother had no more tears to implore; the child, its eyes enlarged by hunger and its lips parted in a broken-hearted smile, asked a succour which it was impossible for us to give. The mother had walked until she dropped with her burthen.

"And the others, those who dragged themselves on still—their walk was staggering, their steps uncertain, like those of drunkards. At every pace they looked back, fearing that an inhuman conductor was coming with his pitiless lash, to bleed their shoulders to hasten their slackened pace.

"More pitiful still was the spectacle of the ascent

of the heights. The unfortunates clung on to the roots and weeds, but their hands, already paralysed, let go, and they let themselves slip down and roll back. I saw some of them advancing on their hands and knees, their dried-up chests emitting whistling moans, their mouths twisted into a cry, always the same, 'I am starving,' and their haggard eyes fixed on me in supplication. Alas, these unfortunate creatures were dying of hunger! They had thrown the provisions I gave them at the moment of departure into the grass, too weak to carry even such a light burthen. I had them given all that remained to me—half a loaf of bread, some slices of pork, the remains of some vegetables. All, cooked together in a sort of soup, was devoured in the twinkling of an eye, and gave these wretched creatures a little strength and courage.

"This lamentable journey lasted two days. Of the thirty-six I had ransomed, seven perished. The others are now cared for in our hospital, and, considering their condition, in the best possible position for their bodies and souls. Happier than they ever were before, they wait without fear the approach of a death which cannot be slow in coming.

"A crabbed person might object that I did wrong in bringing the sick people with me, the death of many of whom, at least, on the journey I could have foreseen. Why not have left them at their village?

"Because it would have been much more cruel to have left them there. They would have driven them out with blows of sticks, to suffer the taunts of the passers-by before dying of starvation in the bush. That they might go quicker they would have thrown them, still living, into the river, where their corpses would have carried the contagion far. While with us, their suffering at the last moments will be softened by a compassionate word, and they will not die without their passports to Heaven."

In the Vicariate of the Independent State the story of difficulties and successes is repeated. The establishments of the Pères de Scheut in this vicariate in 1903 consisted of nineteen chief stations, in each of which three missionaries resided permanently, twenty-nine secondary stations, and a hundred and forty farm-chapels. To each of the farm-chapels there was attached at least one elementary school, while superior schools were attached to each of the missionary stations. The total number of the schools directed by the missionaries in the Vicariate, elementary and superior, was at that time 159, and there were in the missionary district 6,066 Christians, and 13,721 catechumens, besides 2,166 children in the orphan schools of the missionaries.

In addition to the farm-chapels in the vicariate, many villages, inhabited entirely by Christians, have sprung up around each of the stations. The number of Christians and pupils at the villages and farms of the missionaries has increased considerably within the year, notwithstanding the fearful ravages of the sleeping sickness. Since its first appearance that sickness has swept the whole of the country with unlessening and irresistible force. The flourishing, well-built and well-cared-for villages of the Christians have been swept by it as fatally as the foul and fœtid hamlets of the savage natives.

Berghe Ste. Marie, a Christian settlement, in which Monseigneur van Ronslé, the superior of the mission, has his headquarters, and in which, to quote his words, "the hundred (native) families which were collected there lived happily under almost ideal conditions," was blotted out of existence by the disease, its native inhabitants dying to the last man. The inhabitants of this station were contaminated by contact with the Bobangi tribes. Wherever the sickness makes its appearance, says Monseigneur van Ronslé, it lays low, slowly but surely, all the inhabitants, and remains,

COTTAGES OF THE WHITE RESIDENTS, COQUILHATVILLE.

OFFICE OF THE GOVERNMENT SURVEY STAFF, BOMA.

whatever may be done, master of the soil, the conditions of well-being, peace and tranquillity, and labour all being ineffective against it. Nevertheless, all that can be done in the hope of checking it is done by the missionaries. The sick are isolated in villages in which they are tended by the priests ; while at the same time the missionary labour amongst the healthy is continued with unabated zeal.

Since the disappearance of Berghe Ste. Marie, Leopoldville has become the headquarters of the mission. At that station in 1902 the catechumens numbered 1,859 men and 653 women, and the number baptised 12,000. The population of Leopoldville is a floating one, and Christian natives employed in the service of the State or on the steamboats are continually coming to and fro between it and the other posts of the State. In addition to their work amongst these natives, and that in the schools, the missionaries at Leopoldville also serve the military camp at Jumbi, and the post at Kinchassa. The missionaries of Scheut at New Antwerp also serve the post of the State ; and at that station, notwithstanding the depopulation caused by the sleeping sickness, their congregation of converts remains so numerous that the average number attending the High Mass on Sundays is not less than two thousand. The missionaries have other flourishing stations on the Congo above New Antwerp ; but everywhere they have the same dreadful plague of the sleeping sickness to contend against.

Following the river downwards from Leopoldville, their next important station is that at Kangu, Moll Ste. Marie, in the Mayumbe country, which was founded in 1898. At the commencement the Mayumbes, who wanted no connection with the State, showed themselves hostile to the missionaries. It was with difficulty that the missionaries gathered a few children into their school ; but they gradually worked their way amongst the people. When they had fourteen children sufficiently instructed they sent them out as catechumens into the villages, where they succeeded beyond all hopes, until, at the time of preparing the returns for 1902, there were two thousand children in the Christian schools of the two hundred villages in the district, which the missionaries visited regularly, eighteen hundred of which children were to be seen attending Mass at Moll Ste. Marie on Sundays.

At Boma the missionaries of the Scheut congregation have a boys' school, in addition to which they manage the military and technical colony of the State which is situated at that post, and in which there are three hundred children.

Finally, to bring this long list of the missionary stations of the Pères of Scheut to an end, there is a station of the congregation of Moanda at the sea coast, which was founded in 1893 as a sanitarium. At Moanda these fathers had originally an orphanage for boys brought from the Upper Congo, in addition to the girls' orphanage situated at the same place ; but it was found that the voyage down the great river was too long for the children, and that their presence at Moanda aroused the jealousy of the native tribes of the district. The boys' orphanage has therefore been removed from that station, the orphan children of the Upper Congo being now kept at the schools established in their own districts. The girls' orphanage, under the direction of the nuns, is maintained, the girls educated in it being married to the young men of the colony at Boma. This change has removed the jealousy of the natives, who now send their children to be taught in the missionaries' schools, and to show their affection they call the missionaries of the congregation of Scheut " Mpelo Bafiote " (" Fathers of the Natives ").

The remaining ecclesiastical district, the Apostolic Prefecture of Kwango, embraces the whole of the Kwango

THE CONGO MISSIONS. 213

district and portion of the Stanley Pool district, and extends from Leopoldville to the boundaries of the State, where they touch the Portuguese territories. This district is evangelised by the Jesuits, and, again of this order, it has to be recorded that their missionary labours in the Congo were undertaken at the invitation and on the insistent demands of King Leopold. The railway which connects the great waterway of the Upper Congo with the ocean runs through this district, which consequently is one of much importance; and never was a judgment more wisely exercised than that which summoned to the charge of this wide district the missionaries of the great order whose wonderful organisation, deep learning, and profound knowledge of mankind place it first in the field in which every labourer is devoted and zealous; whose self-sacrificing and successful toil amongst the heathen and the savage have long since won for it the admiration and the respect not only of those to whom the name of Christ is sacred, but of all who know its achievements, and rejoice at the spread of humanity and civilisation.

In the Kwango district, heavily burthened and impoverished though it was, the education of the natives has already been raised to a high point. The chief station of the missionaries in the district—Bergeyck St. Ignace, at Kisantu—resembles, in the perfection of its buildings and appointments, an institution flourishing in the midst of European civilisation. All that is to be seen there is the work of the native children, directed by the missionaries. They made the bricks with which the buildings were constructed, built the large church which holds fifteen hundred people, the houses of the missionaries and workmen, the class-rooms and dormitories of the schools, the workshops for the tailors, the bootmakers and the carpenters, the printing office, the soap works, the brewery, the dispensary; and the native children are themselves the workmen in all of the manufactories and workshops they have built.

There is also at Ki Santu a normal school for the catechists, an elementary school, a great farm in which the children learn to cultivate vegetables and fruits, and a botanic garden, one of the glories of the Congo State.

The missionaries have five other chief stations in the Kwango district, established in the same manner. In the neighbourhood of each station Christian villages have sprung up, and there are, besides, scattered throughout the district, over three hundred farm-chapels, the number of which is continually increasing. The Jesuits commenced their missionary labours in the Kwango district in 1893. The reports for 1902 place the number of Christians in the district at 2,045, that of catechumens at 2,095, and that of school-children at 4,294. The Congo mission of the Jesuits is yet young, but it already gives promise of the greatest things. The native Christians in this district, as throughout the whole of the Congo State, are in the majority of cases men and women reared from childhood in the Christian schools.

Experience proved, as has been recorded, that, humanly speaking, it is impossible to make a new idea penetrate into the brain of an adult negro of the Central African race; but it would be wrong to conclude that because of this the missionaries, who have a perfect trust in the workings of Providence and the action of Divine Grace, neglect the adult while training the child. On the contrary, they bring all around them, and preach Christianity in season and out of season—or, rather, at all times—to men and women as well as to the little children.

They do not act, however, as if prayer and preaching were their only duties; and as if they only looked for the miraculous conversion and civilisation of millions of savage negroes steeped in ignorance, and filth, and sin. Rather, they seek to fit the black to raise himself

SHIPBUILDING AT LEOPOLDVILLE.

LAUNCH OF A STEAMER.

by persevering industry. The greatest instrument of civilisation which they wield is that of the Christian families established in the farm-chapels. These are the oases of civilisation in the midst of savage desolation; but unlike the oases of the desert, they are forever increasing and forever multiplying; so that, if the progress of recent years be continued, the whole land will be covered with them at no far distant date. The contrast between these farm-chapels and the localities in which they are placed is as vivid as that between the oasis and the desert.

"In all the farm-chapels of the interior," says Père Butaye in an interesting letter published in the *Missions Belge* for September, 1902, already quoted from in this chapter, "the Christians have well-kept fields; in the native villages the hoe is only wielded by the women; the men hunt a little, they promenade much, and they rest still more. It is only in our farm-chapels that the masculine sex gives itself up to the work of the fields, that one sees men labouring from morning to night; it is therefore only in our farm-chapels that constant labour can be obtained, and that the culture of crops can be carried on. If you press them little they will do nothing; if you press them much they will hide themselves, separate, or emigrate. Who will find for me that just medium, *suaviter et fortiter*, for the guidance of the savages?

"In my opinion there is only one entirely efficacious means to this end; it is that of resuscitating these people by religion. In becoming Christians they become obedient; they learn to work, and by work will come all the benefits of civilisation. Even now the contrast is striking; at the farm-chapels the spirit of work reigns, at the natives' homes idleness and indolence continue to reign. At the farm-chapels cattle breeding is carried on, the Christians contribute to the nourishment not only of the *personnel* of the mission, but also of the railway and of the State. Amongst the natives there is hardly any cattle breeding; they gave it up since the porterage. At the farm-chapels they read and write, they commence to have utensils and furniture, and to dress themselves better. All the natives have in their homes is a greasy cloth and a porringer of wood; they let themselves be mystified by a boy of six years, the bearer of a scrap of paper picked up on the road. It is evident these contrasts will accentuate themselves more and more, always to the detriment of the native abandoned to himself or keeping himself from the influence of the white man, and in favour of our Christians, guided by the missionaries, voluntarily submitting to the civilising action of religion and the State, and by doing so progressing always in the way of civilisation."

Father Butaye declares—and every other missionary who has experience of the Congo natives holds as he does—that the natives are in no way incapacitated from furnishing a good amount of work, or from reaching a high degree of intellectual development. He believes that neither their want of constancy nor their intellectual indolence form insurmountable obstacles, but he fully realises that the work of educating them must be a work of time.

"Two years ago," he says, "we had less hope than now. I am happy to think that in two years their constancy will have again progressed. Why not? There are those amongst them who have quite freely engaged to remain at their desks during three years—that is to say, three times twelve moons, thirty-six moons; or, rather, as they say, forty less four. For them it is an eternity; and the little tots say to me, 'And after those forty moons we shall have beards already, shall we not?'"

It is to the future of the race springing up around them that these missionaries look, and in their efforts to civilise the natives by planting Christian households

THE CONGO MISSIONS. 217

and schools in their midst they are materially assisted by the various orders of nuns which work in each of the missions. These orders are: the Sisters of Notre Dame de Namur, the Franciscan Nuns, the Sœurs Blancs, the Cistercians (or Trappistines), and the Sisters of the Sacré-Cœur de Berlaer.

In addition to their visiting and teaching in the native villages, the nuns have special charge of the girls' schools and orphanages, of the hospitals, and of the sick. They give the native girls a religious and technical training similar to that given by the missionary priests to the boys, and it is from their schools that the Christian girls are drawn who become the wives of the native catechists in the villages and farm-chapels founded by the missionaries. In these Christian homes lies the future hope of the Congo; and here it is not out of place to correct an error into which the opponents of Christian missionary enterprise seek to lead the public.

The statement that the observance of the rules of Christian morality in Central Africa would entail the extinction of the negro race is proved by the experience of the Congo State to be entirely false. Christian villages and farm-chapels, in which native families live, strictly observing the rule of monogamy, have now been long enough in existence to show that monogamy neither lessens the birth-rate nor injures the physique of the native races. An aspect of polygamy, overlooked by every advocate of that system, is this: that while each husband had many wives under the native *régime*, there were very many men who never had, and never could hope to have, a wife. A wife, amongst the savages, being nothing more nor less than a labouring drudge, a tiller of the soil, a drawer of water, had a certain value as a worker—more even than that of a slave; and as such wives were bought, as they still are where the native customs are unchanged, only rich men could afford to have wives. Slaves had none; and in the heart of darkest Africa, before the coming of the white man, the great majority of the male population were the slaves, as the majority of the females were the concubines of a comparatively small number of ferocious and debauched chieftains. The customs of negro mothers in the Congo are the outcome, not the cause, of polygamy ; and neither they, nor the polygamy they exist under, are more natural to the negro women of Central Africa than they are to the negro women of North America, to the Caucasian, or to the Mongolian. The Christian families reared in the mission stations are as ready to abandon their native customs regarding married life as they are to abandon cannibalism ; and in each case the result is equally happy for them and for their race.

Negro women do not bear many children ; but the reports of the missionaries show that child-bearing is as frequent amongst the monogamic families of the Christian settlements as it is amongst the polygamous families which surround them. Every missionary station has its babies born of native Christian parents ; the record of births in Christian households is the same from the Uele to Tanganyika, from Tanganyika to Kwango, and from Kwango to Boma ; and Ki Santu is not the only place in the Congo which is at times so crowded by Christian mothers and their babies that the housing room of the large convents proves inadequate for them, as happened during the Easter festival of 1903 ; nor is the well-filled store-room of the generous nun who rules over that convent the only one emptied of all its contents by the giving of small presents to a crowd of Christian mothers on a like occasion.

Notwithstanding all that the missionaries have achieved in the Congo up to the present, it is still to the fruit of the seeds they are now sowing, rather than to any instant fruction, that they look for the triumph of Christian civilisation in the State. They see that long-continued labour is still necessary before Christianity can be fully acclimatised to that alien soil. In a report on the Congo Missions in the *Missions Belge* of February, 1904, Father Goossens says: "The really serious work will only commence when we have under our hands the children of the Christians whom we are actually forming, and who are, for the most part, too much in touch with the native pagans. Their children, more accustomed to the white man, will apply themselves more closely to following the guidance of the missionary. Moreover, they themselves, Christian parents, will sustain us in the work of educating their children, which their own parents, still pagans, hardly do to-day."

It is not because the Christian teaching does not already bear fruit amongst the savage children that Father Goossens says this. On the contrary, he says that though the native children remain for a long time liars, and nearly always improvident, the improvement in their morals is most noticeable. The reason for the statement of the missionary that the work of civilisation, instead of being done is only commencing, is that he sees that long training is still necessary before the deep-rooted instability of the African savage is overcome. He says: "One of their great faults—that which, perhaps, places the greatest obstacle in the way of carrying on vigorously their scholastic and technical training—is the incredible need of change which manifests itself in them from adolescence. The majority of them, after one or two years at the same occupation, have had enough of it; they aspire to something new; whatever it is, better or worse, does not matter: school-children want to become workmen, carpenters try to become masons, and cooks long to be gardeners or carpenters."

To change the habits of improvidence, centuries old, and the natures formed by these habits, cannot be the work of a moment. All that can be looked for, all that should be looked for, is a gradual change, for none other can be lasting. Every day the signs increase that that change is being brought to pass. The change is most marked in the districts in which regular labour goes hand in hand with Christian teaching. The tribes which lived along the great routes had, of necessity, heavy labours imposed on them in the early days of the State's existence, before the railroads were built. From these labours, constantly and regularly imposed, they have emerged new men, and now that the necessity of porterage is no longer imposed on them they turn readily to other work, which they carry on with a steadiness and constancy which prove that the custom of labouring has entered into their natures, with the desire to gain wages and profit by the comforts of civilisation. These tribes, moreover, are the tribes amongst whom Christianity has made the widest progress.

To sum up the present situation of the Catholic missions in the Congo the following are the official statistics regarding them, published in the report of the Governor-General of the Congo to the Secretary of State in June, 1904 : 59 fixed posts and 29 posts of passage ; 386 missionaries and nuns ; 528 farm-chapels ; 113 churches and chapels ; 523 oratories ; 3 secondary schools ; 75 primary schools ; 440 elementary schools (where black instructors teach the elements of reading, writing, and arithmetic) ; 7 hospitals ; 71 Christian villages ; 72,382 Christians and catechumens.

The Protestant missionary societies, inspired by the great name of Livingstone, commenced their evangelising labours in the interior of the Congo State in the same year as the Catholic missionaries. Protestant missionary organisations working in the same field suffer always from the fact that, while they all desire with equal sincerity to spread the knowledge of Christianity, they differ widely amongst themselves as to the tenets of the Christian faith, and where their congregations mingle insist on accentuating their differences, rather than dwelling solely on the great truths which all Christians

THE CHURCH, KISANTU.

MISSIONARIES' HOUSE, KISANTU.

THE CONGO MISSIONS. 221

hold in common, and on the one end for which every Christian missionary strives.

The extent of the territories in which the missionaries labour has, however, caused this fact to be less injurious to the Protestant missions in that State than elsewhere ; and the polemical weaknesses of the Protestant missionaries in the Congo might be said to do little to retard the cause they wish to advance, were it not, that instead of giving loyal praise to the actions of their Catholic fellow-workers in the cause of Christianity, numbers of them are forever decrying the priests, seeking to undermine their work and to poison the minds of the natives against them, until one is forced to ask himself if the natives can possibly realise that the religion these antagonistic missionaries teach is the same, or if they do not rather think the Christians believe in different Gods, and look on the God of the white men who speak French and bear the Crucifix in their hands to be quite another God from the God of the white men who speak English, and bear no sign.

This attitude of men who speak of Anti-Christ to those who have not heard of Christ, and who, instead of instructing the natives to bow down before the Cross wherever it is preached, teach Christian neophytes " to contend with the three forms of darkness which they will meet in Africa : Heathenism, Mahomedanism, and Popery," is so harmful to the cause of Christianity in the Congo that it is impossible to avoid dwelling upon it in any appreciation of their work. It is an attitude which ill-befits a Christian, wherever his lot be cast, and one the Protestant missionaries in the Congo would do well to abandon and to follow the wise example of the Methodists of the United States, who, at their Congress of 1904, resolved that they would neither contend against nor impede the work of the Catholic missionaries. It is probable that the slow advance of the evangelising work of the Protestant missionaries is due in a very great part to their wasting of energies in stirring up the natives' hate, instead of teaching them the love they need so much. That it cannot be attributed to any action of the Congo Government or of the King seems to be proved by the very explicit wording of the address presented to King Leopold by the British Baptist Missionary Society in January, 1903. The text of this address, which has already been quoted in this chapter, is as follows :—

"The Committee of the British Baptist Missionary Society of London desire most respectfully to address your Majesty as Sovereign of the Congo Free State, and to express their grateful acknowledgments for your Majesty's gracious and helpful sympathy with all wisely considered efforts put forth for the enlightenment and uplifting of your Majesty's native subjects living within the territories of the Congo Free State.

" In the prosecution of these labours, the Committee of the Baptist Missionary Society desire gratefully to acknowledge the many signal and helpful proofs they have received of your Gracious Majesty's approval and support ; and very specially at this juncture they are anxious to express to your Majesty their respectful appreciation of the great boon granted ' to all religious, scientific, and charitable institutions ' by the reduction of direct and personal taxes by 50 per cent., from, on, and after the first day of July last, as proclaimed by your Majesty's command in the May and June issues of the *Bulletin Officiel de l'État independant du Congo*, which the Committee regard as a further and significant proof of your Majesty's desire to promote the truest welfare of your Majesty's Congo subjects, and to help forward all institutions calculated to produce enduring and beneficial results."

The Baptist Missionary Society is the longest established of the Protestant missionary societies in the Congo. It is also the society which has the largest number of posts—numbering fifteen—and, further, it is a society honoured by the services in the Congo of able and learned men such as the Rev. Mr. Grenfell, who allows his Christian zeal to be marred neither by sectarian hatred nor jealousy of the State he lives under. The posts of the Baptist Missionary Society are situated on the Congo commencing at Matadi, and following the river as it mounts, at Lufu, Lukungu, Gombe-Lutete, Kinchasa, Bolobo, Lukela, Monsembi, Bopoto, Yakusu (Falls).

The American Baptist Missionary Union, an organisation established in the Congo in 1883, which has its headquarters at Boston, is also active in the Congo State, in which it has fourteen posts, situated at Boma, Matadi, Palaballa, Kenge, Banza-Manteka, Lukungu, Kifua, Kimpese—all in the Lower Congo; and at Leopoldville, Kingila, Bolengi, Irebu, Ikoko, Bwema.

Another American association—the International Missionary Association—is, of the Protestant missions, that which possesses the largest number of workers in the Congo, where it was established in 1889. This society, which limits its action to the Lower Congo, has in it thirteen stations, principally grouped about Matadi and Boma, where it possesses flourishing schools.

The Swedish Missionary Society, the Svenska, also confines itself to the Lower Congo, where it has eight stations, four in the district of the Cataracts—one at Londe (Matadi), one at Mukibungu, one at Kibunzi, and one at Nganda—and one at Diadia.

The American Southern Presbyterian Mission commenced its labours in the Congo in 1890. This society, which has its American headquarters at Nashville, Tennessee, has now three stations in the Congo, Kenge, in the Lower Congo, Lulebo.

Besides the greater missions there are several entirely independent Protestant missionaries with stations in the Congo State, and associations which have but one station : the Foreign Missionary Society, William Oscar

White, Daniel Crawford, the Westcott Brothers, and Campbell and George.

There is one of the American missions which stands out from the others from the fact that, instead of trusting for its existence to the subscriptions of American and European Christians, it is, in principle and in fact, absolutely self-supporting. This is Bishop Taylor's Mission, founded by the American Bishop Taylor in 1886. This mission, whose sphere of activity is not confined to the Congo State, provides its missionaries with their outfits and their travelling expenses to the place in which they are to work, and with no more. In the Congo, as the Catholic missionaries and the Christians in the farm-chapels prove, it is easy for a Christian, while carrying on the work of evangelising, to cultivate the soil sufficiently for his support and that of his household. The example of the missionaries of Bishop Taylor's mission, which has now seven stations in the State, who support themselves by the produce of the chase aided by that of the fields which they cultivate, shows that Protestant missionaries can also exist, if they will, in the Congo without making incessant demands on European charity, and continually draining the purses of their friends.

The English Protestant missions in the Congo started, indeed, with some such promise of becoming self-supporting. The English missionaries, whose work in the Congo is most prominently before the public—those connected with Congo Baolo Mission—insisted most forcibly at the commencement of their work on not alone the desirability, but the necessity, of the Protestant missions on the Congo being "self-sustaining and self-extending." Yet this mission has not to any extent become one or the other, since, after thirty years of existence, it has only seven stations in the Congo; and while its secretary admits that with it, it "is still the day of small things," its expenses in the Congo, paid from

THE CONGO MISSIONS. 225

the funds of the Regions Beyond Missionary Union—a body with an income of nearly £26,000—amount in one year to £13,458.

The following particulars regarding the staff of this mission are given in "These Thirty Years," a special number of " Regions Beyond," for January and February, 1903, edited by Dr. Harry Guinness, the head of the Missionary Union in England :—

" During the past thirteen years ninety-six missionaries have been sent out, of whom thirty have laid down their lives, thirty-five remain to-day on the missionary staff, and, of the remaining thirty-one, six are in connection with the home side of our work, eight have joined other missions, nine retired through ill-health, and eight proved unsatisfactory. All the latter, however, were members either of the engineering, building, or transport department of the mission."

According to the statistics published in " These Thirty Years," " There are to-day 211 Protestant missionaries on the Congo, belonging to eight various societies. There are 283 native evangelists, 327 native teachers ; 40 main stations, and 192 out-stations ; 6,521 communicants, and 1,470 catechumens ; Sunday school attendance, 5,641 ; and day school, 10,162.

" The majority of the communicants are found in the Cataract region of the Congo, in the ranks of the American and Swedish missions, whose church roll together numbers 4,876."

Compared with the wide-spreading work of the Catholic missions, this statement of the result of thirty years' work of the Protestant missions is astoundingly small. Nearly the whole of the native converts made by the Protestant missionaries are, it is stated, to be found in the one small district of the Cararacts, a district near the coast, the one of all in the Congo, perhaps, the most easily in touch with civilisation and its comforts. It is not easy to understand why missionary societies so richly endowed with money as the Protestant missionary societies should remain grouped in the same localities in the Lower Congo without making a more serious effort to found missions in the real centre of savagery on the upper river. The Congo Baolo Mission has at least sent its missionaries far up the Congo. The society which subsidises this mission was originally represented on the Congo by a mission the care of which was handed over by it to the American Baptist Missionary Union in 1884. The present Baolo mission of the Regions Beyond Missionary Union was founded in 1889 as a mission " to the Mongo section of the great Bantu race inhabiting the horseshoe bend of the Congo. The new mission," says the account in " These Thirty Years," " has since that time been prosecuted with vigour. It established four transport stations in the Cataract region during the years that elapsed before the completion of the railway in 1898. Of these only Matadi and Leopoldville are now required, and at the latter centre our mission undertakes at the present time the storage and transshipment work of two other Protestant missions engaged on the upper river."

It is, perhaps, by no means a matter of regret that this mission remains dependent for its existence on the very large donations it receives from England instead of carrying out its implied promise to establish itself in a self-supporting manner; for, judging from the passages which refer to missionary trading in the work of Mrs. M. Grattan Guinness, "The First Christian Mission on the Congo," the manner in which the missionaries proposed to support themselves was not by the cultivation of their land, but by trading. " Men can do business to earn money, and serve God in the Gospel of His Son, at one and the same time here; and why not ultimately in Africa also ? " says Mrs. Guinness. " Why not in the land where the very doing of business with the natives is, in itself, a most material benefit to them, as well as the very best way of getting them under direct spiritual influence ? "

Unfortunately, these questions are too easily answered. There have been instances in which Protestant missionaries in the Congo traded while seeking to carry on their missionary labours, and there have been other cases in which keeping only the name of missionaries as convenient cloaks, men who had gone out as missionaries to the Congo were discovered red-handed carrying on a shameful trade, bartering forbidden arms with the natives for stolen goods. Even in the small and more or less necessary way in which the Protestant missionaries carry on a trade in barter with the natives to-day it is difficult to see how any person can dream of suggesting that these missionaries' dealings bring the natives either "material benefit," or in any way get them under "direct spiritual influence." "One of the missionaries opens the store," says the description in "These Thirty Years," "and hands out to the expectant natives cloth, cowries, beads, brass rods, knives, spoons, or anything else they may require in exchange for the building materials or food they bring. This is not a very pleasing task—very often a dirty, disagreeable one ; but the natives enjoy it thoroughly."

The missionary may say to this that he is not responsible for the fact that it is beads or shells the native seeks ; but at least he should not think, or pretend to think, that such a trade—a traffic of trash for things of intrinsic value—is to the improvement, moral or material, of the native, or to his own credit. In truth, in the publications of the missionary societies too much is written—and, it is greatly to be feared, in the intercourse of these missionaries with the natives too much is said—which has no foundation except that of bathos, of which neither religion nor intelligence can approve, and through the flimsy pretence of which the downright mind of the savage must often penetrate.

Many of the Protestant missionaries are fatally liable to allow themselves to be led away by cheap sentiment. The training of many of them for the mission field, when it extends beyond learning the words of the Scriptures, lies chiefly in lessons of appeal to hysteria. In the description of "Harley's Daily Round," in the work just quoted, it is told that with his studies in English, of which he discovers he knows little, Greek, and other subjects, the study of all of which is subordinated to the study of the Bible, "evangelistic work also forms an essential part of every student's training. Every Lord's Day the men scatter here and there, proclaiming the glad tidings in highways and byways; in lodging-house or chapel; fit training for the day when they shall go forth bearing precious seed, weeping, it may be, but having the glad assurance that they shall doubtless come again rejoicing, bringing their sheaves with them."

There is but too much reason to believe that the Protestant missionaries carry with them the methods of religious hysteria, which the picture conjured up in the lines just quoted suggests, when they seek to convert the blacks. These are the methods of the Salvation Army: methods successful enough when used by the Salvation Army in England, because it seeks there to waken up dormant feelings in those who are Christians at bottom, but methods most hopelessly wrong when applied to untutored savages. To seek to convert the savage by exciting his passions to frenzy is worse than reprehensible; it is criminal. But such an attempt at conversion is all that can be hoped for from missionaries who, for their training, have received instructions in how to rant at street corners.

These observations apply in no way to the qualified clergymen who are to be found amongst the Protestant missionaries in the Congo. Unfortunately, such clergymen form the very smallest proportion of the Protestant

THE CONGO MISSIONS.

missionaries there. " Educate your missionaries " should be the first and the most often repeated injunction given by all of those who wish for the success of the Protestant efforts in the African missions. The works of some of the Protestant missionaries show them to be educated men. In literature they have made important contributions to the Bantu tongue, the chief language of the Congo ; but even amongst those engaged on literary undertakings, and therefore presumably amongst the best educated of the missionaries, the most astounding ignorance is found, and the most extraordinary confessions of inability to convey the lessons of Christianity which they are in the Congo to teach to the natives whom they have been for years " converting." In " These Thirty Years," to quote one instance, a certain missionary, who is said to have devoted himself for years to the arduous task of reducing to writing the native tongue of the people amongst whom he lives, deliberately states of the language that " after persistent study and sustained application we have discovered that it is not adapted to convey Christian ideas, or to express the highest thoughts and worthiest feelings of the intellect and heart."

Conjecture is bankrupt when one seeks to discover how a missionary converts savages to Christianity when he is unable to convey Christian ideas to them. Clearly, many Protestant missionaries in the Congo still need instruction themselves before they can reap the harvest they promised their supporters at home.

The Protestant missionaries in the Congo seek to draw the savages to Christianity solely by their preaching and by scholastic education. If they do not ignore its advantages they do not make any use of technical education for the elevation of the savage, and they leave the necessity of regular work on one side as something beyond their sphere. It is in this that lies their failure to make more than a superficial and quickly passing impression on the negro. School teaching without the formation of the labour instinct is ruinous, instead of being helpful, to the blacks. Fortunately in the Congo State there are many influences at work besides those of the missionaries to force the natives to abandon the lives of sloth into which they are inclined to fall since the coming of the white men has put an end to their lives of strife and warfare; and since the State teaches the natives to work, the missionary schools, in which nothing but reading and arithmetic are taught, may become useful adjuncts to the work of civilisation; but these schools should be regularly conducted institutions—not haphazard undertakings which the negro child approaches for frolic, and where he remains for pay, not for learning. " There are three or four town schools in connection with some of our stations," says the report in " These Thirty Years." " The arrangements for these are very primitive. A chief lends us a palaver house, or the little ones meet in the open air. A native teacher starts off, bell in hand, ringing as he goes, and the children follow him by twos and threes, and he arrives at his destination with a long tail behind him."

This is mockery of education. It contrasts strangely with the description given of the schools of the Catholic missionaries, and wonder grows why such a system, or want of system, which the missionaries almost complaisantly describe as very primitive, is carried on by a mission which has been working for " these thirty years," and the expenses of which in the Congo are over thirteen thousand pounds for one year.

Looking at the situation and the history of the Protestant missions in the Congo, it becomes clear that if these missions are to make a permanent impression on the natives there should be added to the zeal which is already there, and to the very ample funds of which the missionaries dispose, a good education and fit preliminary training for the lay missionaries, as well as

AGRICULTURE BY THE PUPILS OF THE MISSION SCHOOL, KISANTU.

GIRLS' SCHOOL, MOANDA.

for those who are clerics, and a proper organisation and association in their work. It would be well also, not only for the sake of the missionaries themselves, but for that of the natives, who cannot but watch the examples they set, if the Protestant missionaries taught themselves a more generous perception of the work of the Catholic missionaries, and more Christian charity towards them.

It is perfectly appalling to one who, holding aloof from the war of creeds, prays only for the advancement of Christianity and the training of the natives to lead Christian lives, to find the following statement made by English missionaries as the happiest summary of the present outlook amongst the native pupils of the Protestant missions : " They have proved themselves again and again well able to hold their own against heathenism, and also against Romanism. There are many encounters between Catholic and Protestant adherents, but in most cases it is a very unequal contest, as the native Catholic is grossly ignorant of Christian truth, while the Protestant is able to appeal to the law and the testimony, and can wield the sword of the Spirit with success." This is a deplorable picture. The native Catholic has a prodigious memory no less than the native Protestant, could also learn whole passages of scripture—all the law and all the prophets ; but his teachers seek to endow him with the spirit, rather than to stuff him with the letter, and it is evident from the passage quoted here that he is never taught to consider the Christian religion as a thing debatable. To do the work they have set out to do the Protestant missionaries should act quite otherwise than they are doing ; they should cease to make sectarians of their converts, and make Christians of them instead.

There is another point on which the Protestant missionaries, in order to lead the Christian lives to which they aspire, should alter their ways. They should render unto Cæsar the things which are Cæsar's. It is beyond doubt that, whether driven by unchristian—if unconscious—jealousy of their fellow evangelisers who are Catholics and Belgians, or led by the desire to see the country in the hands of English-speaking people, the Protestant missionaries are, as a rule, fomenting hatred of their rulers amongst the natives. They know the natives to be liars, yet they listen to their tales of fictitious woes, and repeat these tales as true. It was Mary Kingsley who said they did this to gain subscriptions for their missions. It is more charitable to suppose that the missionaries, not always the most logical of men, are carried away by misplaced sympathies, or give credence to false tales because sacred names are invoked to prove them true. It is possible, even, that horrified at the brutalities they actually see in savage and brutal Africa, and forgetful that crime exists as well in brutal New York and brutal London, in Texas and in Yorkshire, they think that such things never were before, and would not be but for the men they themselves dislike, until they are obsessed by a phantom of Congo crime, and call—strange thing—for the punishment not of the criminals, but of the judge. These, however, are mere hypotheses and excuses. The fact remains that many Protestant missionaries in the Congo, in direct contravention of Scripture precept, are stirring up rebellion in the State against its lawful rulers; and this fact, coupled with the other fact that the Protestant missionaries, after decades of residence in the Congo, being able to claim no more than a few thousand converts out of the thirty million of inhabitants, have not advanced Christianity as those whose manifold contributions have flowed into the coffers of their societies were entitled to expect they would have advanced it, makes the situation of the Protestant missionaries in the Congo a serious one—one calling for examination and revision on the part of the peoples who sent them out.

CHAPTER XIV.

THE PROGRESS OF THE INDEPENDENT STATE.

THE Independent State of the Congo has been in existence for no more than nineteen years. It is not more than ten years since, after a sanguinary war, it overthrew the massed forces of Arab Mahomedanism, and drove the slave raiders from the land; nor more than five years since it still depended for the means of its financial existence on the grants made to it from the private purse of its sovereign or the loans of Belgium. From the first it has been impeded at its every step by savage and vindictive foes within the State, and from the first it has found itself unaided by a single civilised Government without.

Yet, unaided and hampered as it was, the State of the Congo has already achieved the most stupendous results within its immense territories. The suppression of the slave trade, in which its success has been beyond the possibility of denial, would alone have been a glorious and an all-sufficing return for the labour of its nineteen years of existence and the streams of the Belgians' blood and of their sovereign's money which within these years have been poured out for the civilisation of the State. Alone, the suppression of cannibalism would have been a sufficient attainment to justify the State's existence as an ameliorator of the native's lot.

These two achievements united go far to prove it the most successful of all the civilising governments of our time. With these great successes in the suppression of evil, there are joined other and no less great successes in the creation of good, which must establish its right to be recognised as the most successful of the civilising governments of this age in the eyes of all who are not blinded by jealousy of others' success beside their own failure, by the lust of gold, or the lust of land.

With slave raiding and with cannibalism, the Congo Government — which, to use a phrase the enemies of Belgium are fond of using, is the King—has suppressed the barbarous customs of Fetichism, by which hundreds of slaves were sacrificed on the graves of dead chiefs, and hundreds of innocent people were murdered at the daily trials by poison of the witch doctors. It has forbidden the importation or manufacture of alcoholic liquor throughout all but a very small portion of its territories; it has made stringent regulations regarding the introduction of firearms, and forbidden the sale of arms of precision to natives; and it rigorously enforces these laws. It has suppressed the intertribal wars of the natives, substituting peaceful labour for them, as it is substituting Christianity for Fetichism.

First amongst the creative works by which the Congo State has opened up the way for its civilisation of Equatorial Africa there must be counted the railways and the high roads of the State. Stanley, in his work on the Congo, has written a moving history of the herculean labours he carried out in constructing the first waggon road past the Cataracts: the story of the construction of the railway from Matadi to Leopoldville would not disgrace an epic. As early as 1878 a syndicate was formed on the inspiration of King Leopold to examine the question of a way of communication by railway and steamboats between the Lower and Upper Congo. The construction of a railway had naturally, however, to be postponed until the political organisation of the State was completed, and it was not until 1887 that the King found it possible to entrust the construction of the railway connecting the Lower Congo with Stanley Pool to the Congo Company of Commerce and Industry. Even then technical and financial difficulties

STEAM MOTOR.

AUTOMOBILE ROAD NEAR KWANGO.

STEAM MOTOR WITH TRUCK.

THE PROGRESS OF THE STATE. 235

lay in the way, and it was not until the middle of 1889 that the concessionaire company was definitely constructed with a capital of twenty-five millions of francs, and nine years more of unceasing labour were necessary before the building of the railway line was carried to a successful conclusion.

Everything, it has been said, seemed at the first to conspire against the success of the undertaking : the ground with its abrupt slopes which it was necessary to cross, the absence of labour, the contagious sickness, the discouragement of the directing staff decimated by death. Out of four thousand five hundred men employed on the works from January, 1890, to May, 1892, nine hundred succumbed. In such circumstances demoralisation could not but become general ; there were desertions from the working gangs, and even revolts amongst the labourers. On June 30th, 1892, the railway had only reached its ninth kilometre, and already eleven and a half millions of francs—nearly half of the company's capital—was spent. Still the work was carried on unchecked. " We have in France for other colonial railways—for the line, still unfinished, which is to connect Senegal with the Niger—the same obstacles, the same discomfitures in previsions that seemed seriously founded," says M. Eugène Etienne, the Vice-President of the French Chamber of Deputies, writing in the *Revue Politique et Parlementaire* on " The Congo and the Berlin General Act." " We triumphed over them only after long pauses, after periods of halt which have been irreparable losses of time and money. Therefore we cannot render enough homage to the energy and tenacity of which the promoters of the Congolese work have given proof." It was owing to the co-operation of the Belgian Parliament that the constructors of the railway were able to complete their task.

When it became apparent that more money would be required for it than had been originally estimated, the Parliament raised its subscription from ten to fifteen millions of francs, and authorised the issue of bonds for ten millions, for which it gave a Treasury guarantee. Ample capital having been thus found, the work was pushed on with wonderful rapidity. The half-way station at Tumba, at the hundred and eighty-eighth kilometre, was inaugurated in July, 1896, and on March 16th, 1898, the first locomotive arrived at Dolo, on the shore of Stanley Pool. In the commencement of the following July the ceremony of the opening of the line was presided over by Colonel Thys, Director-General of the railway, in the presence of delegates of the Governments of England, France, Austria, Italy, Spain, Germany, Russia, and Portugal. This railway through the region of the Cataracts is four hundred kilometres long. Its track is a narrow gauge of 0.75 metres. From first to last its construction cost seventy-five million francs.

No sooner was the work on the building of the Cataracts railway concluded than the State turned its attention to the construction of further lines of railway in the districts where river navigation was impossible or difficult. The Mayumbe railway, the second built, which connects Boma with Lukula, was commenced in the same year, 1898. This railway, which is eighty kilometres long, and has a gauge of 0.60 metres, took three years to build, and has been working since 1901. On the completion of the Mayumbe railway, the State laid down the plans of the railway which the Compagnie des chemins de fer du Congo supérieur aux Grands Lacs Africans is now building on a 1.0 metre gauge.

This comprises three lines, which will have a total length of about 1,600 kilometres. The first of these, from Stanleyville to Mahagi, will run through the whole of the northern part of the Province Orientale. The second of the lines of the railway of the great lakes will also have its terminus at Stanleyville. It will run

THE PROGRESS OF THE STATE. 237

from thence southward to Pointhierville, following closely the course of the Congo. Its chief aim will be to connect the navigable portions of the Lulaba River. The third of the great lakes lines will connect the river above Nyangwe-Kasongo with Lake Tanganyika. Already extensions of these lines have been projected, and surveyors are busy laying out the country between Mahagi and Redjaf on the Nile, for a continuation of the first mentioned of these lines from Mahagi to the Nile, a distance of three hundred kilometres. The extension of the second line beyond Pointhierville will depend on the extent to which the river is found to be navigable for large steamers. It is intended to join this second line as soon as possible with the third railway now also projected in the State, the Katanga railway, in order to reach the rich copper, gold, silver, and platina fields which are said to exist in that district. The extent of the Katanga railway itself will be four hundred and fifty kilometres.

The work on these railways is being pushed forward vigorously. Reports of the Great Lakes Railway Company state that in the spring of 1904 that company had already transported seven engines, fifty-eight waggons, three thousand tons of rails and accessories, and a complete repairing workshop; and that the station at the terminus—Stanley Falls—and five hundred metres of quay, were then already completed. At the work seventy white men and two thousand blacks are employed, and no difficulty is found in obtaining native labour. The blacks, finding themselves well fed and paid, offer themselves in great numbers for the work. Neither is there any difficulty found in supplying food for the large body of workmen employed. A quantity of cattle having been introduced, fresh meat is always to be had for the white men, while rice for the native workmen is obtained easily in large quantities.

The great aim of the railway is not to make the carriage of goods possible, but to substitute steam-traction for the porterage by which traffic was formerly carried, and which weighed so heavily on the native carriers. In order to abolish entirely such native porterage, the Government is supplementing the carriage by railways and steamers by means of carriage by motor-cars, and for this purpose it is cutting new roads in several directions, while enlarging and improving the existing caravan roads. Already motor-cars are running on specially constructed roads, from three hundred and fifty to four hundred kilometres long, in the districts of Uele and the Cataracts.

The Cataracts railway connects the lower waters of the Congo and the ocean with the immense network of waterways which stretches over the territories of the State. This network of navigable waters contains a length of no less than ten thousand miles. On the Congo there is a stretch of a thousand miles from Leopoldville to Stanley Falls; on the Mobangi there is one of seven hundred and fifty miles; on the Kasai one of five hundred miles; on the Ruki there is another of five hundred miles; while the Sankuru and the Juma have each stretches of four hundred miles; and many other rivers have navigable stretches of hundreds of miles each.

To profit by these immense stretches of waterways the State has put a fleet of steamers on the Congo, which are put together in the shipyards at Leopoldville. This fleet consists of thirty steamers, varying in tonnage from five to a hundred and fifty tons, and having in all a tonnage of 1,675 tons. The smaller steamers are relics of the days when the railroad was not yet built, and the vessels for the upper waters of the Congo had to be hauled over the Cataract region by manual labour.

At present, after many careful trials, the Congo Government has adopted a special type of narrow draught, stern-wheeled steamers as best adapted to the

THE PROGRESS OF THE STATE.   239

navigation of its rivers, and, in addition to the vessels already enumerated, two steamers built to its design, of five hundred tons each, are now plying on the waters of the upper river. Steamers of considerable burthen have been also launched on the waters of the other chief rivers of the State, and a sailing vessel has been launched on the Tanganyika, and a steamer on the Nile. There are employed in the naval service of the State one hundred and sixty-six white men and one thousand three hundred blacks. A regular steamer service has been established between Leopoldville, Stanley Falls, and the intermediate stations since 1896, and this service is now arranged in such a manner as to suit the arrivals and departures of the mails from Belgium.

Beside the Government fleet there is a flotilla of steamers belonging to traders and private individuals on the upper waters of the Congo, consisting of about forty vessels, but of a lesser tonnage than the flotilla of the State. These vessels are generally used for the transport of the goods of their owners on the affluents of the Congo, use of the Government service being made, in nearly all cases, for transport on the Congo itself. All the steamers use wood as fuel, and are supplied with it from the forests on the banks of the rivers. Special posts are placed along the river for the supply of fuel to the steamers of the State, where wood is kept ready cut, and special regulations are made for the replanting of the localities from which the trees are cut, that the forests may run no danger of being exhausted. Further, the Congo and its principal affluents in their most intricate parts have been buoyed and charted, a pilot service has been established at Banana, the lower river is dredged to remove the deposits of sand and gravel which accumulate in it, and lighthouses erected near Banana Point cast their light eleven nautical miles out to sea, and serve as a safe guidance for in-coming mariners.

The postal and telegraph services come next to the railway in the State organisation. To those who have studied the progress of the State so far it will not come with astonishment to learn that an admirably maintained telegraph runs through twelve hundred kilometres of the centre of what was once the Dark Continent, or that there is in the Congo State a telephone service which extends for four hundred kilometres. It is but natural that a State so advanced in the ways of civilisation should have installed the wireless telegraphy in its territories, as the Congo State has done at Banana, where the station of the wireless telegraph is placed in connection with the station at Ambrizetta, so as to connect the Congo telegraph with the trans-ocean services. Another means of connecting the Congo telegraph lines with the ocean cables is that of the line between Stanley Pool and Brazzaville, the laying of which has been authorised by a recent convention with France.

The postal service of the Independent State was organised in the year of the foundation of the State, when the State joined the Universal Postal Union. The Congo Government has been officially represented at the various postal congresses held since its establishment. At present there are twenty-three post offices in the State, and the number of letters and newspapers carried in it has risen from 33,140 in 1885 to 372,007 in 1902. The postal service in the Congo is carried on with a fixed regularity even in the parts where the carriage of the letters has to be done by couriers. Carefully constructed rules prescribe the hours and dates of the departure of the letter carriers, and the routes to be followed by them; while equally careful regulations prevent the loss of letters and provide against the overburthening of the carriers. Care has also been taken that, while the postal service is protected and ensured in every way, it shall not be used as a means of inter-

AT LEOPOLDVILLE.

ON THE CATARACTS LINE.

SIDINGS ON THE CATARACTS LINE.

THE PROGRESS OF THE STATE. 241

fering with the natives through whose villages the carriers pass; and, lest they should make use of their uniforms to impose on the strange natives with whom they came in contact if they were allowed to march alone through the country with mail bags, or to extract blackmail from the villagers, it has been forbidden to use native soldiers as letter carriers, as, indeed, it is also forbidden to use the soldiers for any work whatever outside their garrisons and their regular duties, in the performance of which they must be at all times under the control of their superiors.

The progress of the Independent State in the settlement of the natives under civilised law and of the labour question, in the spreading of Christianity, and of the establishment of schools, has been recounted in previous chapters. The State has made progress no less great in the utilisation of science for the improvement of the condition of the natives and of their industries, and for the revelation to the world of the physical condition of the Congo and its people, its riches, and its possibilities. In a tropical country swept, as the Congo is, by dreadful diseases, medical and sanitary care are the first necessity, and all the resources of the State are put forward to secure these. The most perfect hygienic conditions possible are insisted on for all the settlements and dwellings of the white inhabitants of the State and those of the natives employed by it, for the double end of securing the health of the people living in them, and of furnishing object-lessons to the natives. Each end is secured. Not only has a marked improvement in the health of the Europeans in the Congo followed the advance of hygiene and sanitation, but also the natives are found everywhere, where they have opportunities of inspecting the dwellings erected by the white men, to be imitating them in the erection of their own habitations. Unfortunately nothing, either in sanitation, medicine, or food, has as yet been found which will check the greatest evil in the Congo, the sleeping sickness. The medical service of the State has been organised, so that there is a doctor established in each district under the directions of the chief of the medical service, who is stationed at Boma. Besides the official doctors, there are several private practitioners in the Independent State in the employment of the various trading companies, of the railway companies, and of other like bodies; and further, every European going to the Congo is pressed into the medical service, being given portable medicine chests and instructions regarding them for use during travels in distant parts. The doctors at the chief stations, who have each a certain number of native infermarians under their directions, travel throughout their districts wherever their attentions are required. In each of the chief stations there are pharmacies and hospitals, in which the natives are cared for; and at Boma and Leopoldville there are hospitals for white patients established by the Congolese and African Association of the Red Cross; the one at Boma being tended by nuns, and that at Leopoldville by native infermarians. The Association of the Red Cross has also instituted a flying ambulance service which has rendered the greatest services to the expeditions and missions sent out to the farther portions of the State. In addition to these institutions there is also at Boma a Bacteriological Institution installed in 1899 by the Société d'Études Coloniales, in which the various African maladies are studied.

Smallpox prevails in the Congo with a virulence almost as great as that of the sleeping sickness. To combat this disease the Government has installed Instituts Vaccinogènes in the centre as well as in the outer parts of the State, from which regular supplies of vaccine are sent to all the posts of the State. The agents in the employment of the State are instructed in the methods of vaccination and of cultivating vaccine,

THE PROGRESS OF THE STATE. 243

and they are required to exert every means of spreading vaccination amongst the natives. These efforts for the check of smallpox have proved most successful, and the Governor-General of the Congo, in his report in June, 1904, states that the natives, recognising the benefit of vaccination, come themselves in great numbers to ask for it.

The report of the Governor-General gives particulars of the efforts to counteract the sleeping sickness. Up to the present, it states, science has found itself powerless to combat the disease; but recent discoveries have led those studying the disease to conclude that it is due to the penetration of a microbe, the essential propagating agent of which is the Tse-tse fly. Science having found the cause, it is not beyond hope that it will before long discover a remedy for the disease. Doctors of the Liverpool School of Tropical Medicine, an institution subsidised by King Leopold, are at present studying it on the spot; and while remedies are being sought, all that can be done for prevention by isolating patients affected by the disease, and destroying the houses and clothes of those who have died from the disease, is being done.

Social science has occupied the Congo Government from the moment of its foundation, and its progress in this and kindred sciences is attested by a splendid collection of publications and reports, the value of which to the scientific world, and to those scholars on the result of whose studies all wise legislation of the future must be founded, it is impossible to over-estimate. Besides several valuable monographs on the subjects written at the instance of the State, the State has undertaken through its agents a wide ethnologic and anthropologic inquiry throughout its territory. Methodically drawn-up inquiry forms were sent to every official in the State, and their replies form a mine of information. There is hardly an inch of territory in the Independent State which has not been explored by one or several of the many scientific explorers who have travelled in the State either with the assistance or as the agents of the Congo Government ; and as a result of the work of whom a practically perfect map has been prepared of the whole Congo basin. Amongst the principal missions of a special scientific character organised by the State, Baron Descamps cites the following in his work on New Africa :—

  Dupont : Geology (1887).
  Delporte and Gillis : Trigonometrical survey (1890–1892).
  Gorin and Grenfell : Astronomical survey (1893–1896).
  Laurent : Botany (1893–1894).
  Wilverth : Pisciculture (1893–1896).
  Dewevre : Botany (1895–1897).
  Michel : Photography and natural sciences (1895).
  Luja and Dechesne : Botany (1898–1899).
  Delhez : Pisciculture (1898–1899).
  Weyna : Zoology (1898–1899).
  Cabra : Trigonometrical survey, astronomical surveying, and natural sciences (1895–1899).
  Lemaire : Trigonometrical survey, zoology, mineralogy, botany (1897–1899).
  Bastien : Trigonometrical survey, astronomical surveying (1891).
  Cabra : Astronomical surveying and natural sciences (1901–1902).
  Royaux : Mineralogical studies and natural sciences (1902).
  Lemaire : Astronomical surveying (1902).

Besides the various scientific expeditions which it has sent out, the Government has established in the Congo nineteen scientific stations provided with all the necessary materials for their work. In Belgium the Museum of the Independent State at Tervuren contains

THE PROGRESS OF THE STATE. 245

7,796 exhibits in ethnological collections, especially with respect to industry and art amongst the primitive races. That museum has also a useful commercial division, and possesses several thousand zoologic, mineralogic, and geologic specimens.

The great scientific masterpiece of the Independent State may be justly said to be the " Annales du Musée du Congo, publiées par ordre du Secrétaire d'État," a superb work edited for the State by world-renowned scientists. In this work, the glory due to the publication of which the oldest and richest Governments may well envy, the flora of the Congo occupies no less than eighteen volumes, with over a hundred and fifty large plates. Six volumes of the annals are devoted to the description of newly discovered fishes, and are equally richly illustrated ; one volume is devoted to musical instruments, and subsidiary volumes to Congo architecture, the condition of the people, and the Government works.

Learned works have also been published on the climatology of the Congo, and, indeed, on every other scientific subject the study of which could be encouraged by the Government with advantage, immediate or future, to the inhabitants of the Independent State. A whole literature has sprung up in the native tongues, both in the form of books and periodicals, in the printing of which several printing presses are kept busy in the Congo. In Europe the literature relating to the Congo has long passed the bounds of a swift summary, as will be understood from the fact that the " Bibliographie du Congo," by M. M. A. Wauters, although published as long ago as 1895, contains no less than three thousand eight hundred items. All this literature, broadly speaking, was called into existence by the energies of the Independent State, and a very great part of it, which is due directly to the State, is of the greatest scientific value.

Before the foundation of the Independent State the

chief manufacturing industry in the Congo was that of the smith, who forged the arms of the warriors and the knives of the executioners. To-day the principal handicrafts at which the natives are employed are those of the carpenter, the brick-maker, and the builder. In the orphan and deserted children of the State, and in the children whom their parents and chiefs hand over voluntarily for education in the Christian schools, the Government finds a large and always increasing body of apprentices to the useful trades which are taught under its supervision. The sanguinary slave raids of the Arabs and the war which was necessary to suppress them having left great numbers of orphans desolate in that land whose barbarity knew nothing of kindness to the weak, the State nominated itself the guardian of the Congo foundlings. A decree of July, 1890, having recited that "whereas measures of protection are necessary in favour of children who have suffered from the slave trade, and whereas it is the general duty of the State to provide for the guardianship of abandoned children, and of those whose parents are not fulfilling their natural obligations," ordered that the guardianship of such children should be assumed by the State, that "means of subsistence shall be furnished to them, and care taken to provide them with a practical education in order to enable them to earn their living," and that "agricultural and technical settlements shall be established to receive, firstly, the children qualified according to Article I. (those orphaned and deserted), and secondly, as far as may be, the children who apply for admittance." The decree further provided that the children should remain under the guardianship of the State, and be bound to do the work set them, until the completion of their twenty-fifth year, in return for their maintenance, board, lodging, and medical attendance—a provision, it may be observed, similar to those made in the statutes of the orphanage of civilised

PLOUGHING AT EALA MODEL FARM.

CORNER OF THE STUD FARM, EALA.

THE PROGRESS OF THE STATE. 247

countries, and approved of by all civilised Governments, but one particularly suitable and admirable in a country like the Congo, where the orphans are being rescued from barbarity, and where long years are necessary to form them into regular and persevering workers.

Experience proved to the Government, as similar experience has proved all the world over, that the most powerful adjuncts a Government could have in the spread of civilisation were the Christian missionaries; and a further decree, made in March, 1892, provided that "the legal representatives of philanthropic and religious societies may, by submitting an application to the Governor-General, be allowed to receive those native children whose guardianship belongs to the State in the agricultural and technical settlements under their management." This decree also provides that the application for permission to receive the children shall contain the programme of the technical instruction to be given to the children, and that the settlement shall be placed under the supervision of the Governor-General or of his deputy.

In the foregoing chapter details have been given of the trades taught in the orphan schools, and of the developing influence which these schools exert on the intelligence and the moral character of the native children and youths. It only remains to be added here that the children are perfectly free to go and come as they wish in these schools; nothing but their preference for the schools, and their loyalty to their promises to remain in them, standing between them and the liberty of the trackless forest.

The introduction of European trades and methods of workmanship into the Congo has not killed, nor has it been sought to kill, by them, the ancient savage handicrafts, in which the amount of skill and artistic sensibility attained to by the natives is manifested. Although lances and swords and iron-tipped arrows are no longer of prime necessity for the native whose sole right to live in past times lay in his ability to murder his fellows, the metallurgic industry has not fallen into decay. The native workers continue to turn out with their primitive instruments knives for agricultural use, as well as lances, which may be used in the chase when warfare is no longer possible; and with these razors, hatchets, nails, horse-shoes, bells, collars, hairpins, and the rings of copper and iron which still not infrequently form the chief portion of the attire of rich natives. The output of the native workers has increased considerably since they learned from the white men how to extract and cast metals in an improved manner far different from the primitive methods they were accustomed to employ. The native craft next in importance to metal working is that of weaving. With looms similar to the handlooms used by European workmen up to the end of last century, the Congo weavers manufacture cloth of a close and resistant quality, cords which stand every strain, and hats which are not without elegance in their design. In some districts they also manufacture fine fabrics for clothing, which they dye many bright colours.

The natives are also skilful basket-workers, mat-makers, and potters. Grotesque carvings in wood and ivory are common amongst them, and though these are losing the savage merits they possessed before the instruction of the white men, the manufacture of carved chairs and stools is gaining much from that instruction and the spread of civilisation with its demand for household furniture. The natives still work assiduously at the manufacture of musical instruments, of which they have many varieties; but this manufacture is one which seems destined to be killed, or at least modified considerably, by the spread of commerce with Europe. Already brass bands are superseding their primitive lutes and mandolins in the fancy of the natives.

THE PROGRESS OF THE STATE. 249

One of their industries, which is as flourishing as those of the metal workers and weavers, is that of the manufacture of fishing-tackle. A continuous trade is done in the various native industries, which represents a considerable amount of wealth. This trade progresses as the authority of the State, and the peace it brings with it, advances; but as it is a trade done almost exclusively between the natives themselves, it is not possible to arrive at an exact estimate of the development to which it has attained.

The progress of the Independent State in the department of agriculture is as marked as it is in every other direction. It is to the State that the introduction of regular and sufficient methods of agriculture amongst the native races is due. For long centuries the natives of the Congo have lived from hand to mouth, with the result that even in that generous land famine was a common experience amongst them. A scratching of the soil was all that was necessary to produce a harvest, and a sorry scratching was all that the natives gave it. Since they laid nothing by for a future day, and cultivated no more than was exactly sufficient for their needs, the slightest failure of their harvest left them without a resource. Moreover, each race had a tendency to rely exclusively on some staple article of food. They knew nothing of cultivating various crops, so that should one be blighted or destroyed—as by the locust pest—another would sustain them. This again was the continual cause of suffering amongst them, and in this fact is to be found the explanation of how famine so often swept whole villages away, while tribes not distant from them lived in plenty, and while the land teemed with fruits. In introducing wiser methods of agriculture, the State had to overcome not only ignorance and laziness, but prejudice, rooted in superstition.

The success which has followed its efforts is due to the most patient perseverance. It has been obtained by continually setting before the eyes of the natives the example of the agricultural stations of the Government. Through the agency of these stations the State is gradually extending throughout the whole of its territories the cultivation of valuable products, which were only known in certain districts. For example, rice, unknown before outside of the Manymema district, is now cultivated in nearly every district, and so successfully that the natives living near the Government stations are able to supply them with many tons of rice at a time. The agents of the State have spread the cultivation of manioc through the districts in which it was previously unknown, and they have imported sweet potatoes and earth nuts into the north-east districts and along the borders of Lake Tanganyika. They have also imported and scattered over the country Indian bananas, which are better than those formerly cultivated in the country.

The work of the agents of the State in spreading agriculture is aided by the action of the discharged soldiers and workmen who, on completing their terms of service, return to village life, and by the Christian families which have been educated in the missionaries' schools. These, profiting by the lessons they have received, cultivate many kinds of European vegetables, tomatoes, cabbage, onions, beans, potatoes, lettuce, spinach. The natives who cultivate these European vegetables have in many cases not as yet begun to eat them themselves, and cultivate them only for sale to the Europeans at the stations; but once the cultivation of a vegetable or fruit becomes common in the Congo, it is certain that in time its use will be adopted by the negroes, in whom the spirit of inquisitiveness and imitation is sufficiently strong to overcome the most deeply rooted prejudice.

Although the spread of new plants throughout the State by the Congo Government dates from the earliest

THE KITCHEN GARDEN, LOFOI.

CULTIVATED FIELDS, LOFOI.

THE PROGRESS OF THE STATE. 251

days of its existence, the foundation of a central State-managed botanic garden did not take place until 1900. Previously, however, a trial garden had been established at Boma in 1895, and at various other posts in the Lower Congo, at which posts the cultivation of plants suitable to the district is continued. Eala, a spot at the confluence of the Congo and the Ruki, was chosen as the situation of the Botanic Garden of the State on account of the fertility of its soil, of its nearness to the great centre of cultivation at Coquilhatville, and the facility with which its products can be conveyed to distant parts of the State. Its situation further permits of the passage through it of the agents of the agricultural service of the State when on their way to their stations in the Upper Congo, and it is customary for these agents, as well as private individuals interested in agriculture, while *en route* to remain for some time at this station in order to study the methods of agriculture which are carried on at it. The Government establishment at Eala consists of a botanic garden, a trial garden, glass houses for propagation, hot-beds, and a model farm. It has in all twenty-nine buildings, and a hundred acres of plantations in addition to its pasture lands. Five hundred different vegetables are cultivated at it, of which over two hundred have been imported. This botanic garden at Eala is the first place in Equatorial Africa at which the propagation of plants by slips has been carried on. Before the installation of its glass houses and hot-beds, cultivation from seeds was the only means used there for the multiplication of vegetables.

During several years the efforts of the Congo Government to import plants into the State proved fruitless, owing to the inability of the plants to bear the long voyage from the countries to which they were indigenous to the Congo. During ten years continuous attempts were made to transport the gutta-percha plant from the Dutch East Indies to the Congo, but each attempt was a failure. Of eleven hundred of these plants imported in 1893 not one lived. Four subsequent attempts to introduce plants of the same species were equally complete failures. Of the fifth lot imported in 1899 two plants survived, while twenty-seven survived of the number imported in 1900.

These continuous failures to introduce new species of plants into the Congo, instead of disheartening the Government, caused it rather to consider if a method before untried could not be found which would turn the failure which attended the importation of plants into success. Since the want of success was caused by the failure of the plants to bear the long voyages to the Congo, it was determined to try the method of resting the plants for a time in a special establishment, or rest-house, at Brussels. For this purpose the colonial garden at Laeken was founded. Its use has already produced the desired effect, and the State is now enabled to import into the Congo plants of every species and from the most distant parts.

All the plants destined for importation to the botanical gardens at Eala are now cultivated at Laeken, and transported from there to the Congo in whatever condition is found to be best for their propagation. There are actually twenty thousand plants under cultivation for the Independent State in its Laeken agricultural rest-house. From this rest-house there were forwarded in 1902–1903 three hundred and twenty shipments, containing fifteen thousand plants, to the Congo; and from the year 1903 the Congo Government has commenced from this place, and from Boma, where the exports from it are unshipped, the distribution of plants on a large scale to companies, to private individuals, and to the natives. Its distributions include plants of tobacco, bananas, cotton, rubber, and fruit trees, as well as vegetables.

The agents engaged for the agricultural service of

NATIVES PREPARING RUBBER.

NATIVES COLLECTING RUBBER, LUSAMBO.

the State are instructed at Laeken in the management of tropical gardens and pastures before their departure. These agents are drawn in a large part from the excellent agricultural schools of Belgium, and their number increases daily. Besides the establishment at Eala, there are now seventy large agricultural stations of the Government in the Independent State, to each of which a specially trained agricultural staff is attached.

The principal vegetable products cultivated and gathered at these Government stations are indiarubber, coffee, copal, cacao, palm nuts, palm oil, ground nuts, and wood. Not one of these, with the exception of the ground nuts and palms, was gathered by the natives, or traded in by Europeans before the foundation of the Independent State. Rubber, amongst the others, was unknown to the natives before the State showed them its existence and instructed them in its value. A few tribes of the north or south coated the ends of their drum-sticks with rubber, and used it to fix the iron heads of their arrows; but even these set no value whatever on the rubber more than any other resinous matter, and they simply used the rubber when no other sticky substance was nearer to their hands.

The collection of rubber in the State commenced in the year 1887, in the Kasai district. In the development of the rubber industry since its commencement many precautions have been necessary to prevent the destruction of this great source of riches by the attempts of traders to exploit the rubber, or the carelessness of natives in cutting down plants instead of tapping them. Replantation, to replace the rubber collected, is insisted on at the rate of five hundred feet of creepers or trees for every ton of rubber collected. The State sets the example in this matter by planting millions of rubber creepers annually. In the Cataracts district alone, where the rubber creepers had almost disappeared, there are now growing more than a million rubber creepers, planted by the Government. The smallest clump of trees, plantations, and woods have been utilised for the planting of these creepers, in the spreading of which the Government has been given ready assistance by the native chiefs.

As has been explained in the chapter on the Congo law and the natives' future, the natives, while obliged to gather as a tax a certain amount of rubber from the Crown lands outside of their forests—as much as each man can gather in forty hours' work, at the outside, each month—are paid a small but sufficient sum for gathering it, in order that they may have a money inducement to work for in addition to protection, and the many other material benefits the State affords them in return for their tax. The natives, as has also been related in the chapter referred to, are secured in the possession of their villages and of their native plantations ; and in seeking to improve the condition of agriculture the State naturally pays the greatest attention to the improvement of these plantations and cultivated fields, on the produce of which the inhabitants of the country live. It is not content, however, to allow the natives' activities, or their interests, to cease at the boundaries of their fields. Instead of this, it calls for their co-operation in the work of advancing agriculture all over the land, the immediate profits from which it shares with them, and by the future benefits from which they must profit largely. Regulations regarding the cultivation of coffee and cocoa were made on April 30th, 1897, in the following decree :—

" The chiefs recognised by the Government shall be bound to create and keep coffee and cocoa tree plantations on the vacant lands pertaining to the State in the regions submitted to their authority.

" The area of the plantations to be created will be established by the district commissioner or his delegate, according to the density of the population under

THE PROGRESS OF THE STATE. 255

the authority of each chief, and calculated on an average of one twentieth part of the work that can be produced each year by the said population.

"The plantations are under the management and control of the scientific agriculturist of the State, who will give the necessary instructions to the chiefs, both as regards the choice and the clearing of the land and as regards the planting and the tending of the cultures.

"The chiefs will receive a bounty of ten centimes for each coffee or cocoa tree properly planted, and measuring seventy-five centimetres in height.

"The product of the said plantations shall be handed over to the State in the localities indicated by it, at a price fixed each year by the Governor-General, and corresponding to one-half of the value of the product in Belgium after deducting the outlays necessitated by transport from the place of origin to the place of destination.

"The chiefs shall have a right of fruition on the plantations created and worked by them according to the present decree. They may transmit this right of fruition to their successors. In no case can the right be alienated or encumbered with mortgage or charge without the consent and authority of the State."

There are twenty-one inspectors charged with the execution of the decrees relating to re-planting. Under their directions there have been planted in five years in the territories of the State two millions of feet of coffee plants, three hundred thousand cocoas, five million two hundred and fifty thousand feet of rubber plants, and four thousand feet of gutta-percha.

Amongst the agricultural developments of the Independent State, that of cotton culture requires special notice, although it is still in its infancy. Cotton is indigenous to the soil, and the natives in several districts have been in the habit of making some use of it for the manufacture of hammocks, bags, hats, and clothes. Besides this native cotton, the State has imported cotton seeds and planted cotton fields at the Eala botanic gardens, with the view of studying the different varieties in order to discover which is the best for cultivation for trade purposes, and what is the best method of growing and gathering it. The study of cotton growing made in the Congo has already proved so encouraging that it has been determined to undertake the cultivation of cotton in the territories of the State on the largest scale; and Sir Alfred Jones, the President of the British Cotton Growing Association, who declares that the Independent State has " millions of acres of picked land suitable for cotton growing," predicts of it that " it is quite possible that we shall yet see in our time that Africans in Africa will supply the world with cotton."

Another industry fostered by the State, and, though still in its infancy, advancing rapidly towards what promises to be a most prosperous future, is the timber trade. The great forests of the Congo contain many different kinds of timber. Certain species dominate the different regions, but, with the exception of the elaïs, it is rare to find any one species growing in large clumps not intermixed with many trees of other species. This is looked upon as a happy circumstance, as when the timber trade of the Congo becomes enlarged as regards the species most suitable for exportation, it will prevent the rapid disafforesting, such as other virgin forests have suffered from in the past. The Government arrangements for the working of the forests date from the year 1894. In 1895 a station for the cutting and forwarding of the forest trees was established at Shinganga, on the left bank of the Shiloango, in the centre of the forest of Mayumbe; and six months afterwards the first shipment of Congo timber arrived in Europe. The timber is floated down the stream from Shinganga in rafts

NATIVES SAWING TIMBER.

HAPING TIMBER BY HAND.

THE PROGRESS OF THE STATE. 257

so constructed that the heaviest trees are kept afloat by being tied to other trees of a remarkable lightness and buoyancy, which are found in quantities on the banks of the Shiloango. The timber principally exported from the Congo at present is the " Ngula Maza," or *Sarcocephalus Diderrichii*, which is called the " Yellow Congo Mahogany," a straight, slender tree, which shoots up to a considerable height. This tree, which is of a beautiful golden colour, and of a grain which permits of the finest working, is already much used for cabinet making and house carpentry in Belgium.

The industry of cattle breeding is joined to that of agriculture by the Congo Government. Fifteen years ago, with the exception of goats, which were found in every part of the State, and occasionally of sheep, there was not a beast to be found in any part of the immense territories of the Congo outside of the north-east region and the extreme south. Now, there is not a station of any importance in the Lower, the Middle, or the Upper Congo without flourishing herds of cattle. In the Lower Congo the first attempts at cattle breeding were made by the Compagnie de Roubaix, in Mateba Island. These attempts proved successful, and the work has been carried on by the Compagnie des Produits du Congo, which succeeded that company. From the beasts imported from the south and west coasts of Africa and from Europe, thousands of heads of cattle have been raised, which are to be found in the establishments of the Lower Congo. In the Middle Congo the increase in the stocks is equally great, that at Stanleyville, for example, being 40 per cent. in recent years, notwithstanding the fact that there, as in all the stations of the Lower and Middle Congo, an abundance of butchers' meat is regularly supplied. In the other stations of the State, although the breeding of cattle progresses equally successfully, the slaughter of any animals for food is forbidden up to the present, in order that the herds may increase as rapidly as possible, their rapid increase being particularly desirable from the fact that it is the cattle themselves which must form their pasture lands by continually eating the grass, which otherwise would grow too long to be fit for their nourishment. As soon as the heads of cattle grow sufficiently large, a regular revictualment service for the stations of the Upper Congo will be organised, similar to that already established in the Lower and Middle Congo.

The Catholic missionaries give potent aid to the officials of the State in spreading the knowledge of cattle breeding as well as of agriculture amongst the natives. At each of the hundreds of farm-chapels established by the Jesuits the farm-yards, orchards, and vegetable gardens of Europe are found reproduced with their familiar animals, fowl, fruit, and vegetables. It is the same at the great agricultural schools of the Pères de Scheut at New Antwerp and Luluabourg; while at La Trappe of Bamania, where a thousand natives are employed in the farm and workshops, the industry of the fields and farms has made a paradise where there had been a wilderness at the famous mother-house of the Cistercian order.

In the Lualaba-Kasai district the native chiefs possess large herds of cattle, and the Europeans at the stations in these localities have succeeded in breaking their oxen to burthen.

In addition to its cattle, the model farm at Eala possesses a fair number of harness horses, imported from Senegal, the transport of which from the coast lasted a whole year, so carefully was the journey performed, and so many the measures taken to acclimatise the horses to the country. In the Uele district there are also horses to be found in the posts of the State, descended from those imported from Lake Chad by the Government in 1895. At New Antwerp the State breeds horses, asses, and mules, with which most of the stations

THE PROGRESS OF THE STATE. 259

above Eala are supplied. In the grass country of the Ubangi-Uele district there are great herds of cattle, many stations of the State possessing over a thousand head, and several native chiefs possessing twice that number each.

The stations of the State are supplied at present not only with milk from their own cows, but also with butter of their own making, for the manufacture of which the Government has supplied them with churns of the most improved description, thus enabling the agents of the State to instruct the natives in the proper manufacture of milk-products, of which they were ignorant before.

Side by side with the familiar domestic animals of Europe, the Congo Government is breaking in to its use the wild beasts and fowl of Africa, ostriches, dromedaries, zebras, and elephants. A special mission is at present engaged on breaking in zebras, not only for the purpose of using these animals in harness or as beasts of burthen, but also for that of crossing them with horses and asses, with the object of obtaining a breed capable of resisting the attacks of tse-tse fly. Another mission is employed at the present time in rearing a number of young African elephants, which the Government intends to use when trained for the capture of numbers of other young elephants, after the method employed in India. These young elephants thrive in captivity, and show themselves easy to train ; and the Congo Government boasts that before many years it will have in its service troops of trained African elephants, such as no man has had since the days of Cæsar.

Turning from agriculture to commerce the tale is the same—one of wonderful and continued progress, due to the untiring labour of the State for the furtherance of the country's good. With the yearly returns of the commerce of the Congo before them, none can be blind to its growth—a growth which attained to the figure of 87,888,775 francs for its general commerce in 1903; but it is easy to forget the past which does not stare one in the face, and many forget that it is to King Leopold alone, and his action in the years which followed the foundation of the State, that the advance of the Congo commerce and its now assured prosperity are due.

It is not enough to found States in lands teeming with possibilities of development, and to endow them with laws or trade rules, in order to bring about their development. Even the richest land needs the labour of years or the expenditure of millions to open it up to trade. It was King Leopold who gave the Independent State the means it needed. Had he not advanced to the State the sum of nearly two millions sterling from his private purse, and had not his enthusiasm led the Belgian Parliament to aid when his own resources ran low, the "Belgian Congo" would be to-day as the French Congo beside it is—without a railway, without a steamer service, without great motor roads. Most assuredly it would still be without a commerce sufficient to attract the jealousy of the greatest nations, and sufficient—a thing its creator thinks of more—to bring to the inhabitants of the Independent State the benefits which, through wise government, it has brought, and which have been enumerated in this chapter.

The French Congo and the Independent State came into existence almost on the same day. The two explorers, Brazza and Stanley, it will be remembered, raced each other through the virgin forest to gain possession of the great river and of the coast line; and, it will also be remembered, the boundaries of the two States were fixed by treaties between France and representatives of King Leopold, by which the French and Belgians settled down amicably in the possession of either side of the great river. Not only were the two contiguous States founded at the same time, but they have been governed since by practically the same laws.

CATTLE AT STANLEYVILLE.

STABLE AT EALA

CATTLE AT VANKERCKHOVENVILLE.

In what refers to the suppression of the slave trade, and the freedom of trade, each country is bound by the Act of Berlin, France as a signatory to the Act, and the Independent State as having adhered to it; while for the interior government of the countries, the rights of the people and the rights of the State, the government of each is modelled on the Code Napoléon—a code between the rules of which as applied in France, Belgium, and the Independent State there is no material difference. There has been only one difference between the two countries, but that difference was one that was all-important from the point of view of their prosperity. It was this: that while France, having accepted her new colony *sans dot*, to quote the words of M. Etienne, " seriously believed that a colony could live, prosper, and be developed without the expenses of its foundation being undertaken to supply it with ways of communication, and without the necessary economic equipment for the improvement of its natural riches," King Leopold saw that great works were necessary for the development of the Congo, and boldly flung out his money that they might be completed. It is to King Leopold's foresight and determination in carrying out the public works of the Congo that the commercial progress of the State is due.

King Leopold's beneficial action for the commercial development of the Congo was twofold: it opened up the Congo, even to its inmost recesses, to the freedom of the trade of all nations on the one hand; while on the other it warded off plunderers and marauders, those pirates of commerce who, " trading " gin and powder with the savages for the rich products of the country, would have swept the country bare, hacked down its forests, slaughtered all its beasts, and debased its natives but for the King's restraining hand.

The law which preserved the country from pillage in the name of commerce was made, as has been told in the chapter on the Congo law, in the same month as that in which King Leopold assumed the sovereignty of the Congo, when a decree was published prescribing that "no one has a right to occupy, without title, any vacant land, or to dispossess the natives from the land which they occupy; the vacant land must be considered as belonging to the State." The vesting of vacant land in the Crown is a principle of law universally acknowledged and universally acted on. Between its adoption and anarchy there could be no medium in the Congo. If the rights of property in its territories were abandoned by the Congo State, nothing could obtain in that country, as the Congo Government has itself pointed out; but "the system of the sweepstakes where the first occupier, since the property would be a forbidden monopoly, would be logically dispossessed by others who were new comers would result at the end of the account in insecurity for all, in the devastation of the forests, and in their inevitable and rapid disappearance, and in destroying all possibility for the whites on the Congo to preserve the legitimate fruits of their labour."

The truth of this cannot be disproved. No one has been found sufficiently imbecile to pretend that the natives could of themselves, undirected or uninstructed by the white men, enter into effective occupation or cultivation of the immense tracts of untrodden forest and prairie which formed the Congo State. No one, not blinded by self-interest, can be found sufficiently ignorant to believe that the abandonment of the land to the pillage of adventurers could end otherwise than in the destruction of the native races. Pillage is not commerce, although those who desire to carry it on naturally pretend it is, and although it is difficult to find in the dealings of European traders with savage races where pillage ends and trade begins; but even as regards commerce, none can be found who regard the lessons of history who dare pretend that unregulated

THE PROGRESS OF THE STATE. 263

commerce has ever yet proved beneficial to a savage race with whom Europeans dealt. The history of America, the history of Australia, the history of Africa itself, all show the ruin that is wrought in the sacred name of trade.

Long before the Independent State was founded traders were settled at the mouth of the Congo, whence they carried on unrestricted intercourse with the natives; but no good came from their settlement. Rather, it was disgraced by crimes against the blacks before which the most terrible "atrocities" of later days pale into insignificance—crimes committed not centuries since, but on the very eve of the foundation of the Independent State; and it bore a reputation for the debauchery and degradation of the natives which has not yet faded. Long after the foundation of the Independent State traders continued to penetrate, unhindered by the authorities, into the French Congo; but the only benefits the natives got from them in return for the goods that they gave were those of gin and gunpowder. No honest man can deny that if King Leopold had permitted unregulated trade in the Congo, that trade would have been a trade in the same articles of gin and gunpowder.

Yet the traders of gin and powder have dared to protest, in the name of humanity and of the native interest, against King Leopold's wise regulations of trade and cultivation in the Congo, and honest men have been found simple enough to listen to them. They protest that King Leopold's regulations regarding the cultivation of the lands of the Crown are a violation of the clause of the Act of Berlin which stipulates that freedom of trade shall exist in the conventional basin of the Congo. Nothing can be more false or more absurd than such a contention. Regulation is not restriction, nor is cultivation commerce, however much the ignorant or the interested may cry out that it is.

Following up the decree by which he preserved the land of the Congo from the marauder, King Leopold proceeded to regulate the manner in which the land vested in the Crown should be managed and cultivated. Portion of the domain he decided should be managed directly by the State itself, and of the manner in which the State manages its property, and carries on its cultivation, much has already been told in this chapter. Part of the domain he entrusted to the hands of concessionaires, following in doing so the example of England, who, to quote a few instances, granted 1,425,000 acres in Lower Canada to sixty people, who granted 15,000,000 acres to concessionaires in Upper Canada, and who distributed the land in gratuitous concessions in Australia; and a portion he left open to the exploitation of traders, with, however, the restrictions retained that neither alcoholic liquor nor powder should be imported for trade with the natives. In another portion of the domain he decreed that the collection of its fruits should not be undertaken until a later period.

King Leopold's decrees divide the country into three zones, in which these separate forms of managing the domain lands are practised. The first comprises the basins of the M'Bomou, the Uele, the Mongolla, the Itimbiri, the Aruwimi, the Lopori, and the Maringa, of Lakes Leopold II. and Tumba, and of the Lukenia. In this zone the State alone collects the ivory and rubber of the domain lands, either by itself or with the co-operation of the companies in which it has large interests. The second zone comprises Mayumba and the region of the Falls, the banks of the Upper Congo from Stanley Pool to as far as Stanley Falls—excepting the banks in the districts of the Equator and Aruwimi, and the left bank of the Ubanghi below its confluence with the M'Bomou—the basins of the Ruki, Ikelamba, Lulonga, below the confluence of the Lopori and the

Kasai. In this zone, which contains more than a quarter of the vacant lands of the State independently of all the region below Stanley Pool, the State has left the land at the public disposal, and abandoned the exclusive right of collecting rubber on its property in it to private individuals. The third zone comprises the eccentric territories of the basins of the Congo-Lualaba, and the Upper Loamami, of the Urua, and of the Katanga. The decree of October, 1892, by which these zones were fixed decides that the collection of rubber shall be regulated in the latter district " when circumstances permit of it," a moment which has not yet come, and the rubber in this district consequently remains as yet uncollected.

These regulations regarding the management of the domain lands and the collection of its fruits interfered in no way with the freedom of trade in the Independent State, which the Congo Government has fostered from the first. Opponents of the Independent State make the ridiculous complaint that trade is impossible within its limits, since the Government itself gathers the fruits of the land, which are the only articles for which Europeans can trade in the Congo. The trade returns give an instant refutation to this allegation.

These returns form also a complete refutation of the other false statement, that only Belgian firms can trade in the Congo. Merchants of all countries not only can, but do, trade, and trade prosperously, all over the territories of the Independent State. The trade of the foreign merchants increases no less than that of the Belgians. Of this the Congo Government gave an example in its report for June, 1903, when it cited the case of the Dutch Society, whose exportations in 1897 reached a total of nearly £30,000, while in 1901 its exportations amounted to more than £120,000 ; and similar instances could be multiplied, were it not that the published statistics of the Congo trade make elaboration of the point superfluous. The Governor-General of the Congo in his report in June, 1904, declares that the policy of the Independent State is the policy of the Open Door, and his declaration is justified by facts. He is equally right in the declaration that " the traders of every nationality can sell in the Congo the objects of their commerce and buy the natural products from the proprietors of the soil ; no limit, no hindrance is placed to this traffic, and this is really commercial liberty."

The adventurers and plunderers whose desire it was to obtain the rich fruits of the soil from ignorant savages in return for a trade in beads and buttons and suchlike valuable considerations are, it is true, but little content at this. It does not fit in with their ideas of equity to find that if they want to buy they must deal with proprietors who know the value of the goods they have to sell, and expect to be paid it ; but this is an aspect of the case which must recommend itself to every lover of justice, and all the more so since the State, as owner of the domain lands, is acting entirely as the people's trustee, and returning to them directly and indirectly every farthing of profit gained by the sale of the fruits of the soil. So true is this, that not only is much of the money received from the sale of the products of the domain spent on the public works and institutions of the State, but a very large proportion of it is actually handed to the natives in payment for their labour.

It must be remembered that while the labour of forty hours a month of the natives in gathering the rubber is required from them as a labour tax, nevertheless, that labour may be made acceptable to them, they are actually paid for the work they perform. The amount of money paid in this way to the natives, and the further revenue which they earn from the public service, apart from their large profits on the transport of goods, is calculated at over 26 per cent. of the expenditure of the State. In the returns for 1904, while the revenue from the working of the domain is calculated at £657,500, that of the natives from the State is returned at £320,000. From this it must be seen that so far from having nothing to trade with, owing to the action of the State in requiring the collection of the rubber in payment of the labour tax of forty hours' work each month, and in itself selling the rubber, the natives are in a position, financially speaking, far better than any they could be supposed to hold if they and the land were left to exploitation of rubber hunters from over the seas.

The action of the Congo Government in marking out the country into zones, and in allowing the fruits of the soil in the greater part of these to be gathered only by the agents of the State or by concessionaires, each—agents and concessionaires—acting within certain well-defined limits, and each bound to replant rubber in the place of all they cut, did away with the possibility of the denuding of the forests, such as was carried on then, and for years later, in the French Congo, until the French Government in its turn put an end to their liberty of havoc by the agents of the irresponsible European purchasers. The characteristic of these traders was to allow of fixed establishments only on the coast, at which the trader attended in his factory the result of the deals effected by his agents, who, in their turn, traversed the country and collected the rubber from the natives. Under this system, the trader was absolutely without responsibility. He discharged his full legal duty to the country, which in his estimation was his only duty to it, by the payment of a light export tax—against which export tax, moreover, he continually grumbled; he interested himself in no way in the methods used by his agents to obtain the rubber from the natives, but contented himself in giving these agents the most fiery gin, the cheapest powder, and the trashiest "trade goods" to barter with the natives for the valuable products of the soil.

The system of granting concessions to traders for the collection of the rubber in the domain, in return for specified payments to the State and fixed undertakings for the replantation of rubber, did not tempt the traders of sea coast factories, who had not sufficient interest in the prosperity of the country to pay their small export duties without complaint; and although the decree of October, 1889, showed that requests could be introduced by traders of every nationality for concessions for the collection of rubber and other vegetable products in the forests of the domain of the Upper Congo, where these products were not already collected by the native populations, few of the foreign trading companies could be prevailed upon to extend their spheres of action beyond the Lower Congo.

Nor did the decree of October, 1892—which, fixing the limits of the State's activity in the collection of rubber, abandoned the exclusive right of collecting that product in the large areas which have been described to traders—act as an inducement to the foreign companies to engage in the rubber collecting labour in the Upper Congo, probably because with the liberty to collect there was united the obligation to replant; and even in 1897, when a general movement of activity set in and factories were installed in the Kasai, Ikelamba, and Lulonga districts, and on the banks of the Congo, it was, with only one exception, Belgian companies which risked their capital in these enterprises, and braved the hazards of trade pioneering which, in their cases, have been so successfully surmounted.

The reason for the enterprises, both inside and outside of the concessionaire zone, being practically confined to Belgian companies, was not that Belgian companies only were encouraged to embark in them; it was that Belgian companies alone had sufficient confidence in

A CLEARING IN THE BAMBOOS.

DRYING RUBBER.

THE PROGRESS OF THE STATE.

the future of the work to risk their money in it. The field was equally open to all; but while the Belgians entered it, the financiers of other nationalities held back, or even withdrew, as did the English shareholders of one of the most important of the companies formed to collect rubber under the concessionaire system—the Abir, or Anglo-Belgian Indiarubber Exploration Company, which was founded by an English group. Events have proved that the Belgian financiers and traders who answered to King Leopold's call to aid in the development of the country were fully justified in answering to that call as they did. Their own prosperity and the prosperity of the Congo is the result.

The railways, and the regulation of the working of the domain lands, marked what has justly been called a revolution in the economic development of the Congo. Not only were the profits gained by the sale of the country's products increased by immense sums yearly, but the greater share of these profits went—and it was provided that they should continue to go—to the country from which they came, itself, and to its people, instead of going—as by any other arrangement they would have gone—to foreign pillagers and exploiters. The terms by which the concessions were granted to the various companies were in every case practically the same, and they may be summed up in this one sentence: that at least half of the profits of each company should go to the State. In some cases the State holds one-half of the shares in the companies; in others it is paid one-half of the profits. The result is the same in every case—that half of the profits gained by the traders in the Congo go to the Congo; besides which, the traders further payout of their share of the profits additional sums to the State for taxes, patent rights, and other charges. It is this, added to the fact that the whole of the profits gained by the State by selling the fruits of the portion of the domain which it works itself go also to the Congo

Treasury, that has made the Independent State the land of riches and of promise that it is to-day.

The sovereignty of the State is absolute, and King Leopold is the State, to will and to do. The savage chiefs of the Congo, the pioneers of the State, and the Powers of Europe and America have all hailed him as such, and ratified his title; but he is not a sovereign to will that the profits of the State he made, and to which in its dark and struggling days he gave nearly two millions sterling from his private purse, should be his private gain. He has decreed, rather, that every farthing gained from the lands of the domain should be paid into the Independent State Treasury, and used for the public good in the State; and that such is done is proved not alone by the published budgets of the State, but also by the public work done within the State, which is there for all the world to see and for honest men to praise. "These territories, formerly disinherited, opened to civilisation, to evangelisation, and to progress; the populations, formerly troops of slaves, restored to confidence and liberty; the rapid economic machinery; the railways, working and in construction; the flotilla which ploughs the river and its affluents; the roads which open up the most distant regions; the telegraph and telephone lines as far as the upper river; the cultivation extending gradually; the cattle introduced into every district; the missionary establishments installed in all parts; the vaccinological institutions and the medical, sanitary, and hygienic services. These," the Governor-General of the Independent State boasts in his report of June, 1904, " are some of the results of that which has been called the ' system ' of the State—a system which is inspired before all by the wishes of the Conferences of Berlin and of Brussels." This chapter shows how far that boast is justified.

Nothing could be more marked than the bound in the prosperity of the Independent State which followed

THE PROGRESS OF THE STATE. 271

the issue of the regulations regarding the collection of the produce of its land. The exports from the State —which were 1,980,441 francs in 1887, and had risen to 15,146,976 francs in 1897—rose at once, and they have continued to rise since, until they reached in the last year (1903) 54,597,836 francs; and its imports rose likewise, increasing from 9,175,103 francs in 1893 to 20,896,331 francs in 1903. Adverse critics of the Independent State exclaim at the excess of the value of the exports over that of the imports. To this the Governor-General replies that the same state of things existed in the last financial year in the English possessions in India, in Lagos, in Granada, in Guiana, in New Zealand, in the Fiji Islands, in the Bermudas, in Mauritius, in Cochin-China, and in the Dutch East Indies.

The case of the Independent State is, however, different from, and far better than any of, these; and, leaving comparisons aside, it may be replied to the critics that in addition to the value of the imports into the Congo, there must be placed to the credit of the country the value of the fruits of the domain sold on the open market in Antwerp, the money received for which is returned through the State Treasury to the country in the material benefits cited in the quotation from the Governor-General's report—the railways, the steamers, the agricultural stations, the hospitals, the schools, the cattle, the seeds, the labourers' tools, with which, using the outcome of its own riches, the Congo Government has endowed the country, and which marks the real progress of the Independent State assuredly more truly than the importation of a billion francs' worth of beads or a trillion francs' worth of looking-glasses.

CHAPTER XV.

CRIME, CONTROVERSY, AND JUSTICE IN THE INDEPENDENT STATE.

OVER the whole of Equatorial and Central Africa a shadow lies—one black, indeed, but not ominous where it touches the Independent State, for there it is the quickly lifting cloud of the past—the shadow of barbarity.

Much has been written in the earlier chapters of this work of the horrors of savage Africa before King Leopold assumed the sovereignty of the Congo, and of the horrible customs of ignorance and brutality still existing there after that sovereignty was established, which it was the King's first desire, and his duty, successfully performed, to suppress. The horrors of Africa are such as civilised men would fain forget for the honour of their kind, and the day may come when these horrors are nothing but memories of the past, and men may forget them without further shame; but while traces of the horrors still linger, and while the world is still sitting in judgment on the men who committed them, to forget them, or to leave their existence out of count when pronouncing judgment on the work of the founder of civilisation in Equatorial Africa, would be itself a new and a dastardly crime. The fact that his government in the Congo was and is a government over savages never changed or lessened by one tittle the moral obligations of King Leopold. Right is right in the wild forests of Africa; and justice there is justice, changeless and immutable, as it is in Brussels or in London, or as it was in Rome or Greece. But while excusing nothing of wrong done by the civiliser—if any wrong was done by him—the savage state of the country must be allowed its full value in accounting for the brutality which dogged his footsteps and battled against his advance.

It is with no desire to extenuate crime I say that in the Independent State of the Congo those who suffered most from lawless acts were those who were the criminals themselves. The moral obligations of the savage who is bound to no Christian code may be infinitely less than those of the white man; but they exist, nevertheless, and in the scheme of humanity, when the two races come together the black owes duties to the white, as the white man owes duties to the black. Moreover, if civilisation is to prevail, each must be made to perform his duty. This, at least, is obvious; yet each time the Government of the Independent State stretches forth its hand to enforce obedience to its rule, a howl goes forth from its detractors, who rend the heavens, shrieking that it commits atrocity!

If humanity advances as men hold it is advancing, the day must come when the repression of crime no longer entails punishment; but that day is still far distant, and its coming is the most distant of all in the lands newly wrenched from barbarism. In such lands, in the name of mercy itself, justice must be stern, and swift, and mighty. In savage lands crime can never be left unpunished with impunity. Savages are little impressed by mercy, which they regard most often as a faltering of justice; and justice, they think, would never falter were it not too weak to strike. Amongst savages the weakness of others is ever snatched at by the strong as an opportunity for slaughter. Justice, then, amongst them must never seem to falter; and mercy must veil its face, lest the savages, mistaking its portent, rush to their destruction in bestial orgies and unmeasured crime. That King Leopold's justice in the Congo has been stern and swift was, therefore, no more than a necessity; to the fact that it was so, and mighty, is due to-day the tranquillity and spreading civilisation of his African State.

Since the foundation of the Independent State it has had to wage a long and sanguinary war against the Arab sultans in its territories, to repel the invasion of the Mahdist forces, and to repress several mutinies and rebellions. Each one of these actions was a proof of the State's fulfilment of its civilising mission, not of its bloodthirstiness, as its detractors would have us believe. The cause and the result of its war on the Arab slave-raiders have already been told; its repulse of the Mahdists was of the same nature, and had similar results; its suppression of mutiny need not be detailed at length. The causes of each of the mutinies and rebellions with which the State has had to deal were the same; and not only did the whole country gain by their suppression, but even these very causes from which they rose bore tribute to the justice and humanity of the Congo Government.

Such mutinies as there have been in the Congo took place in un-united and scattered districts; they have never been of great importance, but wherever they broke out they have been caused not by the inhumanity but by the humane action of the State. The Congo savages, bred in cannibalism, revolted, whenever they did revolt, not because the white men treated them with brutality, but because their white officers of the Government would not let them continue in the indulgence of worse than bestial habits.

"If we are to proceed on the assumption that the nearer the native or any human being comes to a pig the more desirable is his condition, of course, I have nothing to say," said Mr. Chamberlain in the British House of Commons, while discussing the affairs of West Africa in 1903 as Colonial Secretary. Nothing need have been said, or done, had the Independent State been content to leave the savages of the Congo

CRIME, CONTROVERSY, AND JUSTICE. 275

in the state—worse than that of pigs—to which they had sunk, and in which they wanted to remain. It was because the State was determined to raise them, and because, as a first step, it suppressed their vilest practices, that the natives mutinied. Had the State allowed its soldiers to remain cannibals, with all the loathsome practices of cannibalism, there would have been no Congo mutinies to speak of; but neither would the Independent State have been the civilising State that from the first it has been.

It was not even because the State called on the natives to work that the revolts in the Congo took place. Notwithstanding what has been said to the contrary by foreign writers, the labour tasks, or prestations, imposed on natives never gave rise to any serious trouble. What caused the natives to mutiny was the fact that their indulgence in the vile habits—which can be no more than hinted at—was put an end to with unrelenting sternness, and with a completeness which made the victory won over cannibal barbarity cheap at the price of the blood it cost, as it would have been cheap at ten times the price, had ten times as many punitive expeditions been necessary to win it. In truth, slave-raiding and cannibalism were at the bottom of every engagement fought against the soldiers of the State, and of every rising against its Government. As a result of the action of the State, slave-raiding has completely disappeared from the territories of the Independent State, and cannibalism has disappeared with it from every district where the native is in contact with the white man, or, in other words, throughout the State; for, as has been shown in the preceding chapters, the white man, agent and missionary, has now penetrated to every part, and formed his settlements even in its farthest districts. It was at one time pretended by the critics of King Leopold's Government that the black soldiers of the State, instead of helping to check, actually spread cannibalism. This was never true, and the grossness of its falsity at the present time is shown by the statement of Major Harrison, whose experiences during long travels in the Congo were published in the *Times* of June 24th, and the *Journal of Commerce* of July 25th, 1904. Replying to the allegation of Sir Charles Dilke, that cannibal soldiers are employed by the State, and live as such, Major Harrison declares:

" I can assure Sir Charles that there are now very few cannibal tribes left where soldiers are drawn from, and these are rapidly decreasing. I had interesting talks with many of the officers, and very many soldiers, on this question, and found from the latter that after finishing their term of service, hardly more than one or two per cent. ever reverted to the barbarous custom in which they had been brought up. When once they come into contact with the white man they become ashamed of cannibalistic habits, as, in a similar manner, when once wearing clothes the natives look down on and pity those who wear none."

This declaration—the statements in which are borne out by proof—confirms the assertion that cannibalism, like slave-raiding, has been stamped out of existence in the territories of the Independent State. In saying " there are very few cannibal tribes left where soldiers are drawn from . . . hardly more than one or two per cent. ever reverted to the barbarous custom," Major Harrison knew, and had in mind, the fact that the soldiers of the State are drawn from every part of its territories.

Thus, it is shown that the Independent State has already crushed the two great crimes against civilisation, which for centuries barred the progress of humanity within the regions of the Congo. The crushing of this crime or that, however great the crime, however meritorious its suppression, still does not change at once the nature of those who committed it; and though there are no longer sanguinary slave raids in the Congo, though

CRIME, CONTROVERSY, AND JUSTICE. 277

cannibal orgies are no longer the practice of the land, there yet remains amongst the natives the callous indifference to suffering, the disregard for human life, the absence of the slightest respect for the remains of the dead, which the ever-present murders and horrors of these practices engendered years before the Independent State was founded, and the Congo savages were first taught that human life should be held sacred, and that even after death respect should be paid to the body which the God of the white man and the black man had made for a time the temple of man's soul.

The white men who were settled in the Congo before the pioneers of King Leopold's State came there did nothing to teach these things to the negroes. The Independent State was founded in 1884; the English Parliamentary Papers for 1883 contain detailed accounts of the tortures inflicted on their slaves by the white men trading on the Congo River. In one instance, the English Consul reported that an attempt to burn down a factory having taken place at Ponta da Lenha, the owner of the factory had one of his slave boys seized and tortured until, "under the influence of the great agony he was suffering," he accused first one and afterwards several others of his fellow-slaves of participation in the offence. The slave first accused was at that time many miles away; but he was captured, and, without "being interrogated at all, was bound hand and foot, taken out in a canoe into the middle of the stream, and drowned." The rest of the slaves named by their tortured fellow were treated in the same way. They were conveyed to Boma by "John Scott, a merchant trading there, and a British subject, who caused eleven of them, men, women, and children, to be all attached to an iron crane and drowned in the river in front of his house." "In all, I am assured that about thirty-two unfortunate, helpless beings were murdered," said the English Consul in his report. "I am also informed that the murder of one or more slaves by white men in the Congo is almost a daily occurrence, and that the torture of the thumb-screw was applied to many more besides the boy first alluded to; and in some instances it was so severe that the bones of the fingers of these most unfortunate people were completely crushed before they would implicate others, and beyond a doubt, under their excruciating agony, they accused many innocent people, for children of tender years were included and not spared."

In all that has been alleged of evil practices in the Congo since it came under King Leopold's rule nothing, even where the wildest exaggeration was displayed, was ever pictured which came within measurable distance of the horrors shown in this one glimpse of what happened in that land when European traders exploited the natives, unchecked by a sovereign's justice. The native races of the Congo in their most savage state murdered and ate each other, but it was reserved for these traders to teach them the refinement of cruelty. The mutilating they practised was, in almost every instance, resorted to as punishment for crime. Coquilhat in his work, "Sur le Haut-Congo," published in 1885, shows how the natives proceeded in the districts which the Arabs never reached, and before the arrival of the white men: branding faithless wives with hot irons, and cutting off the hands of robbers. Their savage natures were only stirred to fresh brutalities by the Arab Mahomedans and the debased Europeans, who terrorised them before the foundation of the Independent State, and it has been King Leopold's task, while raising them from their native barbarity, to force them also to unlearn, in ceasing the practice of, the barbarous customs they had adopted from the brutal traders of Europe and of the Soudan. That task King Leopold has performed, and is performing, amidst the howls of execration of the very class in Europe which helped the most to make that task necessary.

CRIME, CONTROVERSY, AND JUSTICE.

There is no page in the history of mankind which is not stained by horrors, just as there is no page in that history which is not brightened by hope, by the story of noble achievement, and by increasing joy. The darkest and the brightest page of the history of our time is that which tells of Equatorial Africa. The darkest lines in it are not those which tell of the barbarity, but those which tell of the debasement of the white traders in that hideous land. To those who studied the history of the Dark Continent up to the date of the foundation of the Independent State, and for years afterwards until the rule of King Leopold was firmly established there, it seemed as if no white man could venture into it without losing his sensibility, without losing his conscience, without losing his civilisation, and without becoming as base as the brutal savages amongst whom he lived. The native thought nothing of human slaughter or of human suffering; the European in Equatorial Africa learned to laugh at it. The native in the regions where the Arab customs had penetrated took a ferocious delight in mutilating those who offended him; the European learned to look without shuddering at men with hands, noses, and ears lopped off, and with even more horrible mutilations. Amidst all the horrors, that which is most horrible in European eyes is the tale of European callousness, and even of European crime.

Few, even amongst the noblest and the most tried, seemed able to escape from the contamination of their evil surroundings. I have spoken with the bravest soldier of the Independent State, a man whose name calumny has never dared to assail—the man who rescued the country from the Arab tyranny: Baron Dhanis; and the tales he told me of the failings of Europeans were not less saddening nor less sickening than the tales of Arab brutality. Baron Dhanis told me of a European, one of the pioneers of the State, a man praised often and deservedly for his heroic and humane services, whose mind in the end became so unstrung by long and solitary residence at a distant station, that one day, when a black girl dared to laugh at him, he seized her in his arms and impaled her on the railings before his house ; after which, when calm and horrified at his act, and fearing punishment, he committed suicide. Baron Dhanis told me of another European, also a tried and respected man, who, unmoved by the scene, sketched the details of a woman's butchery ; and he told me other tales as horrible, and tales which related, as those I have recited did, to trusted officials who were not of Belgian nationality, nor of Latin or Scandinavian race.

From the first the Independent State forbade its officials, under the severest penalties, to permit or countenance the least act of cruelty towards the natives, or to let acts of cruelty go unpunished ; but when the white agents sank beneath barbarity, as those I have told of did, cruelties were practised for which the brutes who committed them hoped to escape punishment. The arm of justice in the Congo is long, however, and it has never hesitated to strike; and to those who examine the workings of justice in the Independent State it must seem that as few escape punishment for their crimes there as in the civilised countries of Europe or America. It is not punishment, however, but prevention that the Congo Government sought for, and that it has long since found, as regards its own officials. King Leopold has found it possible to check the falling into cruel habits of his officers in the Congo by the adoption of two simple rules. One is that a white official shall never be stationed alone at any post—that there shall be at least two white men at the smallest stations ; and the second is that service in the Independent State shall never be for long continuous periods, three years' engagement being the rule for white officials,

THE MOUTH OF THE LILO, PONTHIERVILLE.

INSPECTION OF A JESUITS' AGRICULTURAL SCHOOL.

CRIME, CONTROVERSY, AND JUSTICE.

between which and further services of three years there must be long stays in Europe for every official. Simple as these rules are, they have proved sufficient; and those who read tales of Congo "atrocities" will find that every crime attributed to officers of the State dates from long years past, when the organisation of the State was as yet incomplete, and while the Government had not yet learned to cope otherwise than by punishment with the debasement of white men in savage centres.

The suppression of the Arab-fostered horrors of mutilation were more difficult; and most difficult of all was the suppression of what, in European eyes, is the awful practice of mutilating the dead. It is difficult to convince men whose fathers were accustomed to gnaw the flesh of the foemen they killed, and to fling their bones to the dogs, that it is a heinous crime to cut off the hands of those they have slain in battle and carry them away as trophies of their prowess. It is said that in the early years, at the moment of the Arab war, black soldiers of the State used to bring the hands of the State's enemies they killed to their officers, as a proof that they wasted no cartridges; but the truth of this allegation is specifically denied by Baron Dhanis, the general who commanded the forces of the State in the war. Baron Dhanis neither saw himself nor heard of such a practice. The first moment that natives were enrolled in the Congo Army it was made clear to the dullest soldier that such proceedings would not be tolerated in the soldiers of the State, and the blacks were shown that no mercy would be found by any man who mutilated another, dead or alive. The laws of the Independent State on this point are as clear as laws can be; the practice of the State with regard to it is beyond dispute, and the repetition of the ancient tales of missionaries, themselves long dead and gone, that hand-cutting is practised by the soldiers of the

Independent State is proof now, and has been for many years past, of the densest ignorance of the condition of the Congo, or of reckless mendacity.

Out of the mutilations practised by the natives there has grown a further fiction, that the soldiers of the State practised mutilation on living natives to terrorise them into gathering rubber for the State. This, and tales similar to it, were repeated so often that at last they were carried into the English Parliament. In the House of Commons there is always a party which assumes to itself the protection of the aborigines of savage lands the government of which is not under the English Crown. It is, perhaps, never to be regretted that the weak should find self-appointed defenders, even when their cause stands in no need of defence ; but the justice of attacking a foreign Government on the flimsy evidence of ancient rumours may well be questioned. To attack the Congo Government of to-day on its situation of ten years ago is as just a proceeding as it would be to attack the Government of Mr. Balfour on the first budget of Lord Salisbury, or—since affairs in the Congo march swiftly onwards under King Leopold's rule, and a year of the advance of civilisation there is equal to centuries in Europe— to denounce the Administration of the Independent State in 1904 because of the happenings in the Congo in years gone by is on a par with denunciation of the Irish Administration of Lord Dudley and Mr. Wyndham because of the excesses of Essex or Carew. The English Government seems to have realised this, for, although it accepted the time-worn tales of ancient grievances as sufficient grounds for addressing a note to the Powers which were signatories of the Act of Berlin, it hastened to instruct its consul in the Independent State to undertake a journey through the State in order to see and report on the condition of the country the Government of which it assailed in its note.

CRIME, CONTROVERSY, AND JUSTICE. 283

The charges brought against the Independent State, as summed up in the English note to the Powers, were "that the object of the Administration was not so much the care and government of the natives as the collection of revenue; that this object was pursued by means of a system of forced labour, differing only in name from slavery; that the demands upon each village were exacted with a strictness which constantly degenerated into great cruelty; and that the men composing the armed force of the State were in many cases recruited from the most warlike and savage tribes, who not infrequently terrorised over their own officers and maltreated the natives without regard to discipline or fear of punishment."

With these allegations there was joined in the note the allegation that the regulations regarding the collection of the fruit of the domain lands constituted trade monopolies contrary to the stipulations of the Act of Berlin; and the English Government suggested that the question, either wholly or in part, might be made the subject of a reference to the tribunal at The Hague.

This note was issued on August 18th, 1903. It was addressed to the signatories of the Act of Berlin, and the Independent State, not being a signatory of that Act, no copy of the note was sent officially to it. The Independent State, however, "made itself acquainted with the despatch from the Foreign Office," and on the 17th of the following September it issued its reply to this document. The reply controverted every statement made in the English note. It is not necessary to quote this document here. Each point raised in the attack of England, and each in the refutation which refers to the Congo, has already been dealt with in this work as the matter it related to arose. The question of the alleged "trade monopolies" has been examined in the preceding chapter, as has the charge that "the object of the Administration was not so much the care and government of the natives as the collection of revenue." Those who have read the chapter on the progress of the Independent State will have seen how baseless was this charge—a most extraordinary charge to make in the face of the advance of the government of the Congo, an advance apparent to the whole world, and of the fact that every penny of revenue collected by the State was spent upon that government, and on the material improvement of the country and the people.

The question of forced labour has been examined in the chapter on the Congo laws, as has been that of the demands upon each village, which, it is alleged, constantly degenerated into great cruelty. The forced labour, of which so much complaint is made, is a labour which the law decrees must never exceed forty hours for each man in each month. To liken such light labour to slavery is absurd. It may be true that officials of the Government pressed heavily on the natives in the early days of the labour tax, when these officials were paid a commission, or given a bounty, on the value of the rubber and ivory collected in their districts; but the State quickly saw that the offer of such commissions or rewards was an unwise thing, and stopped the practice, while at the same time intimating to all of its officials that the fault which would be most strictly punished would be that of excess of zeal, if it ever led the officials to exact more from the natives than the strict letter of the law allowed. Since then no official of the State in the Congo can hope for gain from any extra exertion he may use, while he has examples before him to prove that condign punishment is sure to follow on the least excess. Thus it is ensured, as far as human foresight can ensure a thing, that no excess shall be committed in the enforcement of the labour tax in the future, and for that tax itself it must be admitted that it weighs less heavily on the natives, and forces less labour from them, than the hut-tax forces from the natives in the English territories of Africa, which hut-tax, although its collection has led to revolts and the flight of natives, and although it is paid by direct labour or the fruits of labour, has led no party in the House of Commons to cry out that the natives were reduced to slavery by its enforcement.

The last of the allegations in the English note to the Powers, that the armed force of the State was drawn from the most warlike and savage tribes, and that the men composing it not infrequently terrorised their own officers, was a cautious official paraphrase of the statement of Sir Charles Dilke that the soldiers of the Congo State are " cannibal soldiers, and live as such," which statement that leader of the anti-Congo campaign persisted in making, despite all the proofs brought forward to the contrary. The testimony of Major Harrison, already quoted in this chapter, is a sufficient answer to this charge. The charge that the native soldiers of the State terrorise their officers is equally unfounded. So also is the statement that the soldiers maltreat the natives. In an earlier chapter it has been told how the Government, aided by the missionaries, teaches the soldiers, instructs them in the arts of civilisation, offers them inducements to settle down in monogamic life, and provides for their legitimate wives and children. Under the conditions in which they are placed from the moment of their joining the army, they quickly advance out of their native savagery; but they are still no more than a step removed from the untutored savage state, and their lapse would be easy, and their cruelty to their fellow-natives certain, were they allowed to exercise authority armed and apart from their officers in the midst of unarmed savages. The Government of the Independent State is, however, as well aware of this fact as any philanthropist in Parliament can be and it has long since taken precautions to prevent any danger arising from it, by decreeing that no soldier shall be stationed alone in any village or post, or away from the control of his officer, and that no operation, however small, shall be undertaken by native soldiers not commanded by a white officer.

The issue of the English note and of the reply of the Government of the Independent State called forth the publication of a great number of letters and documents of a controversial nature. First amongst these must be reckoned the report of the English Consul, Mr. Roger Casement, of a journey undertaken by him in the Upper Congo during two and a half months in June, July, and September, 1903. The English Government, in issuing this lengthy document, evidently considered it as a document to be used as evidence that an inquiry into the condition of the Upper Congo was desirable, rather than as the conclusive results of an inquiry on which the Congo Administration should be judged, for in every copy of the report which it sent out it suppresses, as far as possible, the names of the people cited and of the localities referred to, thus removing all possibility of verification or disproof of the statements of its representative. The Government of the Independent State was not without reason to complain of this method of presenting grave charges against it which it had no possibility of rebutting specifically; but it was perhaps as well that the English Government adopted this somewhat unusual course, for not alone must the report of Mr. Casement unfortunately be considered as a highly polemical production, but, in the one instance in which names and localities were mentioned in the relation of a charge of the greatest gravity, that of the alleged mutilation of the boy Epondo, it was subsequently proved by admission of the witnesses cited by the Consul that the evidence he produced from these witnesses was false, and that the conclusions he drew from it were erroneous.

This result of the one grave case cited into which

THE *FORCE PUBLIQUE* ON THE MARCH, BOMA.

an investigation was rendered possible by the mention of the names of the alleged criminal and of his pretended victim, makes it difficult to accept entirely other statements of Mr. Casement, in which initials are substituted for proper names. Further, Mr. Casement committed the grave error of performing his journey under the auspices of the declared enemies of the Independent State, on whose steamer he travelled, and by whom he was accompanied and assisted when collecting information from the natives. It may be laudable for parliamentary philanthropists to fling themselves ardently into a quarrel regarding the natives of a distant State ; but the assumption of a partisan *rôle* by one holding a high official position as the representative of a foreign Power, and arrogating to himself a quasi-judicial function, is a thing which cannot be too severely deprecated, and it must be admitted that Mr. Casement, in joining himself with the accusers of the Congo Government— whose adverse opinions of it were already formed— during his investigating tour through the State, placed himself in a position in which an entire impartiality of judgment was not easy.

In the continual struggle against barbarity which the civilising Government of the Independent State is carrying on in the Congo, it has not—and it could not be expected to have—on its side the natives who were grown to man's estate when the white men first came into contact with them. These older natives detest the State that forces them to lead decent lives, and to earn their bread by the sweat of their brow. They cannot be led by reasoning alone into observance of the laws which prohibit the foul practices of the Fetishism in which they still really believe. A strong arm is at all times necessary to restrain them from lapsing into savagery, and to guide them, for they are past the age at which real education or instruction is possible to them ; but if they are past the age of education, they are not past the age of deception, and, with the intense cunning of the savage, they are at all times ready to play on the susceptibilities of these who show themselves innocent enough to be deceived by empty words.

Natives of this description find wonderfully easy victims for their deceit in the Protestant missionaries, whose respect for the words of the Bible leads them to place an undue confidence in every negro who repeats the Scriptures after them. The learning of whole passages of the Bible is the easiest of things for the natives, who possess, in common with all illiterate races, the most extensive memories, and the repetition of such passages is an unalloyed delight to the savages, who rejoice in the singsong repetition of unintelligible words. Adult natives, to whom it is impossible to convey the slightest perception of the majesty and the sublimity of the Christian tradition and ideal, believe readily enough in the hell of an avenging God, and they believe almost as readily in the heaven in which the hymns of their missionaries teach them they will wear golden slippers in a golden street, and where—they gather from the information of the missionaries—they need do no work.

Fortified by the latter intelligence, the adult natives, encouraged by the missionaries to whom I refer, resolve to anticipate Heaven by doing no work in this life for the State or for themselves, if they can help it. In order to further this end they carry to the missionaries long strings of tales of grievances, real sometimes, though more often imaginary, and always exaggerated beyond vraisemblance. To their tales many Protestant missionaries listen not only with sympathetic but with entirely credulous ears. Instead of teaching the natives that labour is the first duty of man, and that labour for the State, the Commonwealth, is the noblest, these missionaries too often sustain them in their repugnance to toil, and seem to teach them that labour for the payment of taxes is a degrading slavery, against which men do right to rebel. So consistent is the attitude of the Protestant missionaries in this regard in the Congo that there has grown up in the Independent State a Labour Party and a No-Labour Party, the leaders of the latter being the missionaries.

A less wise attitude it would be impossible for any white men to take up in a savage land than that the Protestant missionaries have taken up on the question of the labour enforced by the Government in the Independent State. The negro can only be saved in this world, and in the next, if freedom from sin is necessary to salvation, by being made to labour. The missionaries were, doubtless, led to take up the position they did by an honest belief that the native was unduly pressed ; but even had that belief been better founded than upon the extravagant tales of notorious liars, the attitude of encouraging negroes in sloth would have been wrong and dangerous.

Moreover, it is impossible to be blind to the fact that political and religious rivalry has had much to say in influencing the Protestant missionaries in the attitude they took up, and in the teaching they carried on. The Catholic missionaries having loyally adopted the programme of the State for elevating the native races through work, have in every instance set themselves to "make Christians of the blacks by making men of them," and by them the natives are taught to labour and to pray. The Protestant missionaries, it is impossible to deny, have set up the school-room and the chapel in direct opposition to the workshops of the priests; and it is also impossible to deny that in the school-room too many Protestant missionaries teach the native children lessons which are calculated to make them the opposite of loyal or obedient subjects of the Independent State, when they teach them that the State is at present the appanage of Belgium, " an insignificant little chief, very different from England, which is a big chief, owning half the world, with its power extending everywhere, even over Africa, the country of which the Congo is a part."

The reason for the Protestant missionaries acting in this manner is one easy to find. They are filled with a detestation of " Romanism," and think almost any sacrifice desirable which would rescue the natives from the teaching of the priests of Rome. They are not, as a rule, men of much education, and they generally know little of the French language, which is the official language in the Congo, and the language taught in the Government schools and the schools of the priests and nuns to the native children. Their want of understanding the French language keeps them frequently in ignorance of the measures taken by the Government for the improvement of the country, and from coming into touch with the Government officials; and the fact that the European language taught to the native children is not English continually exasperates them.

They quite honestly believe that a French-speaking Government cannot be as good as an English one. For many of them it is enough that the Government is a French-speaking one, and that the teachers in its schools are Catholics, to have them convinced that it is radically bad, and to account for the fact that in its actions they see nothing good.

Whether they intend it or not, the inevitable result of their teaching has been such as to convince the natives that they are working for, and expecting, the transference of the government of the Congo from the King of the Belgians to England, and that the result of that transference will be that all obligation to work on the natives' part will cease, and they will be allowed to sink back into the slothful habits of the days of unchecked barbarity. Belgian agents, passing along the river in their canoe, were greeted on encountering the English Consul, who was voyaging in the Protestant missionaries' steamer, by shouts from the natives crowded on the river bank, " Your violence is over ; the English alone remain ; you others will die ! " And the missionary who was with the English representative at the time explained these shouts by saying, in his evidence at the Epondo inquiry, " The Consul was here at the time, and the people were much excited and evidently thought themselves on top. . . The people have got this idea [that the rubber gathering was finished] into their heads of themselves, consequent, I suppose, upon the Consul's visit."

The nature and result of the inquiries of the English Consul are summed up by Major Harrison in his letter to the *Journal of Commerce* of July 25th, 1904. He says, " To show the effect of Mr. Casement travelling on the mission boat, I found long before I struck the Congo the general native impression was that if they made out a bad enough case the English would take the country, and the inhabitants seemed quite disappointed when they found I was not part of the same show, collecting evidence from the Nile. I fear many people, on hearing that the native tribes are anxious to come under British control, fondly imagine it to be through love of our kind and liberal treatment. Let me quote our Sierra Leone soldiers' views, and advice, to their Congo brethren. They say, ' When you boys become Englishmen, no white man call native d—— fool ; if he do, judge fine him two pounds. If white man kick or strike black man, he get fined five pounds, or go to prison. Sierra Leone boy, he big man ; no do much work.' "

The English note to the Powers stated that " the graver charges against the State relate almost exclusively to the upper valleys of the Congo and of its affluents," in which " the lands forming these vast territories are held either by the State itself or by companies closely connected with the State," and it was in these territories, or rather in a portion of them, hurriedly visited, that the English Consul made his tour, and against the action of the agents of the companies that he made the most serious allegations.

These serious allegations consisted of a repetition of the charges that the servants of the companies mutilated natives by cutting off their hands, in order to terrorise them into collecting rubber. It is not quite easy to understand how the cutting off of a native's hand could make him the better rubber-gatherer; but the English Consul suggests that it was done, as Admiral Byng was shot, "to encourage the others." It is not material whether this explanation is a sufficient one, for the proof brought forward is inadequate. The case of the boy Epondo—cited by Mr. Casement as having been personally investigated by him, and found by him to be proved—is now admitted on all sides to have never happened at all. Mr. Casement, sitting in a quasi-judicial capacity, with two Protestant missionaries assisting as assessors, had the boy Epondo brought before him with the "sentinel" Kelengo of the La Lulonga Company, whom he accused of mutilating him, and, having heard "forty eye-witnesses" of the scene, declared Kelengo convicted of having committed the atrocity of cutting off Epondo's hand, of having chained up women, and stolen ducks and a dog, on which he passed judgment on the "sentinel" by declaring to the assembled crowd of savages, who seemed so vindictively excited against the man, that "Kelengo deserved severe punishment for his illegal and cruel acts."

Further, confident that here he had a case that could be proved up to the hilt, Mr. Casement departed from the practice he followed in every other instance of withholding the particulars of his investigations from the Congo authorities, and informed the Governor-General of the Independent State of the

CRIME, CONTROVERSY, AND JUSTICE.   293

charges against the man Kelengo, and demanded an inquiry into them. The Independent State maintains that the report of a crime has never reached the ears of its officers without being immediately investigated. This alleged crime was immediately inquired into, and in the presence of one of the missionaries who had assisted at the Consul's ultra-judicial court, when it was discovered, by the voluntary confessions of the boy Epondo, the villagers who had figured as eye-witnesses, and all the others on whom Mr. Casement had relied, that the whole story was a fiction, a put-up job, arranged to please the missionaries and hoodwink the English official. The facts of the loss of the boy's hand—which are now perforce accepted by all as true—are these: that the boy's hand having been bitten by a wild boar he was hunting, the wound mortified, and caused the loss of the member.

This charge of the English Consul having been proved false, the other charges brought forward by him—all of which were formulated on hearsay evidence, and most of which relate to distant dates—must be dismissed as not proven. The fact is true that there are mutilated natives in the Congo; but it is no less true that it is in the districts in which the Arab power was dominant that they are chiefly to be found, and the great weight of evidence adduced not only by Belgian or French authorities, but by Englishmen of high intelligence and independence, such as Major Harrison or Dr. Christy, whose personal knowledge of the Congo adds more authority to their words than could be gained by any hurried investigation, leads to the conclusion that where mutilations were committed they were committed by savages removed from the control and influence of white men; and that those who committed them try to conceal from the white men the existence of their crimes by trumping up false tales of why the mutilations took place, and who committed them—tales, in all probability, made expressly for each white auditor, so as to gain whatever may be supposed to be his sympathies.

Side by side with the evidence of the independent travellers in the Congo on the actual condition of the country, the Government of the Independent State has brought forward the evidence of its statute book to prove that severe laws have been made to punish mutilation or ill-treatment of the natives, and it has brought forth the evidence of its courts to prove that these laws are rigorously enforced. The Independent State holds that where its laws and regulations have been violated it cannot be held to be responsible for the commission of crime, but only for the repression and punishment of it.

The Government denies indignantly that its laws and regulations are made for outward show, and that behind them it holds out temptations to the cupidity of its agents which lead them directly to the committal of the most shameful of crimes : the maltreatment of defenceless natives. Its denial is true, and its indignation is most fully justified. It has been shown in this chapter that it removed every inducement from its agents which would lead them to press on the natives by over-exaction of the labour tax, and showed them that punishment, not gain, would be the meed of those who exacted more than the strict forty hours' labour a month, which is the most that can be legally required from any native —whether he gathers rubber or ivory, prepares food for the stations of the State, cuts wood for the Government steamers, or does all three things in discharge of his labour tax.

In the chapters dealing with the Congo laws and on the progress of the Independent State, it has been shown what the real attitude of the State towards the native population of the Congo is, and what it does for their advancement and protection. The tireless exertions of the State for the instruction and education of the natives, for their material and moral advancement, and its success in these exertions, give the Independent State ample grounds for righteous anger at the charge that its object is not the care and government of the natives. Nevertheless, the State would be still open to blame, notwithstanding the fact that in all it does itself its government of the natives was enlightened and beneficial, if white men found themselves able to practise systematic exaction or pillage on the natives under the shadow of its laws. The obligations of the State as regards the white men within its territories and their treatment of the natives, when these white men are not directly officials of the State, vary in what may be called their intensity, though not in their nature, according as to whether these white men are independent traders, missionaries, or travellers, or the servants of the concessionaire companies which are the State's tenants and—since the State owns half the shares in these companies—its co-partners.

Traders, missionaries, and travellers have a right, secured them by the Act of Berlin, to travel in the land, and to treat freely with its inhabitants. The State has found itself able to forbid the most pernicious form of trade, and that which the traders of the greatest European countries are most inclined to, since it is the most quickly—though the most deadly—profitable: the trade in gin, in firearms, and in gunpowder; but beyond this it is not able to interfere with the traffic of the trading class, or with its barter of trumpery for goods of intrinsic value which the customs, and even the laudations of the Great Powers of civilisation, sanctifies under the name of trade. Neither has it been able to interfere with the teaching of pernicious doctrines, conducive to lives of sloth, by missionaries. The obligations of the State with regard to this class, which the Act of Berlin requires it to give free passage through every part of its immense territories, whether these are as yet made effectively subject to the State and policed by it or not, consist solely in its affording the white men such protection as the development of the settlement of the country renders possible, and in the punishment of the white men's crimes where their crimes have been discovered.

These obligations, it must be admitted, have been discharged to the full. Although no one expected that the million square miles of the territories of the Independent State could be rescued from barbarity on the morrow of the proclamation of the sovereignty of King Leopold, or that the King's writ could be made to run within these territories within any short space of years, the determination and vigour of the King worked wonders in the Congo from the first, and no white man has ever complained that the protection of the State was found wanting by him. Even from the first every white malefactor, and every native induced by white scoundrels to act criminally towards his fellows, has been made to cower before the swift, stern, and far-reaching justice of the Congo courts.

The wider obligations of the State with regard to the white men in the employment of the concessionary companies and their intercourse with the natives include the prevention and the punishment of crime, not only in the more settled places, but in every place in which these companies or their servants are established; for, since it is the State which leases the lands to the companies, and permits them to gather the fruits of the domain on them, it is clearly the duty of the State to see that every place into which they penetrate is properly policed. This, again, is a duty which is fully performed. The State has closed against working by its agents or its tenants every district which is not as yet sufficiently settled for orderly management, and it has refused to grant concessions or allow rights of any kind in these districts, the situation of which I have already specified;

CRIME, CONTROVERSY, AND JUSTICE. 297

while it has provided proper measures for the observance of the law and the enforcement of the people's rights in the districts in which it has granted leases, or concessions, for the working of the land.

To say that the Independent State had banished crime from its settled territories would be to court ridicule. It has taken every possible measure for the prevention of crime ; it could do no more. There is no Government so superhumanly perfect, there is no country so civilised that crimes—and crimes of an atrocious nature—are not committed daily and hourly in the best managed and best policed portions of its territories. The Government of the Independent State stands between savages and money hunters, each—the history of all time and of every nation proves it—dosed with man's fullest share of lust and criminality. The State performs its duty by holding the balance evenly, restraining the savages' brutality and the brutality of the white man who would exploit the savage, while making use of the white man's labour and his knowledge to instruct and elevate the savage and transform the land from a neglected wilderness into a settled and a civilised land. It is not by the crimes which are committed in the Congo —in spite of the repressive measures and of the stern punishment of the State—that the Government of the Independent State must be judged, but by the criminality it prevents and by the good it effects. If there is one thing absolutely certain in the history of the Congo, it is the fact that the system of the collection of the rich products of the land by Government-appointed and Government-supervised concessionaries has prevented the commission of many atrocious crimes.

I have told in this chapter of the barbarity of the traders who traffic unchecked in the Congo up to the date of the foundation of the Independent State. It is from murderous brutality such as theirs that the Government of King Leopold has saved the country, from " villages massacred in a madness of destruction which very often did not even spare the human merchandise that it was intended to capture ; men and women attached together like a long chain and drowned to save powder ; children hung, forming pitiful clusters on the trees." Many misdeeds have been committed in the Congo by those who went there for monetary gain since King Leopold became sovereign of the State, as many misdeeds have been committed in Europe during that time ; but no crime has been committed there since his rule was established to equal that of the independent British subject who chained his slaves together and flung them into the Congo to drown because an unfortunate child whom he tortured cried out, to save himself in his agony, that they had tried to burn his store.

It has been proved that servants of the concessionary companies committed crimes towards the natives—crimes even as grave as homicide—and that in some districts they pressed harshly on the natives in order to force them to collect rubber ; but the proof that these crimes were committed came, not from the irresponsible native chatter noted gravely in the report of the English Consul, but from the stern reports of the Congo courts of justice, in which no crime is condoned, and from the power of which no criminal, however high placed, has ever been permitted to shroud himself since first these courts were established.

Mr. Casement in his report criticises the system of the concessionary companies; but he only refers to what he finds evil in them, and he draws no distinct line between the working of these companies and the working of the labour tax. Strangely enough, both he and the other adversaries of the Independent State maintain that that tax has reduced the people to the condition of slavery, from which the State declares it is its chief object to free them, while also alleging that in consequence of the pressure of the tax on the people that

RUBBER CREEPER NURSERY AT LOWA.

FIELD OF SWEET POTATOES
ON THE BANKS OF THE ARUWIMI.

CRIME, CONTROVERSY, AND JUSTICE.

they have fled in large numbers from the localities in which it is imposed, and even from the State. None of those who attack the State seem to see that these two allegations destroy each other. The one supreme mark of slavery is the constraint of the slave's body, by which he is tied down to the spot his master wills him to be on, and the continual moving and shifting of the Congo populations at their own free will, unchecked by the Government, disproves the charge that they have been made bond-slaves of the State. Moreover, the fact that many villages have ceased to exist is due not to the flight or even the change of residence of the natives—though change of residence of whole tribes to distant parts for nothing more than a passing whim is common amongst the savages—but to the fearful ravages of the sleeping sickness which, as yet beyond man's power to check, is depopulating the Congo.

The fact is that the forty hours' labour a month —which is all that the Government requires in payment of the labour tax—cannot weigh heavily on the natives. It may, beyond doubt, be different in the region of the concessions, where the natives, being—in theory, at least—free to engage or not for the collection of the rubber, are also free, in theory, to labour for as many hours a day, or a month, as they wish. Between theory and practice the difference may at all times be vast ; but in weighing statements about the condition of the Congo it must be remembered that the natives of that State are not the timid and defenceless weaklings the European adversaries of the Government of King Leopold seem to desire to have them thought. It is strange that the Congo natives, when they are employed as servants of the State, are invariably described by these persons as bloodthirsty cannibals ; while when they are described as rubber-gatherers they are equally invariably made to appear to be weak, trembling, and spiritless creatures, who cower before the lash or fall defenceless in dozens before the muskets of the solitary "sentinels" or slave drivers whom the rubber-gathering companies leave in their villages to terrorise over them.

Of the two descriptions both are false, for the Congolese servant of the Independent State, whether he be in civil or military employment, is not a cannibal; but of the two the first is by far the nearest to the truth, and it applies to all of the Congo natives, whether they be in the employment of the Government or not. The natives of the Congo are sturdy, warlike, and still ferocious. They may whine to the missionaries, but nothing is more absurd than the picture conjured up of them in the report of Mr. Casement of these barbarous and armed savages standing calmly by while the solitary "sentinel" of a private trading company such as the La Lulonga Company—which is not, it may be observed, one of the concessionary companies at all, and is neither entrusted with police rights or the right of carrying arms of precision—hacks off the hands of their children.

No law of the Independent State has forbidden the natives to arm themselves with their accustomed weapons, and the natives still bear the spears, the darts, and the knives in the use of which generations of savage warfare has made them fatally proficient; but while the savages —who are as a hundred to one, or, it may be, a thousand to one, in proportion to the white men in their midst— are permitted to bear as many of their native weapons as they will, the white men who deal with them as traders, or employ them as concessionaires to gather the products of the portions of the domain which they lease, are forbidden to hold more than twenty-five arms of precision for each of their factories, and, moreover, they are further forbidden to use these arms except for the defence of their factories; while no white man may carry a gun in the State without a special licence from the Governor-General, and without having the gun for which he holds his licence examined, registered, and

CRIME, CONTROVERSY, AND JUSTICE. 301

stamped by specially appointed Government officials. Should he sell his gun within the territories of the State, without having the sale and the transfer approved and registered by the Government, he becomes subject to heavy penalties.

That these laws regarding the carriage and sale of firearms are rigorously enforced is proved by the well-remembered trials and punishments of British and Belgian citizens who infringed them. These laws being such, and the proportion of natives being so infinitely greater than that of the Europeans in their midst, and of the Europeans' native servants, it is but logical to conclude that the contracts entered into by these natives to gather rubber for the companies are as freely made in practice as they must be in theory, and that the amount of rubber the natives collect, and the number of hours in which they labour at its collection for the companies, are decided also in real practice by the free will of the natives themselves and their chiefs, as the laws of the State provide they must.

Agents of the companies, being rapacious as those who adventure in search of fortune into savage lands invariably are, have tried to outwit the law and terrorise the natives in some instances; and in one instance—in the Mongolla district—they have committed crimes against the natives which they prevailed on some officials of the State to countenance, but the Government speedily taught them that the laws of the State could be violated by none with impunity, those who were guilty of the crimes and their accomplices being brought to justice and condemned to long terms of penal servitude, which punishment they are now undergoing. Moreover, as the Congo Government has pointed out, the results which followed the outrages on the natives in the Mongolla district go far to prove that not only are the guilty punished by the State, but that the companies in whose service the malefactors are are bound to lose the services of the natives by such acts of cruelty instead of gaining them, and thus to lose the means of collecting the profitable harvest of their concessions, the loss of the services of the natives to the company implicated in the case of cruelty cited having been so great as to cause a falling off of no less than 98 per cent. in its profits.

The controversy forced on the world by the publication of the English note to the Powers signatory to the Act of Berlin has had one good result in forcing the various Governments to take cognisance of King Leopold's action in Africa, and of its result. So prudent, so enlightened, and on the whole so beneficial, has been this action of the sovereign of the Independent State, that there is hardly a colonising Government which cannot learn valuable lessons from it, and cannot profit by following its example. The various Governments addressed as signatories of the Act of Berlin seem to have recognised the fact that nothing in the administration of the Congo calls for international interference or for international censure. No communication was made public of the replies received by the English Government from the Powers, but it was understood that the only one of the signatory Powers which fully agreed to the suggestion that an inquiry might be desirable was Turkey.

The Independent State, for its part, intimated very clearly in its note, issued in reply to the charges in the English note, that it rejected the suggestion that the matters raised should be carried to the tribunal of The Hague. It is, indeed, somewhat difficult to understand how any of the questions raised in the English note could be carried to that tribunal, for The Hague tribunal is an arbitration court, and no aggrieved parties have ever laid plaint against the Independent State; no dispute on exterior matters has risen between it and any foreign Power, and no foreign trader has complained that he has been deprived of

OSTRICH FARM AT UERE.

DROMEDARIES AT UERE.

BREAKING-IN BABY ELEPHANTS.

his established rights in the State. It is true that the English Government in its note contends that the granting of concessions for the collection of the products of the domain lands—that is, the lands which were held to be vacant, and which were vested in the State by the decree of July, 1885—amounts to the creation of "trade monopolies" in contravention of the clause in the Act of Berlin enjoining freedom of trade; but it does not seem to need the sitting of any arbitration court to disprove the correctness of this contention.

Moreover, the grounds of dispute on this head are rapidly disappearing, for, while the English note admits that "the State has the right to partition the State among *bona fide* occupiers," and that "the natives will, as the land is so divided out among *bona fide* occupiers, lose their right of roaming over it and collecting the natural fruits which it produces," the Independent State can show that its concessionaires have entered in the majority of cases, and are entering in the remainder, into such *bona fide* occupancy. "As a matter of fact, thanks to the enormous progress realised by the multiplication of exploitation centres," said Baron Descamps in his address on the Anglo-Congolese contention, delivered before the Royal Academy of Belgium in 1904, "all lands—or nearly so—are at present reduced into that state of individual occupation which is acknowledged as permanently doing away with the raid system."

The Government of the Independent State is undeniably right in the contention put forward in its rejoinder to the English note, that in the Act of Berlin "there is no provision to be found which would sanction any restriction whatever on the exercise of the rights of property, or which would recognise any right of intervention for the signatory Powers in matters of internal administration amongst themselves"; and no fault can be found with it for its firm declaration, in the further rejoinder it issued on the publication of the report of Mr. Casement, while defending the legitimacy of its labour taxes on the natives, that it " means in this respect to move freely in the exercise of its sovereignty . . . outside of all exterior pressure, or of all foreign meddling, which would be in contempt of its essential rights."

The Government of the Independent State having refused to agree on the matters raised by England being carried to the arbitration tribunal of The Hague, there seems little possibility of the other Powers supporting England's desire in the matter, for as Baron Descamps —who is himself a member of the permanent arbitration court—reminded his hearers, " the Hague court must remain a free court in the midst of independent nations." Neither is there a great likelihood that the Powers will seek to insist on an international inquiry into matters which, as the Independent State truly asserts, are affairs of internal administration. Nevertheless, the Government of the Independent State, while rejecting exterior pressure and foreign meddling, has taken the most unmistakable means of proving that, while guarding its sovereign prerogatives, it courts the investigation of independent foreigners into the condition of the natives in its territories, and desires to have the clearest light of day thrown on the actions of its agents in the Congo.

By a decree signed on June 23rd, 1904, King Leopold appointed a special commission, consisting of three members of different nationalities, to make a full inquiry in the Congo into the alleged acts of ill-treatment of the natives, whether committed by private persons or by agents of the State, and to report on them. This commission, which has now embarked on its mission, is composed of M. Edmond Janssens, Attorney-General of the Cour de Cassation of Belgium, one of the chief members of that most able, upright, and independent body, the Belgian bar, as President ; Baron Nisco, president *ad interim* of the Court of Appeal at Boma ;

CRIME, CONTROVERSY, AND JUSTICE. 305

and Dr. Edmund de Schumacher, Councillor of State, and Chief of the Department of Justice in the Canton of Lucerne. From a commission so composed it is certain that a report will be received setting forth all the facts of the case fully and impartially. With the verdict of the commission on the condition of the natives it is to be hoped that the controversy in which so much has been disgraceful lying, and so much a skilful appeal to avaricious passion hypocritically cloaked as philanthropy, will cease, and that the Independent State will be allowed to continue its great work in the development of its territories, the improvement of its people, and the administration of justice, unhindered by the jealous clamourings of envious adventurers.

It has been shown in the previous chapters of this work how, notwithstanding the clamour of its detractors, the Independent State has progressed, enriching the land and settling it, and elevating the people as its work advanced. Much has also been told of the measures it has taken, by wise laws and regulations, for the protection of the natives and of the foreigners within its territories. In order that these laws might be duly enforced, the State instituted a judicial system, which has performed its functions so well that the Government of the State is able to boast that there has been no allegation of a crime within its jurisdiction which has not been inquired into, and none proved for which the perpetrators, if they could be found, were not fittingly punished. The organisation of the courts of justice in the State is not the least meritorious part of the civilising action of the Government.

The courts-martial, with which, as is customary in unsettled lands, the Government had to be content at first, gave place to regularly constituted civil and criminal tribunals in 1897, and at present the jurisdiction of these tribunals extends all over the territories of the State, and deals with natives as well as white men, and the courts-martial are no longer competent to deal with other than military offenders. The headquarters of the judiciary in the Congo are situated at Boma, where there is a Court of Appeal consisting of a president and two judges, a Crown prosecutor, and a registrar. The president and judges of appeal, who must be doctors of law, and have previously practised at the bar, or lectured on law in a university, are each nominated by a decree for a term of five years. This court of appeal hears and determines all the cases carried to it on appeal from the lower court of Boma, and from the territorial tribunals in every part of the country. The lower court, or Court of First Instance, has also its seat at Boma; but it can remove itself, should a necessity arise, into any other part of the State in order to hear cases on the spot. This court is composed of a judge, a substitute, and a registrar; its judges are appointed for the same length of time, and under the same conditions, as the judges of the Court of Appeal. It has a general competence in civil and criminal matters, and it is before it that every white man must be brought who is charged with offences punishable with death, or presenting a grave character.

In addition to these courts there are twelve territorial tribunals scattered throughout the State, which consist each of a judge, a public prosecutor, and a registrar. These tribunals—the officials of which must hold the degrees of doctors of laws, and have the same qualifications as the judges of the higher courts—have a competence in penal matters to deal with every case brought before them in which the accused lives or can be found in their district, even if the crime alleged has been committed outside of their district, but excepting the cases of a grave nature reserved for the Boma tribunal. There are in all thirty-two judges and twenty-five judicial agents, or Crown prosecutors, in the Independent State; and besides these tribunals in the

THE PORT OF MATADI.

STATE PIER AT BOMA IN 1896.

CRIME, CONTROVERSY, AND JUSTICE.

Congo, the Council of State, or Conseil Supérieur, at Brussels sits as a final court of appeal in cases of exceptional gravity, and has, in addition, jurisdiction to try the judges of the Congo courts should any crime or default be charged against them.

As far as white men are concerned, the court of chief importance in the Congo is that of Boma, since it is before it that every grave charge against white men must be tried. In his report made in July, 1904, the Governor-General of the Congo stated that "it is the principle of the Higher Administration at Boma to report immediately to the competent authorities every case of abuse which is brought under its notice, either by the authorities, by the direct complaint of residents in the Congo, or through the Press," and he adds that these latter accusations are regularly submitted to a minute examination on the spot. It is not altogether surprising to hear that newspaper charges are seldom found to be quite well founded, but, lest any guilty should escape, every charge is inquired into.

Very few of the white men who commit crimes in the Independent State escape denunciation and punishment ; while, as far as white offenders are concerned, if not harsh, most certainly rigid and untempered justice is meted out to every one of them, regardless of who he is or what he was. Mildness towards a white offender finds no place at this time in the law courts of the Congo, and it is right that this is so, for if stern justice now rules in the Independent State, it does so that true mercy may follow, with peace, and with abiding charity.

CHAPTER XVI.

BELGIUM, 1890–1905.

In a memorable speech which he made in 1890, and which has already been quoted in this work, King Leopold declared that "Belgium has conducted her destinies with success, and proved once more that peoples have the histories they merit." These words rang with confidence in the future as well as with pride in the past, and time has proved the King's confidence to be justified. In 1905, when Belgium again calls on her people to celebrate their independence and their prosperity, King Leopold can reiterate his words with the same pride in the past and the same high confidence in the future. Economists please themselves by marking an ebb and flow in the affairs of men, and such can, doubtless, be traced in Belgium with regard to this industry or to that; but for the Belgian nation the advance, noticeable throughout the reign of King Leopold and greater as his reign proceeds, is no tide which even as it swells must ebb, but a steady onward current, which as it goes gathers to itself more volume and greater force.

A Conservative Government had already been five years in office when the celebrations of 1890 were held at which King Leopold pronounced this speech. Since then the party which this Government represented has remained in the majority in the Belgian Chamber and Senate, and for twenty years Conservative ministries have succeeded to each other without interruption. Such a long continuance of power in the hands of one party would be remarkable under any circumstances; it becomes particularly noticeable in this instance from the fact that during it the electorate was changed, and became, from one of the smallest in Europe, one of the largest and most extended. How such a thing came to pass ; above all, how the extension of the franchise did not lessen the hold of the Government on power, bears only one explanation.

It is clear that any party holding office in a free country, under a freely elected Parliament, can only do so for such a length of time in virtue of being an intensely national party, which gives expression to the people's will, and moves as they do with the changing years. Such the Conservative Government has proved itself to be in Belgium in the last twenty years, and such it is at the present moment, when it still holds unlessened power. As a matter of fact, while holding to the name and traditions of Conservatism, the Government so long in office in Belgium is continually recruiting its forces from the fresh blood of the Democratic party, from which it receives a strong propulsion, and with which it has formed so close an alliance that were it not for the fact that questions of religion and anti-religion separate Belgian politicians into hostile camps, the Government of Belgium during these twenty years might well be said to have ceased to be one of party, and to have been one purely national.

Politicians, however, insist on keeping the question of religion in the forefront of their battles in Belgium more than in any other country ; and although the present Government has proved itself, as the electors have again and again certified, to be supremely national and popular, that Government must be viewed, above all things, in accordance with its own claims and its opponents' insistence, as a Catholic Government. At the same time, it must be remembered that the word " Catholic " does not convey the same idea in Belgium as it does in England ; and it must be borne in mind, although there is no Catholic in Belgium who is not ready to affirm his fidelity to the Church of Rome, that at the same time the word Catholic, when used in connection with politics or religion in that country, has the widest and most full significance, and is, in fact, synonymous with Christian. It has been told in an earlier chapter how, by the direct intervention of King Leopold, certain politicians whose policy inclined towards bigotry were compelled to retire from the Cabinet. These politicians, although their ability was of the highest and their honesty of purpose beyond question, never returned to office; and during the continuance of the Conservative rule a perfect regard for the freedom of opinion and of education has marked the action of the Government. At the same time, that Government, while doing nothing to crush the freedom of thought, has continually exerted itself to encourage religion.

The attempt to force religion on a people is assuredly no new thing. It cannot be forgotten that in past centuries rivers of blood were made to flow in Belgium because of it; but the memory of ancient religious feuds stirs up no passions now in Belgium, and excites no inquietude there, for all men know that nothing in the Belgian Government of Leopold II. resembles, or is meant to resemble, the Spanish Government of Philip II. It is not so much that the ideas for which men fight are changed, and that the contest is now between the believers in revealed religion and those who deny the truth of revelation and question the morality which has sprung from it, instead of being between the upholders of different creeds—for a war might be waged by ardent Christians more fiercely on infidels than was ever waged on heretics—as that with the winning of national independence and the establishment of popular government, oppression, against the people's will, became impossible. The bigotry of a dominant class might, indeed, have made itself felt for a time before the power of the whole nation was fully organised and admitted, had not the royal authority itself prevented it; and the tyranny of an anti-Christian Government, sprung to power from an unreal union of jarring elements, will yet be felt for a passing moment ; but it may be looked upon as certain, despite all chance disturbances, that in the future, as long as Belgium retains her freedom, the Government will remain what it has been in the past twenty years—the moderate rule of an enlightened people who will neither impose nor suffer tyranny, but who seek to lead their fellows by the sole force of moral suasion.

Convincing proof of the inherent moderation of the Catholic party of Belgium is found in the nature of the education laws which are in force in the country after twenty years of that party's exercise of power. From first to last compulsion is avoided in them. Adhering to the theory that a child's education is the duty of its parents personally, and not primarily that of the State, the Catholic Government has refused to make education compulsory ; but it has continued to advance the cause of education by the granting of large sums of money to the schools, and it has instituted and maintained the practice of making considerably larger grants to the communal schools, in which every child whose parent desires it is exempt from religious education, than to religious schools, instituted by members of its own party, even though these religious schools are adopted in a great number of cases as public schools by the communes, and have, in such cases, submitted their teaching to the control of the State.

The policy of Belgian Governments has been centred for long, and is likely to remain long centred, around education. It is inevitable that, as the freedom and the power of the masses grow, Governments must seek to influence the people through their education ; but the education of the Belgian people which the Catholic party pursues is not that of the class-room alone ; it is that of the workshop as well. Every day skilled workmanship is called for more and more, and every day machinery replaces unskilled labour more and more, until for every kind of work man's labour tends to centre in his brain; and this being so, it may not be too great a paradox to say that while a certain school of thought, opposed to the Government, clamours for the annexation by the State of all the means of production, the State itself, by its technical education, is placing the real means of production in the inalienable possession of each citizen individually.

Public instruction may, then, be taken as the keynote to the policy of the Government which has held the reins of office for so long in Belgium, and the Ministry of Labour, one of the greatest creations of the Government, must be regarded as an educational institution, devoted to instruction and conciliation more than to restriction and regulation.

The real secret of the power of the Catholic party in Belgium lies in the fact that it is formed from every class of the community, and that it gives ear to the needs and reconciles the desires of every class. What is the policy of the Catholic party and of the parties opposed to it has been summed up with much accuracy by the learned Jesuit Father A. Vermeersch, in his work on "La Législation et les Oeuvres en Belgique." Writing of the labour laws and those of agricultural interest, he says: "One school repels them; that of economic Liberalism, called sometimes Libertaire, of which Bastiat has given the charter in his Harmonies, and the watchword of which has been the famous saying of Gournay, expressing the absolute liberty of competition and exchange, *Laissez faire, laissez passer*. It suffices to the State, according to this school, to guarantee liberty. That will know, like the spear of Achilles, how to cure its own wounds.

"Experience has done good and prompt justice to that error.

"The school diametrically opposed sees safety only in the law. In intervening to legislate on wages, to regulate labour, to limit production and competition, the State has not advanced from its essential *rôle*. For it is it that is the only soul of the social body, the regulator of all the members of that body, their purveyor appointed for all their needs and all their interests, the universal motor which actuates all the looms. That is the State Socialism which is especially in favour in Germany, while Liberalism counts its last partisans in France. It opposes the State Providence to the Liberal conception of the State gendarme.

"These doctrines are hardly professed in their pure or absolute form; but the eagerness to appeal to the State, or the rigour to exclude its action, comes near to one or the other school.

"Between these two extremes an intermediary doctrine is conceived, which, without repudiating the social laws, does not make a panacea of them; which limits the intervention of authority to the case where its efficacy is certain and exclusive, where it alone can procure a general good of the temporal order. In this system the State no longer supplants private initiative; it supplements its defects. It is no longer the official manager of every interest; it is only a guardian—a *subrogé-tuteur*—to whom the common good attributes a subsidiary competence.

"This moderate intervention answers perfectly to the *raison d'être* of civil society. Made to complete the individual and the family, it must put within our reach goods, improvements, and progress to which our private efforts could not bring us.

"This doctrine dominates in Belgium; it is the truth."

It is not difficult to join with Father Vermeersch in his admiration for the doctrine of the Catholic party, as he states it in this passage, since it consists in taking all that is best from every policy and applying it with wise moderation. It is equally easy to join in praise of the actual result of that policy as it can be seen by travel in Belgium, or traced in the statistical returns of Belgian prosperity. With the elaborate returns before one which are published by the Government, and the multitudinous private societies of Belgium, it is impossible to deny that the just medium between Stateism and Individuality has been found and maintained in Belgium. Not only is the country as a whole prospering, but every individual in the country shares its prosperity, and does so by the aid of the Government. While abstaining from the excess of Stateism, which might be ruinous to personal initiative, the Government has succeeded in constructing a body of laws by which the State gives potent aid to the development of the historic Belgian virtues of industry and thrift. Its social laws have become gradually more and more important since the year 1890, when, as has already been pointed out, the initiation by King Leopold of the establishment of a fund for the assistance of wounded workmen marked a great advance in the cause of the protection of workmen. The social legislation of the last fifteen years was, however, not the outcome of any suddenly conceived or specially laid down plan ; it was the logical continuance of the policy of social advancement to which the Catholic party of Belgium, free at all times from the bonds of either Stateism or Liberalism, had adhered from the earliest moment of its formation, but to which it was able to give full effect only when its parliamentary majority freed it from continuous warfare for the freedom of religious teaching.

The parliamentary Government of the party has been marked by the enactment of great social laws since 1890, the laws on the labour of women and children, on the inspection of mines and factories, on old-age pensions, on workmen's dwellings, on employers' liability, the economical measures for the suppression of alcoholism, and the like ; but so much has been thrown by these laws on private initiative that a just estimate of the actions of the Government and of their result cannot be arrived at by a study of statute-books and Government returns alone. Indeed, to estimate fairly what the Government of Belgium has achieved within the last fifteen years, the movement of the great body of extra-parliamentary organisations which have been fostered or called into existence by the passing of the laws referred to, must above all be studied.

Never was there, in any country, a more marvellous or a more perfect organisation than this study discloses, or one better fitted to secure the double end of the material and moral welfare of the people. The organisation commences amongst the children while they are still toddling infants ; it increases at every moment as life advances ; it supports the last steps of the old and the feeble ; it carries the dead to their graves.

Belgium being divided into hostile camps peopled by Catholics on the one side, and by those who declare themselves to be atheists or agnostics on the other, it might be thought that there could be no intermingling in the organisations of the Government or the adherents of the different parties. It is not so, however. The foes approach more nearly to one another than they realise themselves. The belief inherited from centuries of Christianity is not a thing which can be thrown off in a moment, or at will, and amongst the thousands in Belgium who deny the truth of revealed religion, and mock at its morals, there are few who are not in reality still Christians at heart, and possibly not one whose mind is not governed by the Christian code of morals. Therefore, when the Catholic Government restored the teaching of Christian morality to the schools, it found no real opposition to its action amongst the masses of the people who supported its opponents at the polls.

M. Wilmotte, the Liberal historian, seeks to explain

the fact that the country accepted without complaint the passing of the supplementary education law of 1895, which was enacted with the avowed intention of " restoring to religion the place of honour, to which it had right, in all the primary schools," and that the clause which permits the fathers of families to obtain the exemption of their children from religious teaching is availed of nowhere, except in one or two towns " in which a systematic opposition is organised," by declaring that " the father, feeble, dependent, ill-informed, or indifferent, was an assured prey for it (the Catholic party), even if he believed nothing ; the mother belonged to it in advance by confession." Reasoning such as this, based on the ignorance of the population, is antiquated everywhere. In Belgium, joined to arguments drawn from the alleged feebleness and dependence of the male population, it is preposterous. In Belgium, excepting those who are stricken in age or by disease, none are feeble or dependent ; and in that country it is impossible for any man to exist without having the case for and against religious education drummed into his ears, even *ad nauseam.*

Not only was the religious teaching accepted by those of the labouring classes, but it was also accepted by rich and highly-educated leaders of Liberalism and free thought. These, indeed, although they organise opposition to religious education amongst the lesser bourgeois, have never ceased to have recourse to it, in its most perfected and intense form, for their own families ; and M. Wilmotte notes, without seeking to explain by reasons of dependence or ignorance, that " the bourgeois of the first rank, in every occurrence in which private life becomes a sort of spectacle for others, themselves conform to the religious proprieties, the respect of which by their neighbours they can never criticise too vigorously. They confide their sons to the Catholic colleges, cloister their daughters in the

DIMANCHE DES RAMEAUX. BY F. VAN LEEMPUTTENS.
(In the Musée de Bruxelles.)

Sacré-Cœur, have them married before an altar decorated
with flowers and illuminated by candles, and, most
often, demand or accept at the supreme moment of
death the succours of a faith which they have decried
during their whole lives."

Belgium is, then, still Christian in every fibre, and
the study of the Catholic organisations is the study of
the national life.

These organisations commence, as has been said,
amongst the children while they are as yet tiny
toddlers. Children are sent to the day schools in
Belgium as soon as they are able to walk, often before
they are able to talk clearly. Besides the elementary
schools—of which there were 6,886, with 827,165 pupils,
in 1904, and to which infant classes are generally added
—there are 2,500 infant schools with 237,265 pupils.
As technical education is begun in these schools by
kindergarten methods, so also the inculcation of moral
principles is carried on by concrete forms. The child,
while learning his religion from the catechism, is taught
to become charitable and helpful, sober and thrifty,
by the means of the societies which he joins. One of
the first of these is the Society of the Little Protectors
of Animals, called into existence by the suggestions
contained in a ministerial circular issued in February,
1898; there are 3,538 branches of this society,
with 220,634 members in the Belgian schools;
and here it must be observed that the connection
between the Government and the various societies of
school children remains a close one, not only because
these societies have in most instances been founded
or authorised by the Government, but also because the
Government continues to influence their action by the
issue of numerous circulars to the schoolmasters regarding
them, and to grant them subsidies and to send lecturers
to instruct the children on their advantages.

Next to the societies for the protection of animals

come the temperance societies. Amongst the first lessons a child is taught in a Belgian school are those of the evils which arise from the abuse of alcohol. From the first he is taught that the use of alcoholic drink is fraught with danger and destruction; but it is not until he is eleven years old that he is allowed to join the temperance society and to make a solemn declaration, on his honour, that he will abstain from the use of strong liquor, and confine himself to a moderate use of wine and beer until he has reached his twentieth year. Beneficial results have already been found to have resulted from the foundation of this society, which dates from 1887, shortly before the passing of the law on intoxication. The society now numbers 3,538 branches in the schools, with 265,621 members.

The Belgian Government have utilised the love of organisation which the children of the country inherit from their parents in every possible way to counteract the childish passion for destruction, as well as to implant moral and economical habits in them. Another of the societies it has called into existence—the Children's Society for the Protection of Trees, Plantations, and Public Monuments—is a case in point. This society has 1,920 branches and 139,800 members.

Valuable as these societies are, more valuable and more interesting still are the numerous children's societies for mutual aid and for old-age annuities which have been formed through the savings banks. It is only in a country where thrift and habits of provision for the future are bred in the bone that children could be prevailed upon at six years of age to commence the formation of a fund for annuities when their life's work is done, and to continue to subscribe voluntarily to these societies during their youth, with the certainty that they would continue to subscribe to them throughout their lives until the time came for them to cease work and retire on the sufficient pension which their infant forethought had provided. Belgian children are not asked to form old-age annuity societies in the kindergartens, which they attend between the ages of three and six years; but a special law, enacted in 1897, provides that from the time they reach six years of age—the age at which they are admitted to the elementary schools—they may become depositors in the *Caisse de retraite*. The number of school children who availed themselves of this law consisted in the year 1904 of 116,617, who had deposited funds in the *Caisse* amounting to over a million and a quarter francs.

The school children had already become depositors of sums of money, amounting in the aggregate to large sums, in the savings banks, before the mutual societies through which their affiliations to the *Caisse de retraite* are effected were formed for them, and they still continue to place a large amount of their pocket money in the savings bank, 369,779 school children having accounts in it in 1904, when the total of their deposits amounted to 10,042,430 francs. Their contributions to the *Caisse de retraite* are made either through the ordinary mutual societies, to which school children's branches are affiliated, or by means of mutual societies specially established for the various schools. The first of these children's mutual societies was founded in 1896. Their success, which followed immediately on the passing of the law which permitted of children partaking of the advantages of the Government-assisted *Caisse de retraite*, is very largely due to the continual efforts made to excite their natural inclinations for thrift and charity by their teachers in the schools and by the directors of the patronage societies which they frequent, and which latter are exclusively religious institutions.

These patronage societies are the direct equivalents of the Sunday schools of England and America. They also hold their assemblies on Sundays, and in them religion holds the first place. If more gaiety and greater pleasure is to be found in them than in many Sunday schools at the time devoted to play, there is, perhaps, more solemnity at the time of prayer, and no less earnestness and sincerity in their religious instruction. Care is taken to prevent any entrance of politics into these institutions; but the propaganda of religion is carried on zealously by means of them, a thing which Father Vermeersch declares does not prevent " the parents who are unbelievers or Socialists from appreciating the good of a patronage and confiding their children to it," or from having it, like the Louvain patronage for girls, which he cites as an example, " really popular in a workman's quarter badly enough disposed towards religion." The children's mutual societies, which are managed at the patronages, make provision in many instances not only for the payments to the old-age pension fund, but also for the formation of *caisses de jeunesse*, which assure the young subscribers " a present for the establishment of their household," or, in other words, a wedding portion, and contributions towards their funeral expenses. In some cases they provide for medical attendance and medicine for their young members, but this is not done as frequently by the children's mutual societies in Belgium as it is by the kindred societies of France, for the double reason that the paying of doctors' bills does not appeal as much to Belgian children as an incentive to self-denial and saving as the prospect of a future pension, and that most of the children's parents being already affiliated to a mutual society which provides for the needs of all their families in sickness, such provision is not necessary on the child's part.

It is arranged by those who are at the head of the patronages to have the various organisations of the school children—the temperance societies, savings banks, mutual, and the other societies which have been referred to—managed as far as possible directly from the patronages rather than by the schoolmasters, in order that the direct connection between religion and these organisations may be emphasised and assured.

These patronages exist in every important locality, and they are declared by the Catholics to be the fundamental institutions of their social work. Their name of patronages seems to be derived from their being placed under the protection of patron saints rather than the fact that the poor children who frequent them are patronised by the rich. The children of the rich, generally of a somewhat more advanced age than the actual members of the patronages, are, it is true, called on to take part in them; but the part assigned to them is that of leaders in the games, and playfellows, rather than that of patrons. In fact, in the patronages the principle most strongly insisted on is that of fellowship and mutual aid; and the spirit which animates them, says Father Vermeersch, is that expressed in the Walloon saying, "Quand deux pôves s'aidaient, li bon Dieu reie" (When two poor people help each other the good God is pleased).

As the Belgian child grows older he finds new organisations awaiting him which continue to advance his moral and material interests. No less than four hundred and ninety-nine technical schools have been established in the country under the present Government, the total number of these schools—which was eighty in 1884—having now risen to 579. The State subsidises these schools by grants of considerably over a million of francs annually, and over two thousand eight hundred masters are employed in them teaching 46,538 pupils. Very much of the excellent development of these schools is due to the present Minister of Labour, M. Gustave Francotte, who has grounds for his boast that, Belgium being an aristocratic country, he and his colleagues were determined to make aristocrats of its toilers by training them to be master workmen in the perfect knowledge of their crafts. But even before the present development was reached under M. Francotte's administration of the Department of Industry and Labour, a great French specialist—M. Dutilley—found the condition of technical education so far advanced in Belgium that he declared, in 1899, " Belgium will succeed in conquering French industry by means of the industrial science which these technical schools propagate."

In the technical education of Belgium, as in all the other organisations fostered by the present Government, private initiative is called upon to play a considerable part. That that initiative lies almost entirely in the hands of Catholic individuals and bodies is due not to Government favouritism, but to the lethargy of the Liberals who have confined their efforts to the propagation of some branches of higher education, and to the concentration of the Socialists who have limited their exertions to the organisation of their political party by means of co-operatives of consumption ; the action of these parties, which are exhausted by a single effort, being in strange contrast to that of the Catholic party, which has proved itself equally strenuous and equally fertile in every direction.

A list of the various technical schools would be an enumeration of all the trades and occupations of the working classes of Belgium. The subjects taught in them extend from foundry work to fishing, and agriculture for men, from lace-making to housewifery for women. There are schools in every region in which the particular trades of each region are taught ; schools of mechanical engineering, schools for the various iron and wood-working industries, for plumbing, watchmaking, carving, goldsmiths' work, armoury, book-binding, gilding, painting, spinning, dyeing, tanning, basket-making, upholstery, tailoring, joinery, topography, brewing, deep-sea fishing, commercial science, and consular training ; schools of needlework, of dress-making, of bonnet-making, of cooking, of domestic economy—of everything, in fact, on which the skilful hands of a Belgian worker can be employed. The Government, besides special grants towards the purchase of utensils, subsidises schools in which the instruction is purely theoretical by grants of a third of their total expenses; to those which are practical as well as theoretical it grants two-fifths of their expenses; the communes also subsidise the schools in many instances. In most cases, the subsidising authorities restrict their intervention in the actual working of the school to a general supervision of the teaching. The schools themselves very frequently owe their foundation to the zeal of the parish clergy, labouring for the moral and material advancement of their flocks. " Everywhere," says M. Wilmotte, " the curé tucks up the skirts of his soutane. He is commissioner, adviser, recruiter; he encourages, he moderates, or he leads on."

It cannot be denied that the initiative of the clergy in founding technical schools was most fortunate for Belgium, in which, although the Government and the Parliament of to-day are heartily at one with their promoters, the governing class looked for long with unfriendly and suspicious eyes at anything which tended towards the union of workers and the reconstruction of the ancient guilds which the individualism of the French revolution had swept away. The clergy, far more clear-sighted than the legislators of the last generation, were amongst the first to see the danger that lay in flooding the country with youths who knew how to do nothing more than read and sum, and whose only ambition was to fill clerkships in Government offices or counting-houses. It was to counteract this danger, the danger of the sons of workmen learning to despise and detest their fathers' honest trades, that the clergy initiated the movement for technical instruction. In their efforts the secular clergy were joined by the members of the religious orders.

Amongst the most successful and the best of the technical schools in Belgium are St. Luke Schools, in which the Christian and artistic spirit of the master craftsmen of the Middle Ages has been made to live again. These schools, which are managed by the Christian Brothers, were founded in Ghent, under the auspices of the Society of St. Vincent de Paul, as long ago as 1862. They exist now in five centres, and include sixteen hundred pupils, the sons of masters and workmen employed in the building and decorative industries. M. Wilmotte admits that it is to these schools that is due " the development in Flanders of the instinctive taste of the race for colour and the plastic arts," while Father Vermeersch, the Catholic sociologist, seeing in them " the focus of the movement at once artistic and Christian," declares that " they realise thus the quasi-ideal type of the technical school."

From all this which has been told it will be seen that in the present time few men enter upon their life's work under more favourable auspices, or in more happy circumstances, than the Belgian craftsman; and it is not to be wondered at that when he looks around him, self-reliant and confident in his future from the knowledge that he is a skilled master of his craft, the young Belgian workman determines to throw in his political lot with that of the party under whose administration and by whose action the country has been endowed with the institutions by which he has so greatly benefited. Many of the skilled workers of Belgium are, in fact, already earnest members of the Catholic party when the time arrives for them to leave the state of pupilage and apprenticeship, and enter that of workmen and voters, as such fresh organisations await them, this time definitely political as well as religious and social.

The political and social organisations of the Catholic party are grouped around great associations—such as

Mineur au Repos.

La Remonte des Mineurs.

REPRESENTATIVE SCULPTURE.   BY CONSTANTIN MEUNIER.

the Ligue Démocratique and the Federation Ouvriers Catholique de Liége, for those engaged in trade and industry, and the Boerenbond Belge and the Syndicate de Notre Dame des Champs, for those engaged in agriculture. Of these, the foundation of the Boerenbond dates from the year 1890, and that of the Ligue Démocratique from 1891 ; but the Ligue Démocratique is the development of an older association, the Fédération des Sociétés Catholiques Belges, which was founded in 1867, and therefore claims to be the oldest workmen's association founded by any party in Belgium. This league, which took its present form after the issue of the encyclical Rerum Novarum of Pope Leo XIII., pursues a double end according to its statutes, " the advancement, moral and material, of the working class, and the conciliation of capital and labour." Seven hundred and eighty-seven societies, comprising 120,000 members, are affiliated to it. Many of these consist of guilds in which the Catholics seek to revive the spirit of the ancient corporations of trades.

The first of these guilds was established in Louvain in 1878. " It has," says Father Vermeersch, "since 1885, its statutes, and its charter, modelled as much as possible on the ancient corporations." What is the spirit of the guild can be gathered from the motto inscribed over the entrance to its " superb maison de famille," erected in 1887 : " Chacun pour tous, tous pour chacun." Several of the guilds have large memberships ; those at Antwerp, Bruges, and St. Nicholas, for example, having two thousand members each. Each guild is at once a workmen's club and a centre of labour and mutual aid organisation, its aim being, according to the authority just quoted, " the mutual sustenance of the members, the honouring of manual labour and the artistic re-elevation in the town ; and the maintenance of good relations between employers and workmen." The guilds carry on the work of the mutual societies commenced amongst the children in the patronages. Various friendly societies formed in them assure their members medical attendance and indemnities in the case of illness or accident, as well as the old-age pensions, which are ever the aim of the prudent Belgian worker.

In addition to these the guilds are centres of workmen's and masters' syndicates, that of St. Nicholas, for example, having syndicates of weavers, sabot-makers, house painters, bricklayers, and builders' labourers, for the workmen; and masters' syndicates for butchers and kitchen-gardeners, for the latter of whom their syndicate carries on successfully a method of sale in common; while the guilds of Bruges and Courtrai have syndicates of typographists, and that of Courtrai has a large syndicate of tailors, who unite to buy their materials in common.

Further, the guild contains a *cercle ouvrier d'études sociales*, in which priests, lawyers, and working-men take their turn in lecturing on economic questions; a *cercle militaire*, a *secretariat du peuple*, and an *atelier de chemage*, in which craftsmen out of work find temporary employment and pay.

Flourishing as the city guilds of the Catholics are, and wide-inclusive, the agricultural associations, while quite as flourishing, are more inclusive still, for they comprise the whole of the population of the rural districts. The honour of founding the first of these guilds, and of introducing the Raiffeisen system of agricultural banks into Belgium, belongs to a country priest, M. Mellaerts, who remains one of the chief workers in that happy organisation which has preserved Belgian agriculture in a flourishing condition. The agriculturists' guilds, founded on the plan of this good priest, now number four hundred, and included twenty-four thousand heads of families. The aim of these guilds, and of their central organisation, the Boerenbond, is much the same as that of the Ligue Démocratique, except that the agricultural associations, since they can damage none by doing so, make full use of the co-operative system, a thing the Catholics cannot do in the cities, since in them co-operation has been often proved to be ruinous to small industries. On its formation in August, 1890, the Boerenbond Belge issued a manifesto, in which it announced it had assumed a triple mission—the defence of the religious, moral, and material interests of the peasants, the improvement of agrarian legislation, and the corporative organisation of agriculture.

The Boerenbond, by means of a central commission, effects the purchase of raw materials for those affiliated to it, without obliging them to maintain a general storehouse or furnish a common capital. It gives all who apply to it free information regarding prices and qualities, and obtains for its members the analysis of all the stuffs they send to it in the laboratories of the State. It has established amongst the guilds affiliated to it over two hundred mutual societies for assurance against loss by the mortality of cattle ; it provides its members with the means of effecting fire insurances at reduced rates ; it has numerous mutual societies with objects similar to those of the town guilds attached to it ; it has succeeded in obtaining the enactment by the legislature of several laws of great utility to agriculture ; but beyond all these the achievement which its founders look upon as the greatest and most valuable portion of their work is that of the wide extension of agricultural credit by means of the Raiffeisen banks.

The Raiffeisen banks, which were introduced into Belgium in 1892 by the Abbé Mellaerts, were first founded in Germany by the Protestant philanthropist whose name they bear. " They are not simple financial institutions," says Father Vermeersch. " Their founder took a higher point of view ; he wished to found Christian societies, penetrated by the spirit of faith and charity, established on the disinterested patronage of wealth or talent, and on the fraternal co-operation of all." They are primarily intended to provide financial aid to small farmers and cultivators, to whom ordinary banking establishments would not make advances either because of their want of security to offer, or of the smallness of their dealings. They consist of a number of local branches grouped around a central body, each of which local branches forms a separate body, whose operations are distinct from those of every other local branch. The operations of each branch are restrained to as small a sphere of action as possible—a village, a hamlet, or a parish; and while the responsibility of the members of each branch is unlimited for the debts of that branch, it does not extend beyond these debts.

In this responsibility, limited to each one's own district, but unlimited for the transactions carried on in it, lie the strength and the stability of the whole system. It supplies the place of a reserve fund at the commencement by assuring the fact that the affairs of each branch, which are also managed by a local committee, the members of which receive no payment for their services, shall be conducted with prudence. The banks receive deposits from their members, but in no instance do they pay more than three per cent. interest on the money deposited; the profits above that sum, whatever they may be, going towards a reserve fund, which, according to the statutes of the bank, can never be shared amongst the members.

The only person who receives any payment for his services in connection with one of these banks is the clerk or cashier. Each bank is managed by a committee, which is elected by the general meetings of the bank, and which, in its turn, decides on the admission of new members. Advances are made only to members of the banks, but no capital is required to be deposited, and the only payment beyond interest on money lent which is required from the members of the bank is an entrance fee of three francs each. In the idea of the founder of these banks no capital whatever was required; but to satisfy the forms of the Belgian law each bank is established with, and registered as having, the minimum capital which the law recognises, of twenty francs. The advances which are made to members are generally made at about four per cent. interest. They are made on the personal security of the borrowers as well as collateral security, the fact that the managers of the banks are in every case neighbours of the borrowers enabling them to take into account the particular merits of every case, and to advance money freely to those who, although they have no security beyond their words to offer, are known to be honest and industrious people.

Every borrower is required to give particulars of the use to which he intends to put the money he borrows; and a sliding scale regulates the length of time for which each loan is made, that time varying according to the investment made with the money borrowed, and the time in which it may be expected to be realised. The loans are frequently made for long periods extending to ten and even twenty years, the largest amount which may be lent to any borrower being fixed by the general meetings. The want of a subscribed and paid-up capital from which to make loans is supplied by the deposits of the members, the confidence which the inhabitants of each locality have in the committee elected to manage the bank's affairs securing to the banks the deposit of the people's savings.

It is entirely on this confidence that the banks exist; neither in Germany, where the banks have long flourished, nor in Belgium, has it ever been proved misplaced. It has been so great from the first as to be almost a cause of embarrassment for the banks, which, being made the depository of all the savings of the country folk, found themselves loaded with much more money on deposit than they were asked to pay out in loans.

There are six central associations in Belgium to which the local branches of the Raiffeisen banks are affiliated. These central associations are formed by the delegates and managers of the local branches. Like the local branches, they are co-operative societies, but, unlike them, the liability of each member is limited to a thousand francs, and each member is required to pay one hundred francs subscription to them. The central associations supervise the management of the local branches, receive their money on deposit, and act as intermediaries between them and the State savings bank, which the Belgian legislature has placed at the head of all these banks, with authorisation to advance them money at three and a quarter per cent., or to accept their surplus funds on deposit at three per cent.

Besides the Raiffeisen banks, there are two other agricultural credit associations in Belgium of a somewhat similar nature: the Schulze-Delitzchbanks and the Agricultural Counting-houses. But by far the largest organisation is that of the Raiffeisen banks. There are 316 of these banking organisations in existence, and the amount of loans made by them in 1902, mostly on personal security, amounted to 3,592,283 francs.

The establishment of these admirable co-operative loan societies is entirely due, in Belgium, to the exertions of the rural clergy. It is, therefore, of particular interest to learn the advice which their founder and chief organiser, M. Mellaerts, gives his brother clergy with regard to their intervention in their management in his pamphlet on the banks. Holding that the associations "proceed from that Christian virtue which is Charity," he is naturally of the opinion that " the priest has from that fact his place marked out, at least to preserve the Christian spirit in them, to give them a moral direction, and at need the aid of an enlightened and prudent counsel"; but, at the same time, he strongly advises the priests not to accept the office of chairman, member of the committee, or cashier, if they can avoid doing so; though, he adds, there is nothing to prevent an ecclesiastic from presiding over the central association of supervision.

The influence of the organisation of the Catholic party, in addition to the protection afforded by the Government, is seen in every department of rural industry in Belgium. The laws which the Government has made prohibiting or taxing highly the introduction of foreign cattle have something to say to the high price at which Belgian cattle are sold; but it is probable that the maintenance of that high price is more due to the great state of perfection to which cattle-breeding is carried by means of the cattle-rearing syndicates, which, subsidised by the Government, provide prize bulls, and keep a herd-book in which not only the genealogy of each beast is entered, but in which there is also recorded the merits of each beast submitted to examination.

In order that the cattle may be submitted to examination, and that good breeding may be encouraged, the Government grants prizes in money for every animal which reaches a certain standard, the owner of every animal which gains fifty points or more in the adjudication of merit receiving a sum equivalent to sixty centimes or more for each point, and the owner of every animal which gains more than seventy points receiving a larger sum in proportion. So valuable does this system of prize-giving make the best bred cattle, and so keen is the desire to possess them, that prudent farmers who are little likely to make rash investments have been known to pay, within the last few years, as much as fifteen hundred francs each for cows aged four and five years, and as much as nineteen hundred francs for heifers of two years old.

Besides the Boerenbond guilds, and akin to them,

there are in every province numerous co-operative societies for the purchase of seeds, artificial manure, foodstuffs for cattle, and agricultural machinery. The total number of farmers affiliated to these agricultural co-operative societies and Boerenbond leagues in 1892 was 52,228, and the purchases made by them in co-operation that year amounted to the sum of 14,902,781 francs. With these the list of the organisations of the Catholics in the rural districts of Belgium has not even yet been exhausted. The co-operative dairies have yet to be enumerated. There were in 1902 493 co-operative dairies in the country, which sold products of the value of 27,514,729 francs, and of which 50,890 farmers were members, every one of whom was included in the muster rolls of the Catholic party.

It may be objected to this that because a man belongs to a co-operative dairy he need not be a Catholic in religion or belong to the Catholic party in politics. He need not; but in Belgium he does, and the cause is not far to seek. In the creation of the co-operative dairies, as in all of the other organisations which have been enumerated here, it was the Catholic clergy, the parish priests, who were the prime movers, and the farmers and their families feel that it is to them that they owe their rescue from the poverty which at one time seemed to stare them in the face. "The first in date of our Belgian creameries was established in 1887, at Stabreeck," says Father Vermeersch. "Their great multiplication dates from 1896–1897. Thanks to the zeal of the two priests—the Abbé Couturiaux, curé of Orthé, and M. Crousse, director of the college of Virton, they have brought a certain prosperity into the poorest of our provinces, Luxembourg. . . In reality, these creameries exist in almost all of our communes. The Abbé van der Schueren has founded twenty-six of them in two years in Flanders alone. . . Most of our creameries have adopted the rules of the Orthé creamery."

This being so, it is no wonder that the rural population of Belgium are as ready and willing to follow the priests in politics as they are to accept their religious teaching. Yet it does not seem in any instance as if the action of the priests were taken with a political object, or with any object other than that so much insisted on in the statutes of the different societies, "the defence of the religious, moral, and material interests of the people."

Personal ambition cannot with any show of truth be charged against the Belgian priests. They are simple men, strong in nothing but their faith and their energy, and they lead simple lives in full content. Poor as the poorest of the people amongst whom they live, they never seek for, never dream of, wealth. There is hardly one of them who has not made two blades of grass to grow where one has grown before; there is, indeed, hardly one of them who has not doubled, trebled, quadrupled the wealth of his flock; yet no man has been found to say that of all the wealth their energy and organising skill created, one centime has found its way into their pockets, or even into the coffers of the Church.

Salaried by the State, they live on thirty, sixty, or eighty odd pounds a year, without seeking or receiving gifts from their people. Restrained by that sense of sanctity, that certitude of a higher calling which is never distant from the priesthood of the Church of Rome, the lowliest amongst them, those who are most nearly sprung from the peasantry, keep an aloofness remarkable even amongst clergy of their church. Their whole lives, into which no idleness enters, are passed in the discharge of their sacred offices, and in the performance of those works which they conceive to be works of charity. Even in these multitudinous associations and co-operative societies—which, from their union of Catholic voters, make the strength of the Catholic party in Parliament—the priests who have founded them, and whose energy keeps them together, never go farther than to fill the parts of Christian guides and monitors. Unbending in their attitude with regard to questions of religion or morals, they leave all other matters untouched; and, apart from religion and morals, they never seek to interfere with or to sway the civil administration.

Even in the midst of the wide-spreading co-operation they have called into being, each priest restrains his action to his own district, and the general union and organisation for political purposes is the work of the laymen who are the political leaders of the Catholic party. Still since the question which is ever at the forefront of political contests is that of religious education, the question of all others which most closely affects the Church, and since the contest at elections not unfrequently takes place between defenders and assailants of Christianity, the priest's interference is called for in the elections, and his voice and his authority are always on the side of the candidate of the Catholic party.

Thus, without the abandonment of their ecclesiastical *rôle* on the part of the priests, the whole weight of religious influence in Belgium is thrown into the scales on the side of the Catholic party, and every skilled tradesman and every agriculturist in the country finds reason to believe that the education which fits him for his work, and the organisation which protects him in it and enables him to hoard his savings with profit, is due to the present Government and to the political and religious leaders of that party.

M. Wilmotte, writing in 1902, declared: "this most attractive power of association was never better conceived for political and moral ends; never did a more solid network surround a nation with its meshes; and so much so that, instead of being astonished at the persistence of a domination which has already existed for eighteen years, it would be more logical to ask how it is that that domination is not more stable, or more complete still " ; and the Liberal writer adds : " Liberal individualism is only a negative force of political life, which is given off itself, like electricity, in the gleams of electoral combats ; clerical co-operation is a force always present, working ceaselessly, and ceaselessly increasing."

These lines, although written by a leader of Liberalism, are not a quite accurate description of the situation of Belgian Liberalism. It is not only at election times that the great historic party of the opponents of Catholicity displays itself ; and its existence is manifested not in lightning flashes, but in regular work and continuous organisation. If a Liberal can overlook the existence of his party's organisation, those of whom the Belgian Liberals are the foes cannot afford to do so, for the solitary organisation of the Liberals is one for the overthrow of religion.

In English-speaking countries the real aim of the leaders of Belgian Liberals is disguised by the fact that they arrogate to themselves the honoured name of Liberal, and declare their action to be one against the power of Rome ; but, in reality, Rome is dragged into their controversies only to confuse the real issue, and it is against all Christianity that they fight—not against any one Church or creed. Plainly stated, the Liberalism which exists in Belgium is, as far as its leaders go, the Jacobinism of the French Revolution ; a Jacobinism, says M. Emile Faguet, its French Radical admirer, who has written a preface to M. Wilmotte's book, " temperate and polite, but with tendencies of authoritativeness, centralism, and anti-clericalism, very strong and very stubborn." A party in opposition cannot make its centralism or its authoritativism felt ; and the whole energies of Liberalism in Belgium for twenty years have been centred in its anti-clericalism. That anti-clericalism has always been able to prosper, to a certain extent, amongst those who are sufficiently indifferent to find the practices of a religious cult tiresome, or so philosophically incredulous as to look upon them as absurd. Individualism, being the open or secret ideal of all those who work by their brains or their cunning for their own advancement, whether they are writers or doctors, lawyers or shop-keepers, and who see rivals rather than friends in all who are engaged in the same trade or profession, the very fact that the Liberals were opposed to the party which advocated association and union has always been sufficient to gain it the support at the polls of the great body of voters, whose only policy lies in a detestation of co-operation. Great numbers of these amongst the professional and shop-keeping classes, seeing the clergy determined advocates of association, and being themselves indifferent with regard to religion, found no difficulty in joining the anti-clerical policy of the Liberal leaders. The first aim of that policy being to crush the power of the priests, the earliest move of the Liberals, after the re-organisation of religious teaching in the schools in 1884, was to prevail on their followers to use the power the law gave them of forbidding their children who attended the public schools to be taught religion.

The idea of the leaders was to train up in their party a class of more or less educated young men, completely free from religious trammels. To carry out their idea the Liberals organised strong committees in the great towns, the members of which—as employers and in several cases as members of the communal councils—brought pressure to bear on parents to sign the necessary documents calling for the exemption of their children from religious teaching, while at the same time bribing them to sign these documents by presents of clothes and promises of food for their children whom they withdrew from the religious instruction. Rich and determined men are found in the Liberal ranks, and where they organised their anti-clerical policy for the schools they were most successful in all that concerned the suasion or the bribing of the parents. They were, and are, equally successful as regards the education of the children ; and they are able to boast to-day that the public schools of Brussels and Antwerp are manufacturing atheists at the rate of twenty thousand pupils a year ; but, beyond the fact that they have succeeded in withdrawing these children from the religious teaching of the priests, and have allowed nothing to be substituted for it, their educational policy has failed. Although they do not seem to realise it themselves, it is not to the colourless ranks of doctrinaire Liberalism that these young atheists go, but to those of the Socialist party, in which there is both life and colour.

Except for this manufacture of atheists out of a certain proportion of the children of the lesser bourgeois, the Liberals do little or nothing in Belgium to affect the march of events. Many manufacturers and large employers in the country are Liberals by family tradition or by personal inclination, and many of the richest amongst them by boundless generosity have attached the people to them, and are able to lead thousands of electors in their train, like M. Warecque, Deputy for Thuin, who in November, 1904, brought seven thousand at his personal expense from the heart of the country to a Liberal demonstration in Brussels ; but they find themselves hemmed in by the Social laws of the Catholic Government on the one side, and the organisations of the workmen on the other. Their leaders represent the individualistic interest in the Belgian Chamber and Senate; but in very many instances, even since the passing of the law of proportional representation, their return to Parliament has only been effected by what the Liberal historian, who has been so often quoted in this chapter, calls immoral alliances with the Collectivist or Socialist party.

Of all the parties in Belgium, the Socialist party is

the one which has made the most noise within the last twenty years, and by their perpetual clamour its leaders have succeeded in conveying the idea to the world outside that it was they who made the Belgian movement, and that, overturning Catholicity and absorbing Liberalism, they were striding rapidly forward to place and power. This idea is false. In very truth, the Socialists in Belgium have done no more than flies upon the great wheels of government and industry. They date the rise of their party in Belgium from the year 1886, and they try to show that all Belgian social legislation dates also from that year, and is the outcome of the "thunderclap" which, according to them, the strikes of 1886 proved to the governing class.

The story of the development of Belgian social legislation, told in this and the earlier chapters of this work, shows this latter contention to be false. As a matter of fact, the strikes of 1886 taught nothing except that the miners were turbulent, which all the world knew before; and could teach nothing more, for the strikers themselves knew nothing, demanded nothing, and had nothing to teach.

Attempts have been made to trace these strikes to political causes, because the miners amongst whom they began were, for the most part, affiliated to an American organisation—the Knights of Labour; but before the stupendous ignorance and indifference of the miners, which they manifested in the height of the strike itself, these attempts have necessarily failed. While seeking to maintain that the strikes were of a social nature, MM. Vandervelde and Destrée, the leaders and historians of Belgian Socialism, have to admit this in their work on "Le Socialisme en Belgique," where they say, "Those who took part in them cared little for Clerical or Liberal, Progressionist or Doctrinaire; here and there, in an infinitesimal proportion, there were found readers of "The Cathecism of the People" (a Socialist pamphlet), but those even only cared about universal suffrage." In their chapter on the strike, the Socialist leaders tell how, while only one stray miner was found with a complaint about the Belgian civil list, " the profound ignorance of the people was revealed in the cry they raised, ' *Vive la République; à bas Napoléon !* ' " and in this reply of a striker who was crying "Down with Peerboum" (M. Vandenpeerboum was the Minister for Railways): and on being asked who was Peerboum, replied, " Don't know; probably someone who has liards."

These strikes commenced amongst the miners of the Charleroi district, and quickly spread to the glass-blowers of the same district. They cannot have been caused by misery, for even then the miners were paid a wage sufficient for a life of comfort in Belgium ; and the glass-blowers were at that time rich and prosperous— " a sort of aristocracy in the working-class," say the Socialist historians. The strikes of 1886 were nothing, then, but the outcome of the turbulent spirit of the Walloon workers, inherited from long lines of fighting ancestors, who were never for centuries without swords in their hands, and who were celebrated in history for seeking quarrels first and causes for their disputes after.

The strikes of 1886 being quelled, the Government, true to this ancient spirit, proceeded to seek their cause, and a Royal Commission was appointed, which proceeded with the deliberation customary to such commissions, and in due time presented a report of much value, as the reports of Royal Commissions almost always are—to those who read them. Belgian Governments, however, are accustomed, even more than the Governments of England, to appoint Royal Commissions on all possible occasions to inquire into every possible subject, and the appointment of this commission marked the strikes of 1886 with no special significance. Nevertheless, although their influence on Government and

Legislature in Belgium has been misrepresented by gross exaggeration, these strikes have an historical importance which makes their mention necessary, since it was by seizing on the chance they offered that the Socialists were able to establish their party in Belgium.

From the time of the breaking up in discord of the International, Socialism had languished rather than lived in Belgium. It seemed impossible for a party of hate to make headway against the advance of the spirit of union in labour and of co-operation amongst the Catholics; and those who did not shut their eyes to what went on around them must have seen signs of the doom of the war of classes in the formation of the Federation of Catholic workers in 1867, with its quickly multiplying branches, and again in the formation of the Louvain guild in 1878, and of the similar guilds all over the country, the statutes of which were published in 1885 with their significant motto of " Chacun pour tous, tous pour chacun," in the building of the fine *maisons de famille* of the guilds, and in the flooding of the country with co-operative institutions in which all classes worked together for their common prosperity.

The leaders of Socialism, however, were not men to heed what passed at home when they could spy into the future or draw deductions favourable to their theories from the supposed occurrences in distant lands. Despite all that passed in Belgium, there were many who remained convinced, twenty years ago, not only in the truth of the prediction of Karl Marx that the world was sweeping on towards a crisis created by individual monopoly, from the misery born of which Collectivism would emerge triumphant, but also of the accuracy of the supplementary prophecy of Bebel that " the nineteenth century will hardly be at an end before this struggle shall be practically ended." To these apostles of Collectivism the facts that small industries and small farms were multiplying in Belgium went for nothing. They pointed to "the resistless march of the colossal farm in the United States," as John Graham Brooks recalls in his work on "The Social Unrest," as a proof of "the infallibility of Marx's insight," and, amidst the growing and well-guarded prosperity of the Belgian workers, continued to cry out to them that capitalism was advancing, wages were lessening, and the masses sinking into deeper misery and want, from which revolution would alone free them.

It is clear that such exhortations could only be successful when the contentment of the working class was disturbed, and from the moment of the formation of their party the Socialist leaders realised that the best means of disturbing that contentment lay in promoting strikes. They therefore set themselves to assist the destiny which they held was forcing the people into misery by continually exciting strikes all over the country. At the commencement the short-sightedness of certain Liberal employers played into their hands. No sooner was tranquillity restored after the strikes of 1886 than these employers, taking advantage of the introduction of a Government measure into Parliament for taxation on the importation of foreign cattle, actually stirred up a fresh strike in all the industrial centres. The hope of the Liberal employers who acted in this manner was to overturn the Catholic Government and bring the Liberals back to power; the result they attained was none other than a strengthening of the hands of their most dangerous foes.

"It was a new thing," say MM. Destrée and Vandervelde, in their History of Belgian Socialism; "the strike was produced in a great many cases with the consent of the employers; it was not directed against them; it did not demand any increase of wages or any concession from them; but it had the character of a political manifestation destined to constrain the public powers to accord satisfaction to the proletarian demands. This agitation could not succeed in the chaotic conditions in which it was born, but it had the effect of indicating the growth of popular effervescence, and to make evident the certain possibility of a general strike." "The Labour party—which was eventually to co-ordinate the efforts of all the Socialist groups of the country—took consistency in the middle of the vicissitudes of this year 1886."

It is not strange that Socialism spread and flourished in the midst of a time so full of disaster for wage earners. The workmen who had flung down their work without a grievance, and who sought neither higher wages nor " any concession," the miner, whose cry in 1886 was for the downfall of Napoleon, gave easy adherence to the Socialist agitators who taught them at once that they had grievances, and that the moment when the Socialist party would remove these grievances and bring them an undreamt of prosperity and ease was at hand. The Socialist syndicates, say the party's historians in the work just quoted, grew enormous during the period of the strikes, which extended from 1886 to 1894. The fact which these writers add, that after the strikes the syndicates became almost completely disorganised, did not affect the apparent success of the party, for long before the reaction set in the Socialist leaders had found a means much more sure than those of any syndicate or trades union of attaching the workmen of the mining and least skilled classes to them, and of maintaining a party war chest, the funds of which could be at all times used for the propagation of strikes and the spread of Socialism. This means was the formation of the famous Socialist bakeries and shops, which are widely—but far from correctly—known as Socialist co-operatives.

Thrift, a virtue which no Belgian is without, finds its highest expression in the working classes, in the people of which it is so deeply implanted that it may be said to be their master passion. It is to it that the people owe their well-being, and to it in no small degree that the whole country owes its prosperity. This being so, to become the means of enabling the workmen to effect a considerable reduction in their weekly expenses was a sure way of gaining their friendship and their confidence. The Socialist leaders knew this, and acted on their knowledge in establishing the bakeries which are called the co-operative bakeries. Had their desire been simply one to advance the cause of theoretical Socialism, they might have gone very far towards furthering it by making these institutions purely co-operative, and by training the people who joined them, by their use, into habits of co-operation which, it may be conceived, might possibly become so extended in time as to bring about by peaceful development the economic revolution which they declared to be the aim of Socialism. Their desire, however, was not so much to train the people as to rouse and arm them in the Socialist cause; and for this end they made their institutions co-operative for the party and ordinary shops for all the world besides. In fact, instead of inaugurating a war to the death against the limited liability companies, in the existence of which they declared all the evils of civilised mankind to lie, they formed their party into a huge limited liability trading company, which they managed, and continue to manage, so successfully that new shareholders have never ceased to flock into it.

This dealing as ordinary shopkeepers, while destroying the purely theoretic value of the co-operative establishments of the Socialists, has aided largely in the success of the establishments themselves and of the political party which depends on them. The profits gained in ordinary trading with outsiders go to swell the bonuses paid to the members, and the war funds of the party.

The Socialist party, being above all things a party of combat, and not one for the practice of theoretical perfection, has nothing to answer for in setting up trading establishments as it chooses; nevertheless, those who live in a great Belgian town such as Brussels, and see the bread carts of the Socialist Maison du Peuple penetrating daily into its farthest suburbs, with men blowing horns for all who will to come and buy, and who watch the carts stopping to deliver bread at house after house of bourgeois families, cannot fail to be struck by the contrast between the realities of Socialist trading and the boast of the Socialists that they are suppressing middlemen and companies' profits by means of their co-operatives. Moreover, whilst it is absolutely certain that the principles of indiscriminate dealing on which these establishments are worked deprive them of all right to be considered as Collectivist institutions from which trading profit, drawn by shareholders from customers, is banished as the most fundamental rule of their existence, it is most doubtful if, as far as regards the members of the co-operative societies themselves, they differ in any way, except in name, from other large establishments from which the employers draw the greater share of the profits. The Socialist party, in fact, takes the place of the master in every one of the Socialist co-operatives, and, like the ordinary master, draws from them as large a share of the profits for its own use as is possible consistently with sound trading, and the pockets of the "co-operators" or customers are drained as far as can be to pay this profit.

It cannot even be said that this draining of the pockets of the consumers, to pay an unearned dividend to the party-employer, is done with the express consent, or even with the full knowledge, of all those from whom the profit is earned. A very great number of those who buy the bread manufactured by the Socialists because it is cheap, know nothing more about the working of the bakeries than they do about the butchers' shops in which they buy their meat, and trouble as little, and are as little troubled by the managers about how the profits of the co-operative bakeries are disposed of, as they trouble or are troubled about the disposal of their butchers' profits. Leaving the customers who are not members of the co-operatives out of the question, MM. Vandervelde and Destrée estimate the number of the members of the great Brussels co-operative, the Maison du Peuple, who regulate the payment of its share of the profits to the party, as, at the greatest, something less than three per cent. of the total membership.

The fact is, that instead of abolishing the employer who draws huge profits out of all proportion to the work he does in the concern, the Socialist party is itself that employer in every one of its co-operatives, and that it has been able to assume and retain that position under the appearance of co-operation is due to its having practically confined its trading operations to those of bakeries and pharmacies, in which the absence of other great capitalist competitors managing centralised concerns enabled them to realise great profits while reducing the prices and even giving a discount, under the name of co-operative distribution of the gains, to the consumer.

Every function of the ordinary employer is admittedly fulfilled by the Socialist party in its co-operatives; the party made and manages them; it built their establishments, and it found the capital for them; and while fulfilling the functions it exacts the dues of an employer. The capital invested in them is the mainspring of the Socialist co-operatives, just as it is the mainspring of every other trading company, and the idea that this capital was provided by the co-operative subscriptions of members would be a very false one; it has been provided by the heads of the party who either lent it to the co-operatives out of their private fortunes, or pledged their credit for it. In either case interest on the borrowed money is regularly paid, and at the ordinary rates, the amount laid aside for interest and sinking fund at the Maison du Peuple in Brussels for the first six months of 1901 being alone 52,250 francs.

In some instances this money is borrowed from the Government itself; but in any case the interest has to be paid. "The members who loan their own savings to the co-operative know why they take interest," says Professor Brooks in his chapter on "Socialism at Work" in the work already quoted; and in the same chapter that acute and friendly American inquirer tells what that reason is as given to him by one of the managers of the party in Ghent: "Men won't let us have their money without interest."

Besides the interest on the capital lent, the share of the profits which the Socialist party withdraws from the co-operatives for its war chest is enormous. In the six months referred to it amounted to 12,999 francs at the Maison du Peuple at Brussels; and MM. Vandervelde and Destrée say that at the time of strikes or on the approach of elections the co-operatives, four or five hundred out of eighteen thousand, it is true they admit, "lightly vote millions of francs to cover the costs."

It is admitted by every observer that the exceptionally able men of business who are at the head of the Socialist party have made the co-operatives of their party a remarkable success; but many of those who have commented on their success do not seem to notice that that success has been gained by the abandonment of every one of the principles of Socialism.

The dogma that the labourer shall have the whole product is disregarded by the co-operative managers. "We have interest charges, rent, and our managers to pay," explained the Ghent leader to Professor Brooks. An eight-hours' day may be talked of, but the co-operatives do not practise it.

"I next found women working ten hours and men close by, nine hours," reports the same inquirer, whose admiration for the Belgian Socialists is obvious everywhere. "In my Collectivist catechisms, I pointed to the opinion that eight hours should be the maximum for all, that five or six would probably suffice. 'Yes,' he [the Ghent leader] said, 'we have been disappointed.'"

The same contemptuous treatment is given in all the co-operatives of the Socialists to the great law of Socialism that all should be paid according to their needs. "When it was found that the sewing girls in Ghent often produced so little, that the minimum wage took all the profit or even left a loss, it was decided and rigidly enforced that a minimum product should be a condition of the minimum wage—*i.e.* work enough should first be done before this wage principle should be applied." "We could not, it was said, allow a given wage in all kinds of work and with all sorts of workmen," reports Professor Brooks. "I asked in Brussels why a certain man was paid a little more than five times as much as the lowest labourer. 'Because he is worth it,' was the reply."

Instances such as these could be accumulated indefinitely by any inquirer, for there is not a single Socialist co-operative in Belgium in which every practice does not run directly counter to the teachings of the Socialist leaders who are the head of it. Regarding the attitude of those leaders towards labour when they are in the workshops where they are uncontrolled masters, and not on the platform, one further typical quotation from Professor Brooks is, however, sufficient. "I asked if a compulsory eight-hours law would hold. 'No,' he (the Socialist leader) replied; 'not for that kind of work, in which we have found that nine and ten hours will produce more than eight.'"

How, then, it may be asked, does the power of the Socialists grow through these co-operative institutions, if the Socialist party proves itself no different in them from any other capitalist employer? The answer is that these establishments give the Socialists a triple hold on the people; first, that gained by the people's satisfaction at the reduction in the price of bread—a reduction effected by the substitution of large establishments, often worked by machinery, for the small bakeries which before the formation of the Socialist co-operatives were everywhere in Belgium; secondly, by the skilful dressing up of the institutions in co-operative form, and the return of a portion of the profit to the "members," more especially where the return takes the form of *bons de marchandise* or orders for fresh goods, as in the great Ghent co-operative, where all profit given to the shareholders is given in kind on the truck system; and thirdly, by means of the distribution of cash and the party propaganda of every kind, which the millions of profits drawn from the co-operatives to the Socialist war chest enable the leaders of the party to carry on, regardless of the "autonomy of the co-operatives" or of any other Collectivist doctrine whatever, except such as their own will and their own judgment of what is opportune dictates.

The first of these reasons, which is summed up in the words "cheaper bread," drew crowds of the poorer classes in the cities around the new institutions, and gained their votes, as soon as votes were given to all, for the Socialist leaders, not indeed because the majority of those who voted for them were converts to Socialism, but because they held feelings of gratitude and fellowship for the Socialist leaders who had reduced the price of bread.

The second reason—the sharing of some part of the profits, though in reality it is very far off from a real co-operative sharing—brings actual recruits to the Socialist party, and in places like Ghent, where the truck system is practised, keeps within the control of the co-operatives all those who have once joined the Socialist co-operative, to do which they must have declared themselves Socialists. It is this practice of the truck system, indefensible although it is in every way from an economic standpoint, which is one of the strongest links in the Socialist chain. It is it which enables the party to give an air of genuine co-operation to their movement, which the bakeries alone might not give it, by enabling it to keep up the various other co-operatives, like the groceries, cigar manufactories, boot manufactories, tailoring establishments, and suchlike at Ghent, the customers of which are the members of the co-operative bakery whose share in the profits is given to them in orders for goods instead of cash.

It is the use of the truck system, joined to that of the scattering of funds from the overflowing war-chest of the party, which has been given as the third reason for the growth of the Socialists' power. It removes the Socialists' trading experiments from the category of harmless or beneficial experiments, and from that of ordinary shopkeeping, and makes of them a positive evil and a perpetual menace in Belgium. These two things have made many unsuccessful and unnecessary strikes by which Belgian industry has been disturbed within the past fifteen years. On the one hand, the workmen, instead of having their habits of thrift strengthened by the co-operatives, have had them lessened, by coming to look on the *bons de marchandise* which were dealt out to them, in lieu of money, as things to be laid out at once in purchases, whether necessary or not ; and, on the other hand, workmen, once they joined the Socialist party, came to learn that there was nothing to be dreaded from a strike. These very workmen, who got nothing but orders for goods by way of their share of the profits of their co-operative in ordinary times, were assured of generous donations of cash whenever they went out on strike.

It is, then, little wonder that they have been ready to strike on every possible occasion, or that month after month the returns published by the Minister of Labour records hundreds of strikes, the tabulated results of which show that in the great majority of cases the strikers went back to work without having gained any increase of wages or any concession whatever, or produced any result excepting that of a dislocation of trade and a loss of time and money; and, indeed, also excepting the increase to the ranks of the party of hate, which the misery of a strike always brings, which is the cause for which the strikes are excited, and the Socialist strikers paid by the party.

The Socialist party being frankly a party of warfare against the existing classes, the existing society, and the existing beliefs, it would be absurd to reproach it for the tactics of propaganda of strikes which lay at the bottom of its every movement from the formation of its party in Belgium up to the present time, but it would be folly to overlook those tactics or to see—as some amiable critics do—a wise development within the Socialist party in the abandonment by that party of all its doctrines, which is being forced on it from without.

In Belgium, even at the height of its power, when some people thought that through strikes the Socialists might do anything, there were very few indeed who knew what the real tenets of Socialism were. Edmond Picard, the Belgian Senator, who besides being a Socialist leader is well known as one of the leading writers and lawyers of Belgium, limited the number of Socialists who knew the doctrines of their party and their meaning to the small group of some dozen or less leaders. Outside of these the whole strength of the Socialists was made up from the masses of turbulent miners who struck for diversion, whose comparative independence placed them outside of the reach of charitable organisations, and whose stubborn ignorance kept them beyond the reach of instruction, and of the floating mass of city workers, whose shifting habits or whose anti-religious education kept them likewise outside existing organisations.

It was these classes which made up the voting strength of the party. For them no promise was too wild, no theory too vague, no blasphemy too terrible. For a long time it was to them alone that the Socialist leaders played in Belgium, for as long, indeed, as there seemed a possibility of forcing unlimited concessions from the fears of the bourgeoisie ; but when it became apparent that their threats of strikes and risings had begun to lose their effect, and that all classes were determined to make a stand against those self-styled pariahs, the leaders of the party began to see the necessity of educating as well as arming the people, and of winning over to their side as recruits or as allies numbers of the better class of workmen and of the bourgeois themselves, without whose aid at the polls they could effect nothing in peaceful and constitutional contests. It was then that the propaganda by speeches and pamphlets began.

Up to the present that propaganda has produced no great results, though millions of pamphlets have been scattered and thousands of speeches made, each becoming more moderate in its tone than the last. As much in the way of instruction in the tenets of Socialism has not been done as might have been expected by the co-operative organisations. Even the modest claim put forward for them by MM. Destrée and Vandervelde, that " there is good in the co-operatives because the co-operatives, in eating our bread, seasoned with pamphlets and circulars, swallow at the same time some little thing (*quelque peu*) of our principles," is hardly justified. The attitude and mentality of the rank and file of the Belgian Socialists at the present moment are best summed up in the words of an American citizen, who, after long conversations with the chief leader and ablest member of the party, in the intimacy of a trans-Atlantic voyage in the summer of 1904, declared, " The Belgian Socialists are people who don't know what they want—but must have it."

Yet if the rank and file of the Socialist party do not know, the leaders have a very clear idea of what they want. Primarily, it is power. For this end, that they might gain funds to carry on their contests, they abandoned in practice, as has been shown, every one of their theories, and became capitalist exploiters of their fellows' labour in their so-called co-operatives. For this end they have abandoned their open war on religion, and silenced the blasphemies of their partisans as completely as they can, even going to the extent of obtaining a vote from the council of their party that no deputy who is a member of the party shall presume to open his mouth on any subject in the Chamber without first obtaining the leave of the committee of the Parliamentary party; and, finally, for this, they have flung Collectivism overboard.

The leaders of Socialism in Belgium no longer talk of the resistless march of the colossal farm in the United States. On the contrary, they point to the fact that the day of great farms seems to be at an end in America. Their theory, as expressed by MM. Destrée and Vandervelde in the last edition of their work, is that " the collective appropriation imposes itself, from the point of view of social interest, only in the branches of industry where the concentration of capital has caused small property, founded on labour, to disappear "; and they protest that " it is not, then, the Socialists who wish to take his land from the peasant, his shop from the shopkeeper, and his bench from the small employer." They declare that " Collectivism will only, then, be integral if small industry and small commerce happen

UNLOADING POTATOES, LIÈGE.

some day to disappear completely; until which there is a place for private property alongside of Collectivist property, not only for the means of consumption, objects of funiture, the patrimony of the family, but also for all the small means of production"; and while they lay down these theories in their official publications, such as the work on "La Socialism en Belgique," from which the preceding quotations are taken, in their own gatherings "the most loyal members of the party," according to Professor Brooks, "may be heard chafing at the affirmation that the State is 'to absorb all means of production.'"

Collectivism still stands at the head of their programme, to which everyone who joins the Socialist party must subscribe; but for years past the leaders have never ceased protesting to the people whose votes they wish to gain that it means nothing, and has no importance, since it is to be applied only to huge and concentrated industries. "Small industry and small commerce constitute the domain of free association," say MM. Destrée and Vandervelde. "The large industries, on the contrary, should be the domain of Collectivism, and that is why the Labour party demands, and confines itself to demanding, the expropriation for the cause of public utility of mines, quarries, and of the subsoil in general, as well as of the great means of production and of transport."

This change in tactics has failed to produce the desired result. The great mass of the people, the skilled workmen who hope to become masters, the small shopkeepers, and the small farmers, refuse obstinately to believe in the reality of the new-born moderation of the Socialists. In spite of every other change the party has never abandoned the contention that the war it carries on is a class war; and the Belgians, contented with their classes—which, as they mingle, aid, advance, and supplement each other—will have nothing to do with a class war. A very general feeling prevails amongst all the lesser bourgeois whom the Socialists hope to gain that the fair words of the party are meant only to deceive. They hold—to quote a favourite phrase of theirs—that the Socialists have recoiled that they may spring the farther, and their attitude towards the Socialist party remains one of unmitigated suspicion and hostility.

At the same time, while the announcement of a moderate policy and the adoption of a moderate tone has failed to produce any favourable impression on those who are really moderate, it has had the inevitable effect of alienating from the ranks of the Socialist party some of the more fiery spirits who formed its fighting strength, and of damping the ardour of a very great number of people who joined the party because the party leaders promised them, in the most definite terms, a world-wide revolution by which all things would be changed for the proletarians' gain, at a certain fixed and now passed date. As long as the party seemed to be marching forward and gaining victories as it went, even though its performance fell immeasurably short of its promise, desertions from the Socialist ranks did not make themselves felt; and just as the party was surpassingly fortunate in finding the condition of the country such that it was able to cover it with its money-making bakery establishments without trouble or labour, so again chance favoured it exceedingly for over ten years, by the fact that, in its latter stage, the Parliamentary movement towards franchise reform coincided with the Socialist agitation.

Although the movement for reform had commenced long before the Socialists had any party in Belgium, and although the certainty of the reform was manifest before the Socialists' voices were raised, nevertheless it was the easiest thing for the Socialist leaders to make it appear, by timely and violent agitation, as if that reform was won by them. At each move towards reform they did the shouting, and their clamour led many to believe that it was they who won the victory.

In reality, instead of being forced forward by clamour and passed in a panic, the reform of the Belgian electorate was, of all legislative enactments, the one most maturely deliberated and calmly voted. Discussed often in former years, it was actually brought to the front of the programme of the Catholic party in the year 1884, at the annual meeting of the Catholic Federation. The delay in introducing a measure relating to it was due to the fact that, according to the constitution of the country, while a vote of the majority in Parliament was sufficient to have the question opened, a vote of a clear majority of two-thirds of the Chambers was required to settle it.

Naturally, no party was willing to introduce a measure so important as one of reform without some certainty of carrying it, either by the aid of its own majority or of a coalition. This certainty had never been possessed by any Government until the growth of the Catholic majority in Parliament gave grounds for the belief that if it did not secure a majority sufficiently large to carry through the reform itself, that party would at least receive a sufficiently large and unmistakable mandate to settle the question on going to the country on it to enable it to carry the project through the Chambers by the aid of the democratic section of the Liberals, which, being also long pledged to reform, could not openly abandon it on party grounds. The country had long showed itself desirous of a wide extension of the franchise, and a steady movement in favour of it was for long carried on in the popular organisations of the Catholic party; besides which, as the wish of the whole country became more and more apparent, there sprang up a tragio-comic agitation of the Socialist party for universal suffrage, in which, according to the Socialist historians, a system of advertisement was had recourse to which was more outrageous and absurd than any ever attempted by advance agents of Barnum's circus.

To many the actions of the Socialists, with their fictitious referendums, their mock letters to the episcopacy in answer to invented pronouncements, their sorry parody of the oath of Belgian patriots of an earlier time, seemed pure fooling; but in the fooling of Belgian Socialists there has ever lurked the danger of grim tragedy, from their readiness to fly to strikes and bloodshed, and that danger was not wanting in this case. Nevertheless, neither the jesting nor the threatening of the party made any impression on the country, and the party writers admit that when the Chambers finally voted a dissolution in order that the Government might appeal to the country on the question of reform in May, 1892, the vote was taken in a period of profound calm and amidst an appearance of indifference, which had extended from the country to the legislative Chambers themselves.

The general elections which followed were held in an equal calm, and turned on the general principles of the candidates rather than on any of the special systems of reform which were put forward. In the new Chamber the Catholics retained their great majority, having ninety-two votes to sixty Liberals; but they had not gained the two-thirds majority which would have enabled them to carry through a reform of the constitution without the support of some of the Opposition. In these circumstances, several months were inevitably passed in discussion and negotiation —months which the Socialist party utilised for the creation of strikes and riots. The demand of this party was for universal suffrage "pure and simple," and it is not improbable that to the violent unconstitutional manner in which the Socialists sought to force the adoption of that franchise on the Chambers was due the rejection of the measure, although in the previous councils of the Catholic party its acceptance had been advocated by the most able leaders of the younger section, such as M. Henry Carton de Wiart, in whose enlightened guidance the political future of the Belgian Catholics was already seen to lie.

This section of the Catholic party, with which on this matter there were united old and experienced statesmen, such as M. Nothomb, a former Minister of Justice, and whose spokesmen were the Baron de Haulleville and Messrs. Theodor, Alexander Braun, and Carton de Wiart, pressed for manhood suffrage, under which every citizen aged 25 years, and having three years' residence in the electoral district, would have a vote. The more conservative section of the Catholic party, led in the discussion on revision by Messrs. Woeste and de Smet de Nayer, proposed a householder suffrage. As was inevitable in the circumstances, a coalition was forced on these parties, the result of which was that the reform ultimately adopted consisted of universal suffrage tempered by plural votes. According to M. Wilmotte, it is the advanced Liberals and the Socialists who are responsible for the adoption of the system of plural votes; but this statement can hardly be considered as exact in view of the fact that the system adopted was introduced and invented by a Catholic deputy—M. Nyssens, afterwards first Minister of Industry—and carried in the teeth of the most violent threats from the Socialists. This system, which is still in force, gives every male citizen who has attained to the age of twenty-five years one vote; it gives two votes to every father of a family who is thirty-five years of age and pays five francs a year in taxes; and it gives two additional votes to each man who possesses certificates of education, and one additional vote to every male owner of real estate.

At the same time, it provides that no voter can have more than three votes.

The first elections under this system were held on October 14th, 1894. Instead of 137,772 voters, which had been the number at the previous elections, there were at these elections 1,354,891 voters, with 2,085,605 votes. The most remarkable result of these elections was the confirmation of the power of the Catholic Government by the new electorate. Out of one hundred and fifty-two seats, the Catholics gained one hundred and five. The Socialists had, as was to be expected, a considerable footing in the new Chamber, their seats numbering twenty-nine. These gains were made up of Liberal losses, the once powerful party of the Liberals having found in the whole country no more than eighteen seats.

As a consequence of the reform of the parliamentary electorate, it was considered necessary to reform the electorates of all the other governing bodies in the country, provincial and municipal, on the same lines; and the Catholic party boasted that more electorate reforms were introduced, examined, carried, and put into force in the two succeeding years of their government, than in the sixty preceding years. Each reform of the constituencies required new elections to the reformed bodies, and for a considerable period there were elections week after week all over Belgium. All these elections passed over without causing the least interruption to the peaceful life of the country. Their result was such as to confirm the proof given in the Parliamentary elections that the country placed its confidence in the Catholic Government, with the action of which it was satisfied. Indeed, looking calmly and intelligently into the affairs of Belgium from a ratepayer's point of view, it was impossible that any different feeling could manifest itself.

The Liberals, during their administration, from 1878

to 1884, had brought the country to what seemed, with slight exaggeration, to be the verge of bankruptcy. They had succeeded to a Catholic administration which had lasted for seven years, in five of which there had been a surplus in the Budget, and which for the whole of its seven years' administration showed a surplus of thirty-three millions of francs, combined with a reduction of taxation on foodstuffs of two and a half million of francs. Yet, notwithstanding the continued prosperity which such a state of things seemed to show, the first Budget of the Liberal Administration had disclosed a considerable deficit, and every one of their succeeding Budgets had continued to show deficits, in spite of increased taxation, until, at the close of their administration in the year 1884, the total of their deficits had reached the sum of 58,967,186 francs, and their Minister of Finance found himself obliged to call for the imposition of increased taxation to the extent of nineteen millions. It was at the moment of imposing that taxation that the Liberals fell from power, and from that moment, when the administration passed again to the Catholics, prosperity had re-asserted itself in the national finances.

In the first Budget a surplus had replaced the deficit; and when the great reform came the Catholic party were able to boast that, just as the Liberal party had shown a deficit year after year, so, on the other hand, their Government was able to point to an unbroken series of surpluses year after year. Since the Catholics were also able to prove that their surpluses had been obtained without increase of taxation, that they were even lessening all the taxes which weighed upon the people, increasing only (and that from temperance motives) the tax on alcohol; and that the taxation in Belgium was much less than half of that in France and not more than half of that in England, it is no wonder that the voters of Belgium placed their confidence in them. The financial prosperity which the Catholic Government was able to show in 1894, as having resulted directly from their administration, continued in Belgium under the Catholic administration. At the close of each year, despite the increased expenses of the social legislation, the Government was able to produce a surplus ; and at every election the country continued to give fresh proofs of its confidence in the Catholics, and its satisfaction with their administration.

In Belgium, where each member of the Chamber is elected for four years, general elections are replaced—except in the case of a dissolution—by partial elections held every two years, at which one-half of the Chamber is renewed. The first of these partial elections after the great reform was the election of 1896. It resulted in an increase in the Catholic representation, the parties after it standing : Catholics, 111 ; Socialists, 29 ; and Liberals, 12. The next elections, in 1898, produced a similar result ; the Catholics, gaining one seat, had then 112 votes ; the Socialists, losing one, 28 ; and the Liberals remaining stationary at 12. The whole power of the country was clearly in the hands of the Catholics. Both in and out of Parliament the Liberals remained politically impotent, and thought of nothing, aimed at nothing, but an alliance with the Socialists on anti-religious grounds ; while as to the Socialists, their power and action in Parliament was confined to that of making noise and uttering blasphemies ; and it appeared, to those who were the wisest judges, as if, outside of Parliament, their power had reached its height, notwithstanding their continual organisation and the adroit use their leaders made of the funds of the co-operatives for the promotion of strikes for their political end.

It was at this moment, when their power was at its highest, that the Catholics adopted a fresh reform, which embodied the law of proportional representation.

Only an exceedingly patriotic Government, or one sure of its surpassing strength, could have adopted such a measure under similar conditions, for it was certain that its effect would be that of restoring something at least of their lost strength to the Liberals, and at the same time of taking something from the strength of the Government party. While the patriotism of the Catholics need not be denied, it is possible that in passing this measure which assures a representation in Parliament to every party in the country, the Government remained confident that its hold on power would remain unshaken. Events proved that it had the most ample grounds for such belief. The system of proportional election, as adopted in Belgium, gives every party a number of seats in each district proportional to the number of votes it receives, provided that its members receive a certain quorum, or, also proportionally fixed, minimum number of votes. The first elections under it confirmed the hold of the Catholic party on the country, while restoring a number of seats to the Liberals, and leaving the Socialists in the position they already held. The distribution of the seats at these elections, which were held in May, 1900, gave the Catholics eighty-five votes, the Socialists thirty-two, the Liberals thirty-one, the Radicals three, and the party of dissentient Catholics which calls itself Democratic Christians, one.

"The characteristic of these elections," say MM. Destrée and Vandervelde, "evidently sufficiently singular, was that everyone declared himself enchanted with them." Nevertheless, the country was not left long free from agitation. One party in Belgium cannot exist without creating discord, and before very long the Socialists had again declared war to the death against all and sundry who would not join with them in fighting for "universal suffrage, plain and simple" —for men only. Again the threat of general strikes was repeated; again rioting was recommended, and revolution taught with hardly a disguise. A Socialist newspaper practically armed its readers with revolvers, given away as prizes. The leader of the Socialist party, M. Vandervelde, a man of much ability and usually of commendable caution, fell in with the stream, and at the height of the excitement his party created, he cried out from a window of the Maison du Peuple in Brussels, to the Socialist crowd gathered around the red flags in the street below, "The fruit is ripe; it is for you to pluck it."

This was in April, 1902. Never, perhaps, was the description of the Belgian Socialists as men "who do not know what they want—but must have it," more true than at that moment. None of them knew exactly what they wanted—except, vaguely, that they wanted everything; but they were determined, or thought themselves determined, to get what they wanted. The universal suffrage which they demanded—only, however, as a means to the end—they were resolved to force from the country by means of a general strike and street riots, and it would be difficult to say on which they counted most—the strike or the riots. Each weapon failed miserably in their hands.

They believed that the capitalists would surrender before the strikes, and that the peaceful citizens of the towns would be terrorised by the danger of the riots into forcing the capitulation of the Government to their demands. Above all, they believed that none would be found, either Garde Civique, police, or soldiery, to resist their advance, or disperse their gangs. Instead of all this, the employers and people held fast, the great strike was a failure, the soldier-citizens did their duty bravely, and it was the Socialists themselves who fled, dispersed at the first sound of danger.

In those days the world looked on expectant, for the Socialists had made a great noise—so great that their historians declare that at a meeting in Charleroi held during a thunderstorm their voices quelled the thunder; but when the day for the promised revolution came— April 18th—there was nothing. The Brussels companions of the valiant men who had defied the warring elements in Charleroi had already distinguished themselves by breaking up their gathering in panic at the approach of a man leading home from work some old tram horses, whose clattering noise they mistook for that of mounted police; and it was evident that while there were many behind to cry "Forward," there were none before to lead on. Nevertheless, notwithstanding the constant alertness of the inciters, there was some approach to riots by the crowds before the Socialists realised that the defenders of the peace were determined to do their duty, and in these, as always happens, the innocent suffered. Such incidents, however, only added to the discomfiture and discredit of the Socialist party. It was apparent everywhere that what had defeated the strikers and rioters was the patriotism of the people rallied around the Throne.

The abortive riots were quickly followed by Parliamentary elections, which took place in the end of May, 1902. These were again the occasion of the country's re-affirming its confidence in the Catholic Government. The increase in the population had occasioned an increase in the number of representatives to one hundred and sixty-six, and of these, after the new elections, ninety-six were Catholics, thirty-five Socialists, thirty-four Liberals, and one a Democratic Christian.

That the Catholics continued to hold their power was in no way remarkable. The people were more than ever sickened of the Socialists; and though they may have begun to forget the financial mismanagement of the Liberals, and even their envenomed assaults on religion, they could not ignore the proofs which they had under their eyes of the good government and financial soundness of the Catholic administration.

It has been alleged that in their haste to pass labour laws and social measures the Catholics ignored economy. This is not so; it could not be so, indeed, with such a leader at the head of affairs as the present Prime Minister, the Count de Smet de Nayer, of whom it has been said that he has achieved what seemed impossible, and "succeeded in creating in a country saturated with fabrication, as Belgium is, three new industries which are due to him, and which are truly the children of his brain and his will." Under the management of the Count de Smet de Nayer, the financial system of the Belgian Government has been reformed, and a mischievous habit of charging current expenses on the National Debt, by which the real financial situation was disguised, has been abandoned. Under the present Government the debt of the country has been brought into the most satisfactory condition. It now amounts to about three milliards of francs, against which the State possesses immense and valuable property, the railways alone being worth two milliards. So valuable is this property, that although in many instances it is exploited on the lowest scales, the receipts from it of ninety-six millions of francs exceeds the interest payable on the National Debt, at three per cent., by six millions of francs. The Budgets of the Catholic Government, with their annual surpluses, have already been referred to, as has the lowness of taxation in Belgium. Recent comparative statistics show the average amount paid by each inhabitant in taxes to be 34 francs 55 centimes in Belgium, while it is 42 francs 72 centimes in the United States, 65 francs 49 centimes in England, and 76 francs 43 centimes in France.

The actual state of taxation in Belgium being so satisfactory after twenty years' government by one party, it is clear that that party may claim the credit due for it; but the present Government can claim more. Not only can it claim that it has reduced chaos to order, that it has abolished frauds on the taxpayer, such as the issue of loans to pay current expenses, and that it has kept down taxation, but it can also claim that it has adjusted taxation in the most equitable manner, and succeeded, while weighing heavily on none, in giving rebates and advantages to the worth of twenty millions in the reduction of stamp duties in connection with the building of workmen's dwellings and rural properties alone. Moreover, it claims—and its claim is admitted by the Socialist Senator, M. Hector Denis, an eminent sociologist—that the amount of indirect taxation on necessaries, paid under its government by each citizen in Belgium, amounts to one centime and a half a day, or 5 francs 69 centimes—about four shillings and eightpence—a year.

The Belgians are an eminently practical people, and it is facts like this which have kept the present Government in office. It might be thought that the figures disclosed here showed the lowest reduction of taxation possible under a Government which maintains the theory that " each one should carry his obolus to the common treasury, so as to avoid the temptation of augmenting the expenses on the part of those who pay no taxes"; the present Government of Belgium goes farther, however, since it claims that the whole of the money paid by the working classes in indirect taxation is directly returned to the working classes by the Government. This claim is made as follows :

There are in Belgium four million people of the working class : calculating the indirect taxes they pay at 5 francs 59 centimes a head, the total amount of indirect taxes paid by them is about twenty-three millions of francs. Now the Government votes fifteen millions a year for old-age pensions, four millions a year for the rest of the Budget of the Ministry of Labour, which is, in the greater part at least, expended on technical education, in subsidies to mutual societies, and on the inspection of mines and labour, and reduces the railway fares of workmen going to and from their work by nine millions a year—all of which sums put together make up twenty-eight millions of francs, to which might be added the fourteen millions of francs paid every year, under a law made by the present Government, for the remuneration of the soldiers, one half of which fourteen millions is paid to the soldiers, and one half to their parents; so that the Government may contend that the working class, as a class, does not pay one penny of indirect taxation which is not returned to it, as a class, in cash and kind.

In any country these figures would be interesting; in Belgium, where so much is sought to be made out of a class war, they are valuable. More valuable, however, and far more important still, is the knowledge of the great laws on workmen's dwellings, old-age pensions, and employers' liability, which have raised up the people and bound the classes together in mutual aid and friendship.

The workmen's dwellings laws and the old-age pensions laws are the crowning parts of the great edifice of mutual aid and co-operation which the Catholics have built up in Belgium, the commencement of which in schoolboy institutions, technical schools, and co-operative societies has been described in the earlier pages of this chapter.

True to its principles of acting as a benevolent guardian rather than as an all-compelling master, the Government has combined State assistance with private initiative in a most skilful and most happy manner in the administration of these Acts. Their working is carried on, like that of almost all enterprises in Belgium, the land of organisation, by the revolution of wheels within wheels, which, functioned on the outside by private impulse, fit in on the inside into the machinery of the Government, and make part of the great machinery of the State. The General Savings Bank, through which these laws are worked, is itself an independent financial institution, though worked under Government control and guarantee. Its importance in Belgium is seen from the fact that, out of every 100,000 inhabitants in the country, 29,275 people have deposits in it. In 1902 the total number of its depositors was 1,973,480, and the amount of deposits 730,563,054 francs. The confidence of the people in the institutions of the Government being unbounded, the number of the depositors and the amount of their deposits constantly increase, and on a great scale. It is also a significant fact that the amount of deposits increases in exact ratio to that of the depositors. This confidence has naturally increased in the most noticeable degree as the fears which the formation of the Socialist party created died away, and in the six years between 1896 and 1902 the number of the depositors in the savings bank, and the amount of their deposits, was increased by one half.

Even in the best managed of savings banks there is always a danger that the money placed in them will be locked up in what is known as sound securities, where it produces little more benefit to those who deposited it than if they had kept it in their traditional old stockings. This danger has been avoided in Belgium by the wise action of the Government in providing the money lent on workmen's dwellings from the funds of the savings bank, and in working the insurance fund and the old-age pension fund through that bank.

According to the law of 1889, by which loans to workmen for the building or purchase of their dwellings was authorised, the initiative in the matter of each loan must be taken by the workmen, acting through an intermediary, generally one or other of the many mutual societies of the country the statutes of which permit of their interfering in the matter. These intermediaries must submit their plans to one of the fifty-five "patronage committees," which, appointed by the Government, exist all over the country for the purpose, amongst other things, of "making a continuous inquiry into the moral, hygienic, and economic conditions of dwellings." The patronage committees reports being favourable, the savings bank advances eight-tenths of the sum required to the mutual society, generally at four per cent., and the mutual society in turn advances it to the workman at the same amount of interest.

It is generally held that the intervention of the mutual societies between the State and the workmen simplifies instead of complicates matters, and by affording greater security to the State enables the workmen to obtain their loans on better terms than if they applied directly for them. It is unquestionable that the mutual building societies—of which there are at present one hundred and fifty eight—are of great value to the workmen.

In addition to undertaking all the business arrangements connected with the obtaining of the loans, building, and purchasing, these societies generally provide that the workmen shall combine life insurance, also effected through the savings bank, with the purchase of their houses, and for sums equivalent to the amount of their loans; so that if they die before the loans are paid off, the debt is discharged by means of the insurance, and the workman's house becomes the uncharged property of his family; while, should the workman live, his payments to the society are so arranged that while the total he pays each year for reducing his debt, interest, and insurance is always lower than the ordinary rent of a house would be, the debt itself is gradually wiped off, and, at latest, in the great majority of cases, as he approaches the age at which Belgians think of retiring from work on their savings—about sixty-five years—the workman finds

Photo: *Neurdein Frères, Paris.*

PALAIS DE JUSTICE, BRUSSELS.

himself the owner of his house, free from rent or interest, and possessed of a valuable policy of life insurance as well.

The mutual companies also aid the workmen by lending those amongst them who have not saved it previously, the two-fifths of the purchase-money which the State requires them to pay themselves. This is done often on the security of the life insurances. The workman who desires to become possessed of his house, but has no money, effects the necessary insurance and deposits it with the mutual society, which admits him to the house as an ordinary tenant until such time as the insurance policy has acquired a surrender value equivalent to the necessary two-tenths of the purchase money. That sum is then lent to the workman, and he is recognised as the owner of the house, the debt on which he at once commences to wipe off by the payment of the money which would otherwise have gone from him in rent without bringing him any return. The average price which the workmen pay for their houses is estimated to be five thousand francs, and the extent to which the law on workmen's dwellings has been availed of can be seen by the fact that the money lent by the Government through the savings bank under it reached the total of sixty millions of francs in the year 1902.

The laws on old-age pensions, passed in 1900 and 1903, are of a kindred nature to that of workmen's dwellings. The intention of these laws is to give such encouragement to the habits of thrift that every workman will lay aside sufficient money to provide himself with an old-age pension, or annuity, of 360 francs a year, a sufficient sum in that country where the annual expenses of an adult working man are calculated to be, on an average, 222 francs 42 centimes a year. For this end the Government pays into the savings bank into the account of each person who has become affiliated to the old-age pension fund the sum of sixty centimes for every franc he deposits himself, or which is deposited in his name, until there is to his credit a fund sufficient to provide him with an annuity of the amount stated.

In addition, that those who were already advanced in age when the old-age pensions law was passed may benefit by it, a sum of one franc is paid to the account of all who were aged between forty and forty-five when the law of 1900 was passed, one franc fifty centimes to the accounts of all who were then between forty-five and fifty, and two francs for all who were over fifty ; while to those who are already over the age of sixty-five a pension of sixty-five francs a year is allowed. Two hundred thousand of these pensions, involving an annual payment of fifteen millions of francs, are actually paid in the country. The Socialists pretend to despise such pensions ; but, while it is not they but the formation by the thrift of the working-class itself, aided by the Government, of a sufficient fund to ensure every labourer the larger pension of 360 francs, that is the aim of the old-age pension law, it is none the less true that in thrifty Belgium the sum of sixty-five francs a year brings appreciable aid and comfort to many an aged man. The real feeling of the working class towards this law is clearly shown by the multiplication of the number of old-age pension societies, and of the number of their members since the passing of the law. There are at present 4,597 of these societies in existence in Belgium, and over half a million people affiliated to the pension fund.

In these laws, and their acceptance by the people, the Catholic policy of union and conciliation has triumphed. It is they more than anything which have shown the hollowness of the pretended spirit of class hatred in Belgium. Whether they wished to do so or not, the most rabid Socialists were forced to accept them. The Socialist leaders called them laws of pretence, *lois de façade*, and mocked at them ; but they could not prevent their followers from taking advantage of them. These laws gave tangible proof to the working classes of Belgium that the means of their present comfort and that of their old-age lay in their own hands. It is useless to cry out to people who are earning good wages that they are starving, or to tell those in whose hands pensions and house property are being put, that they are ground to the earth; and so it has proved in Belgium. The Socialist workmen have shown themselves eager to accept the benefits of the credit institutions, to buy their own houses through the patronage committees, and to obtain the Government grants towards old-age pensions.

The result was inevitable. The old members of the Socialist party still belong to the "co-operative" bakeries, and the cheap bread of these establishments continues to gain them new customers; but the members no longer "lightly" vote the millions of profits to be dissipated in strikes. They ask, rather, that the gains of the co-operatives shall be shared amongst the benefit societies of their members, and eagerness is no longer shown, amongst those who have begun to own houses and to save up for pensions, for the overturn of society or the disturbance of the country's peace.

Something of this change of the "proletariat" in a country where there are few real proletarians was manifested in 1902, when the attempt at widespread rioting failed; more of it was shown at the elections of 1904, when the Socialist party received a severe set back. These same elections were marked also by an increase in the strength of the Liberals, which was in itself additional proof of the increasing security of the people under the Catholic Government, since the increase in the Liberal vote over that of recent years was due to the return to the Liberal party of many who belonged to it, but who had deserted it in the terror of the Socialist onrush.

The elections of 1904 left the Catholics masters of the country with their vigour unimpaired by twenty years of rule. They can boast as the result of these twenty years of continuous government that they have crushed sedition, not with the sword, but by good laws, and that they have wedded peace to prosperity. Wise measures and great legislation mark the advance of Belgium in these twenty years in which prosperity has been shared by all. In every country these years have been marked as years of social struggle; in Belgium, and, above all, in the latter portion of them, they are even more clearly marked as years of social union. The motto which guided the country through these years, more noble than any a modern hand has writ, and one no Belgian forgets in his heart, or is untrue to for long in his acts, was "Aimez-vous les uns les autres."

It is fitting that the twentieth year of the Government which was moved by such ideals, and achieved so great results, should be marked, as it will be, by the passing into effect of a law the enactment of which has been said to mark an epoch in legislation for the working classes: the law of employers' liability, which was introduced into and carried through Parliament by the Minister of Industry, M. Gustave Francotte.

CHAPTER XVII.

THE FUTURE EMPIRE.

POLITICALLY unknown a hundred years ago, known fifty years ago only as a petty State formed out of dissimilar and often jarring elements, tolerated because of the common jealousy of the Powers, but liable to have her independence swept away the moment that jealousy was quelled or crushed, Belgium is to-day a nation, firm and close-knit, relying on herself for her independence, possessed in reality of all the attributes of greatness, and standing on the threshold of assured empire. Amidst the rush and swirl of the nineteenth century, with its wondrous advances and its appalling retrogressions, its scientific glory, its shame of festering crime and misery, the steady evolution of the Belgian nation shines out a fact most full of promise for patriotic and peace-loving men. Of all the States of Europe, Belgium deserves empire most, for she, alone amongst them, is the one that proves undisputed empire to be possible by the free and willing union under one crown of races differing in language and in blood.

Looking at the existing empires of Europe, torn as every one of them is at the present moment by the internal dissensions of the races which form them, and whose union would make their strength greater than fleets or armies ever could alone, even the most ardent imperialists might be forced to believe that the political union of races is impossible without the domination of one of the races over the others and the crushing down of the others' national inspirations, were not Belgium there to prove the contrary. Belgium, however, proves conclusively that racial independence and national union are not only possible, but that in them lies the power of successful empire at the present time. While proud empires near her seem tottering towards disruption, despite of their armed forces, Belgium stands and grows, not because Fleming rules over Walloon, or because Walloon dominates Fleming; but because Fleming and Walloon remain fiercely independent in their own homes in all that concerns their native languages and customs, and at the same time as fiercely united, in their own land and out of it, in all things national. This union did not spring from the revolution which won the independence of Belgium; it is the result of the wise government which followed the establishment of that independence.

The Flemish and the Walloons were forced into rebellion against Holland by the misgovernment of their provinces by the House of Orange, rather than by any common affection or any desire of political union. They had few ties between them. The memory of their local jealousies and local quarrels was stronger than the memory of ancient union; their races and characters were different; their languages were different; their attitude towards religion was different. Their motives in the revolution itself were widely diverse.

A strong Flemish party sought at first nothing more than a reform of the constitution under the King of Holland; a strong Walloon party worked for a union with France. For a long time this divergence of aim continued, and King Leopold I. ruled for many years before he was able to rid the country of Orange treachery and French intrigue. It seemed as if the equal union of races brought about by their common misgovernment would cease to be an all-inspiring motive when misgovernment was banished, to be replaced by the dominion of one of the races and the gradual extinction or the renewed subjection of the other; but it was not so. That this did not happen was due, in a great measure,

THE FUTURE EMPIRE. 375

at the commencement, to the wisely impartial rule of King Leopold I.; that it can never happen now is due to the patriotic genius of King Leopold II., who, in giving the Belgians an empire, made them a nation.

Were it not for the genius of the King, and his energy in lifting the people up and uniting them for a noble cause, Belgium would still, at the best, be no more than an agglomeration of provinces. The Belgians, having won their independence by daring, were determined to retain it by caution; and it needed all the skill and perseverance of their present King to teach them that that caution was ill-placed. Curiously enough, the rock on which they seemed destined to split was one on which a false reading of English signals was steering them. Having no greater political ambition than to resemble England, the industrious races which inhabited the kingdom of Belgium were content to settle down as a nation of shopkeepers, like England, they thought, oblivious of the fact that England never could have existed as a free country or won her empire had she not been something other than, and very different from, a mere traders' mart. As traders and manufacturers the Belgians were resolved to stick to their shops and their works, regardless of all the world outside. Foreign politics, they thought, were not for them. Certain of their own good faith and peaceful intentions, they believed all Europe to be of equal good faith, equally inclined towards peace, and equally resolved to be swayed by the dictates of reason in seeking the greatest good of the greatest number. They found a sufficient security for their independence in the Treaty of London, and an equal security for the prosperity of their industries, on which the existence of their population depended, in the doctrine of Free Trade, which, they were certain, would open and keep open all the markets of Europe and of America for them.

When King Leopold II. ascended the throne,

Belgium was already the most densely populated country in the world, and her population was still growing, as, indeed, it has been ever since; yet none but the King saw the need of Belgian expansion in this fact, although all knew that no Belgian would even willingly expatriate himself; and none but the King saw in it an imperative necessity for securing widening markets for the goods with which the continuously increasing industry of Belgium was prepared to flood the world.

There are no Belgians who do not think of their country's future to-day as King Leopold does. Already their conception of Belgium as a firm kingdom, self-reliant and self-supporting, stable in its independence as in its peace, has blotted out the earlier idea of a petty State, living on sufferance and leaning for support on the paper promises of foreign Powers. So completely are the people at one with their ruler at the present time regarding the destinies and the duties of Belgium, that they forget they ever held a lower ideal, or hung back when he urged them on. Yet it took many years of urging on the King's part to move the people on.

Long after he came to the Belgian throne, King Leopold I. wrote to one of his ministers, "We must create everything for this country, for private enterprise does almost nothing in it," and this necessity for initiation in the Crown remained throughout the reign of the first King of the Belgians. Nevertheless, the spirit of enterprise, and the character which makes enterprise successful, was never wanting to the Belgians; and it was to awaken the dormant energies of the people, not to endow them with new qualities, that King Leopold II. exerted himself from the moment of his entry into public life as Duke of Brabant. What the Belgians needed was not daring, but the proof that daring should be shown. This proof King Leopold forced home upon them.

THE QUAYS, ANTWERP.

Photo: Stengel & Co., Dresden.

"A young nationality like ours should be daring," he told the Senate in 1855, while Duke of Brabant, "always in progress, and confident in itself. Our resources are immense; I am not afraid to say it, we can draw an incalculable benefit from them. To succeed it is sufficient to dare." As Prince and as King, he repeated these words again and again, until the Belgians from listening came to believing, and until they not alone believed in them and repeated them themselves, but they acted on them, and found in their action the success he foretold.

From the first moment that the power lay in his hands, King Leopold was not content with speech alone; he himself has ever been throughout his reign the leader in Belgian enterprise. Son of the wisest prince in Christendom, he taught himself the needs of Belgium at an early age, and set himself to bring them within the country's reach, and to assure their attainment. He saw that chief amongst these needs were markets for Belgian goods, and room for Belgian expansion. Even when the star of Free Trade shone brightest, he realised that for a country like Belgium to trust alone to the excellence of its manufactures and the cheapness of its prices was to place that country at the mercy of the more powerful nations which surrounded it. He saw—and he repeated in his speeches—that the doors of these nations might close at any moment to Belgian trade. France out of petulance, Germany from a desire to force Belgium within the circle of her empire, England wishful of trading only with her colonies, might at any moment place prohibitive tariffs on Belgian goods, and Belgium had no means of forcing her trade on these countries.

The treaties which guarantee Belgium's independence tied her hands with regard to trade. They forced Belgium to declare she would never enter on an offensive war, but they did practically nothing to protect her commercial rights. Belgian statesmen seem to have taken little heed of this fact; but its significance was not lost to the King. Twice at least, during the reign of his predecessor, great Powers had declared to Belgium that the completion by that country of projected treaties of commerce would be looked on by them as a cause for war; but Belgium stood bound, by her pledge of perpetual neutrality, never to threaten compulsion, however much her equitable rights were trampled on. In these circumstances, King Leopold saw that Belgium, to be secure, should spread her commercial interests far beyond the boundaries of Europe, and carry her goods to her customers in their own lands instead of sitting down at ease at home, waiting for customers to come, under the police protection of the Great Powers—whose protecting policemen might be transformed at any moment into threatening soldiers.

The obstinate manner in which those who led Belgian thought and controlled the movements of Belgian commerce clung to the belief that the work of the country was done when its manufactures and industries were fostered at home, would have discouraged anyone less ardent and less determined than the Prince who now rules over Belgium. The only effect that obstinacy had on him was to cause him to advance from words to acts, and to do himself for Belgium what the Belgian traders did not think of doing of themselves. " The doors of the neighbouring countries may close against us, but the ocean is for ever open to our ships "—this was the continual burthen of his speeches. To prove its truth was the end of his geographical studies in his studious youth; it was the object of his travels in his early manhood; it has been his constant labour ever since—a labour so heavy that it has won for him the reputation of being the most laborious citizen in labour-loving Belgium, and one which has won for Belgium the success which all the world sees.

Never was there a success more wonderful; never was there a success more directly due to the efforts of one man. It is not in the territories he has gained, nor in the riches he has built up for Belgium, that King Leopold's greatest success lies. It is in the minds of the Belgian people. Little Belgium is no longer heard of in the country which King Leopold rules. People no longer talk in that country of the square roods of Belgian soil; they speak, rather, of the Belgian interests and Belgian enterprises in distant lands, in China and Siam, in Russia, and in Africa. The Belgians have learned that power is not measured by the acreage of a mother country; they have found the truth of their Prince's declaration that the peaceful conquest of the world was possible for those who had the courage to attempt it and the energy to persevere; that for Belgians " to succeed it is sufficient to dare."

The widening of the horizon of Belgium has brought an incalculable benefit to the Belgians in the widening of their minds. With the coming of larger and more generous aims, provincialism and petty jealousy have died amongst them. Deadly enmities cannot spring up around the village pump when men are planning, at the invitations of these countries' rulers, the re-organisation of the judicial systems of Asiatic States, or, out of their own Christian charity, equipping missionary expeditions for labour amongst the Africans. Men cannot lose their patriotism when their country assures them work at home or careers under Belgian direction in lands near and far. Trade depression may come at times, but lasting despondency there cannot be amongst a people whose King has established a foothold for them in the three great centres of Europe, Asia, and Africa.

This is what King Leopold has done—this has been his life's work ; and it is not Belgium alone, but all Europe which stands his debtor. Europe needs men—strong men and daring. King Leopold has assured them to her, while securing Belgium from the misery which would follow disruption, the famine of over-production, and the sad decadence which fear for the future begets ; the effects of which are seen in a continually dwindling population in one of the greatest countries near to Belgium.

The pride of his race, beyond doubt, as well as his patriotism, spurred King Leopold on in all his endeavours for the advancement of the interests of the Belgian kingdom ; and it is more than strange, not indeed that he should be assailed—for success has ever its detractors—but that assaults on him should be allowed to pass amongst the people of the country who should know the race of Coburg best. Mud may be flung by those who grovel in it ; but in England, amongst men whose hands are clean, scorn should be the meed of those who slander a Coburg King. England was right when she hailed King Leopold's work in Africa as one for humanity ; she will be right in still hailing it as such.

The King of the Belgians did no more than his bounden duty in uniting the success of his Congo State to that of the Belgian kingdom. The fact that he has done so makes the gain that he has won none the less Europe's. Amidst all the slanders that have been poured out on him, the King's motives and his actions stand out clear and unmistakable. Personal gain has never entered into them. King Leopold has poured his own money into the Congo ; the money that came from the Congo, from the sale of products which, rich though they are, were valueless there, is poured back by the King into the Congo, and made to fructify a million-fold in the public works of that most nobly planned of States.

Had the Independent State of the Congo been left open to the plunder of adventurers, evil, not good, would assuredly have resulted from the establishment of that State, at the moment that the Congo was found to possess valuable products. King Leopold, in ordering his government of the State as he did, saved it. The proof of his wise government is found in the marvellous progress of the State, even now, while it is still in its infancy. So great and so beneficial has been that progress that there is not a country of Europe, however old its colonies, which could not learn something to its advantage from King Leopold's administration of the Congo. As is natural in every country in which civilisation has but lately set its foot, the machinery of the Congo Government is being perfected every day. That machinery was set up by King Leopold alone.

In the hardest days of his struggle to plant civilisation in Central Africa none aided him, except those who came directly under his personal influence, and felt the inspiration of his determination to succeed. Now all the world is willing to aid or share, but none can deny the King's right and his wisdom in accepting aid chiefly from his own Belgian people. None can deny, either, the King's right in decreeing that in the future the Congo State shall be merged as a colony in the Belgian Crown, nor his wisdom in postponing the transference of the Congo administration to Belgium until the settlement of the State is somewhat advanced.

Amid all the virtues of parliamentary government patience is not the greatest, and continental Parliaments are not quite without a suspicion of being prone to try hazardous experiments in colonial administration. The date, however, at which the great colony of the Congo can, with safety to its population, native and foreign, be handed over to the Government of Belgium, is not now far distant in the eyes of its founder. The transference of the Congo to Belgium will do nothing to affect the situation of Belgium in Europe as a neutral State, but it will strengthen Belgium immensely in its independence. That gain will itself be a gain for Europe, for Belgium's independence stands for peace; and peaceful Belgium is a prosperous land. Since ages long since past, Belgium has been a pioneer of Christianity; in future ages, even in the immediate future, her people's success may make her one of the strongest bulwarks of European civilisation. In the present reign her flag has been carried into the farthest countries of the world; wherever it has been carried success has followed it, and that success in every instance has been due to the King, who initiated, who sustained and animated the peaceful expeditions which displayed it.

Like every other country, Belgium has difficulties to contend with at home and abroad; but those who foresee most clearly what her difficulties will be in the coming time, see also most clearly that she possesses the means and the will to surmount them. Independent peoples whose hearts are united in a nation, and the great majority of whom strive together for the common good, need fear no foes, within or without. The peoples of Belgium are such. They have been guided to union in great endeavour by their King, and it is to their King, Leopold II., that they owe the fact that they stand to-day a nation strong and prosperous, on the threshold of a glorious future.

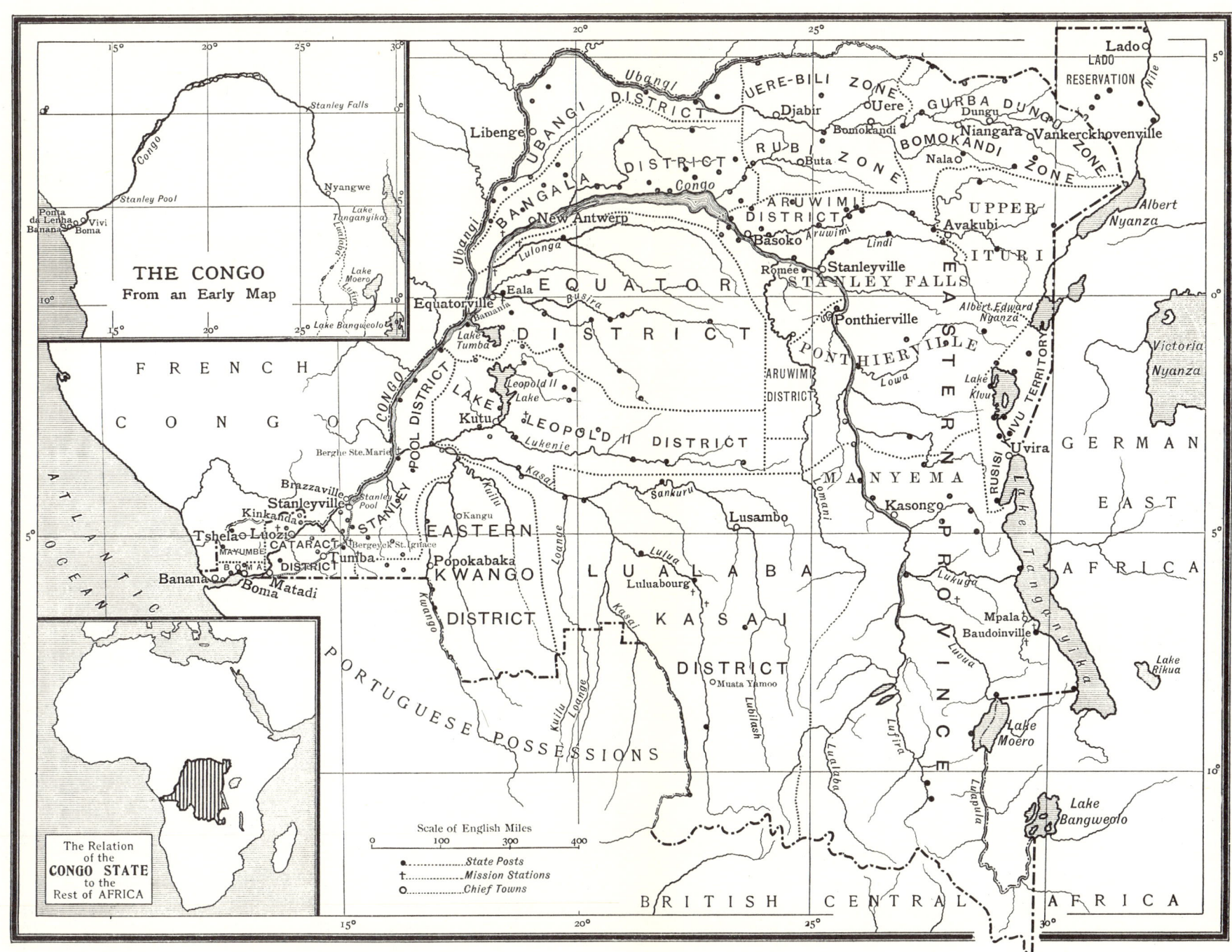

GENERAL MAP OF THE INDEPENDENT STATE.

INDEX.

A

Africa, Proposed civilisation of Central, 89, 97; International Association for opening up, 108; battle ground of Europe, 126 (*see also* Congo River and Congo State)
Agriculture in Congo State, 249—253
Alcohol and native races, 145
Alkemade, General Cousebant d', Resignation of, 77
Alvez, slave hunter, 101, 102
Alviella, Count Goblet d' (*see* d'Alviella)
American Missions in Congo State, 223
Anglo-Congolese Convention, 303
Anti-Slavery Congress at Brussels, 66
Anti-Slavery Crusade, 156
Antwerp, Convention of, 31; fortification of, 69, 79
Apostolic Vicariate of Congo State, Creation of, 192
Arab chiefs: of Manyemba district, 155; rising of, 160, 192
Army, Belgian, Parliament rejects proposal for personal service in, 72
Army of Congo State, 170; civilisation of its native soldiers, 285
Aspremont-Lynden, Count d' (*see* d'Aspremont-Lynden)
Augier, Father, Death of, 192
Austria, Archduchess Marie Henriette of, Marriage of, 9

B

Bamania, Abbey of, 203
Bamboula, African negro, 118
Banning, M. Emile, on slave trade, 99
Baptist Missionaries, 222
Basoko, Mission station at, 201
Baudouinville, Missionaries in, 198
Belgians' love of pageants, 14
Belgium; under Leopold I., 1, 9; her expansion under Leopold II., 5—9, 13; her commercial alliance with China, 10; her parliament and people, 14—46; her constitution, 21; celebrates twenty-fifth anniversary of accession of Leopold II., 51; and Foreign Powers, 54—87; as a buffer State, 56; Napoleon III.'s designs on, 57—65; her army budget increased, 63; proposed sale of her railways, 63; and Franco-German war, 64; cockpit of Europe, 66; perfects her fortifications and army, 69—72; Parliament rejects proposal to institute personal service in army, 72; England's attacks on, 82; expansion of, 88—92; grants loan to Congo State, 159; her progress from 1890 to 1905, 308—372; social legislation in, 314; education in, 316—327; Raiffeisen banks, 327—330; co-operative societies and dairies, 332; Liberalism in, 335—337; Socialist party in, 337—355; strikes of 1886, 338, 341; co-operative institutions, 343; electoral reform, 354—358, 360; her financial prosperity under Catholic government, 360; proportional election, 361; reform of

384   INDEX.

financial system, 364; taxation in, 365; General Savings Bank, 367; mutual societies, 368; old-age pensions, 369; future of, 373—382
Benedetti, M., 58
Bergeyck St. Ignace, Mission Station at, 213
Berghe Ste. Marie, Mission station at, 210
Berlin, Congress of, 138, 141—151
Bishop Taylor's mission, 224
Bismarck, Prince, 138, 141
Blyden, Dr., 182
Boerenbond Belge, 325, 326, 327
Boma, Mission station at, 212; court of, 307
Botanic garden at Eala, 251
Brabant, Duke of (*see* Leopold II.)
Brazza, M. de, at Stanley Pool, 123
Brazzaville, Establishment of, 124
Breydel, Jean, 72
British Baptist Missionary Society, 222
Brooks, Prof., on Socialism, 346, 347
Bruges, King Leopold's speech at, 72—75
Brussels, Leopold II.'s improvement of, 5, 16; King's entry into, 14; King visits Hôtel de Ville to receive congratulations, 52; reception of British volunteers at, 61; Congresses held at, 66; Geographical Conference at, 93—96, 103—106; Socialistic meeting at, 363
Brussels General Act for suppressing slave trade, 157
Bulletin Officiel de l'État Indépendant du Congo, 165, 176, 222
Bureau of Bienfaisance and private schools, 40
Butaye, Père, on Congo missions, 215

C

Caisse de retraite, 319
Cameron, Captain, on slave hunting, 101—103
Cannibalism in Congo State, Suppression of, 275—277

Casement, Mr., Report of, 286, 291, 292, 298, 300, 304
Catholic clergy and State schools, 39
Catholic missions in Congo State (*see* Missions, Congo)
Catholic missionaries in Congo State, 189—220, 258; and civilisation of negroes, 289 (*see also*, Missions, Congo)
Catholic party in Belgium, 21—46, 309—327; and electoral reform, 355, 358; financial prosperity under, 359
Catholic priests, Simple life of Belgian, 333
Cattle breeding: in Congo State, 257—259; in Belgium, 331
Cemeteries, Release from clerical control of, 25
Chamberlain, Mr., 274
Charleroi, Socialistic meeting at, 363
Children, Law for protection of, 46 (*see also* Education and Schools)
Children's Society for protection of trees, 318
China, Belgium's commercial alliance with, 10
Christianity in Congo State (*see* Missions, Congo)
Church and State, Battle between, 21
Cocoa, Cultivation in Congo State of, 254
Coffee, Cultivation in Congo State of, 254
Collectivism (*see* Socialism)
Colmbra, slave hunter, 101
Commerce in Congo State, 259—271
Commission for inquiry into alleged ill-treatment of natives, 304
Compagnie d'Ostende, 10
Conference, Geographical, at Brussels, 93—96, 103—106
Congo Baolo mission, 224, 226
Congo River, Freedom of trade on, 147; regulations for trading in basin of, 150; steamers on, 238
Congo State, England's attacks on, 82, 86; slave hunting in, 98—106; first

INDEX. 385

French expedition to, 123; Portuguese claims in, 128—130; its sovereignty recognised by Powers, 138; freedom of trade in, 146; resolutions of Berlin Congress concerning, 148; suppression of slavery in, 152—161; proclamation of constitution of, 152; receives loan from Belgium, 159; war with Arabs, 160; Leopold II. announces his sovereignty of, 165; its code of laws, 166; number of recruits for army, 169; number of volunteers, 170; formation of national army, 170; freedom of religion, 171; collection of rubber, 173, 253, 268; history of its tribes, 176; Leopold II.'s subsidies to, 177; provisions for natives to retain their lands, 178; governing power given to native chiefs, 179; its missions, 181—232; creation of Apostolic Vicariate, 192; trades, 196, 246—249; number of missionary stations in, 197; construction of railways, 234—238; postal, telegraph, and telephone services, 240; medical science, 242; sciences, 243—245; literature, 245; agriculture, 249—253; botanic garden at Eala, 251; cultivation of coffee, cocoa, and cotton, 254—256; timber trade, 256; cattle breeding, 257—259; commerce, 259—271; exports, 271; crime, controversy, and justice, 272—307; false charges of cruelty against its officials, 280—289; civilisation of native soldiers, 285; its Courts of Appeal, 306; its tribunals, 306

Congress, National, of 1830, 21
Congress for suppression of slave hunting, 157
Congress of Berlin, 138, 141—151
Congress of Brussels, 1874, 67
Congress of London, 1830, 55
Coninck, Pierre de, 72
  Z

Conservative Government in Belgium, 308
Constitution, Belgian, 21
Convention of Antwerp, 31
Co-operative institutions in Belgium, 332, 343—354
Cotton, Cultivation in Congo State of, 255
Court of Appeal in Congo State, 306
Court of Boma, 307
Court of First Instance, 306
Creameries, Belgian, 332
Crime in Congo State, 272—307
Criminals, Belgian law for conditional condemnation of, 46

D

Davis, Alexander, on collection of rubber, 175; on African missions, 182
d'Alkemade, General Cousebant, Resignation of, 77
d'Alviella, Count Goblet, on Liberal party, 27, 29; on generosity of Belgian Catholics, 39
d'Aspremont-Lynden, Count, on Belgium's international obligations, 67
de Brazza, M., at Stanley Pool, 123
de Coninck, Pierre, 72
de la Valette, M., 59
de Lhuys, M. Drouyn, 57
de Neyer, Count de Smet, 364
de Schumacher, Dr. Edmund, 305
de Semenow, M., at Geographical Congress at Brussels, 105
de Winton, Sir Francis, 176
Debt, National, of Belgium, 364
Déniaud, Father, Death of, 192
Descamps, Baron, on Act of Berlin, 149; on Brussels General Act, 157; on collection of rubber, 175; on Anglo-Congolese Convention, 303
Destrée, M., on strikes of 1886, 338, 341, 346; on co-operatives, 351, 353; on proportional election, 361

Dhanis, Baron, 160; on brutality of Europeans in Congo State, 279; denies practice of mutilation, 281
Dhoop, soldier, Death of, 191
Dilke, Sir Charles, and Congo State soldiers, 285
Drink question and native races, 145
Duclerc, M., letter to King Leopold II., 125
Dutch Society, Exports from Congo State by, 265
Dutilley, M., on technical education, 322

E

Eala, Botanic garden at, 251; model farm at, 258
Education: Law on secondary, 25; primary, 30; intermediate, 31; higher, 32; Bill of elementary, 1879, 38; religious and technical, 316—327 (*see also* Schools)
Elections: of 1892, 356, 363; of 1894, 358, 371; of 1896, 360; system of proportional, 361
Eliot, President Charles W., on treatment of backward races, 167 (*note*)
Elton, Consul, on slave trade, 100
Emin Pasha, Murder of, 160
England: Reception of her volunteers in Brussels, 61; warns Belgium not to count on aid of English army, 71; her attacks on Belgium, 82; King Leopold's friendship for, 85—87; withdraws from International Association for Suppression of Slave Trade, 110; and Portuguese claims in Africa, 128—130; and charges of cruelty in Congo State, 282—304
English-Portuguese Treaty, 1884, 130, 137
English Protestant missions in Congo State, 224
Epondo, Alleged mutilation of boy, 286, 292
Etienne, M. Eugène, 235, 261

Exports of Congo State, 265, 271

F

Faguet, M. Emile, on Belgian Liberalism, 335
Fédération des Sociétés Catholiques Belges, 325
Fire-arms in Congo State, Laws concerning, 301
Flemings and Walloons, Union of, 374
Flemish Academy, Establishment of, 46
Flemish citizens relieved from pleading in French, 46
Flemish race, Characteristics of, 45
Foreign Powers and Belgium, 54—87
France: her designs on Belgium, 57—65; her first expedition to the Congo, 123; and Portuguese claims in Africa, 129, 135
Franchise, Parliamentary, 22—24; extension of, 354—358, 360
Franco-German war and Belgium, 64, 80
Francotte, M. Gustave, 321
Frere, Sir Bartle, at Geographical Congress at Brussels, 104; resigns membership of International Association for Suppression of Slave Trade, 110
Frère-Orban, Walthère, Policy of, 20, 32, 33

G

Geographical Conference at Brussels in 1876, 93—96, 103—106
Geographical Congress at Brussels, 66
Germany, Napoleon's proposed secret treaty with, 58; and Belgian bishops, 67; her wooing of Belgium, 84; formation of territories in East Africa, 131; acknowledges sovereignty of International Association, 138
Goossens, Father, on teaching natives, 219
Gordon, General, and Leopold II., 153

INDEX.   387

Granville, Lord, and Portuguese claims in Africa, 128, 129, 137
Grison, Reverend Gabriel, 199
Guilds, Catholic, 325
Guinness, Dr. Harry, 225
Guinness, Mrs. M. Grattan, 226

H

Hand-cutting in Congo State, 281
Handekyn, Père, on Congo missions, 200—209
Harrison, Major, on Congo soldiers and cannibalism, 276; on report of Mr. Casement, 291
Higher education in Belgium, 32
Hinde, Dr., on Arab rebellion, 160
Hodister, M., Murder of, 160

I

Injured workmen, Fund for, 50
Instruction, Ministry of Public, 39
Intermediate education, 31
International African Association, Growth of, 127, 133; its sovereignty acknowledged by Foreign Powers, 138
International Association for Suppression of Slave Trade, 108—118
International Commission for Suppression of Slave Trade, 108; its meeting in 1877, 114
International Missionary Association, 223

J

Janssens, M. Edmond, 304
Jesuits, Missionary labours of, 213, 258
Journal of Commerce, 276, 291
Justice in Congo State, 271—307

K

Kangu, Mission station at, 211
Kasai, Upper, Mission stations at, 205
Kassongo, Slave hunting in, 101
Kelengo, Accusations of mutilation against, 292

Kingsley, Miss, 182
Kinkanda, Mission station at, 203, 204
Kisantu, Mission station at, 213; schools at, 214
Kwango, Apostolic Prefecture of, 212

L

Labour Commission, 46
Labour tax in Congo State, 299
Laeken, Colonial garden at, 252
Lambermont, Baron, 98; at Berlin Congress, 149
Lavigerie, Cardinal, Anti-slavery crusade of, 156; and Pères Blancs d'Afrique, 190
Leo XIII. on Belgian constitution, 38; on condition of Africa, 156
Leopold I., Belgium under, 1, 9, 19, 54; and Queen Victoria, 85; his impartial rule over Walloons and Flemings, 374
Leopold II., Birth of, 3; his entry into Parliament as Duke of Brabant, 4; what he has done for Belgium, 5—9, 13; his marriage and travels, 9; urges expansion of Belgian trade, 10—13, 376; ascends the throne, 14; his speech to Parliament on his accession, 16—18; and Walthére Frère-Orban, 20; insists on Government carrying out wishes of nation, 37, 44; celebration of his twenty-fifth anniversary of accession, 46—53; defeats Napoleon III.'s designs on Belgium, 59—65; his appeal to patriotism of citizens, 72—75; his letter to Cousebant d'Alkemade, 77; his friendship for England, 85—87; his interest in expansion of Belgium, 89; his address to Geographical Conference at Brussels, 93—96; his address on slave trade, 111—113; his diplomatic victories in forming Congo State, 119—131, 135; his love for France, 136; at Berlin Congress,

INDEX.

138; his desire to suppress slavery, 143; suppresses slave trade in Congo State, 151—161; and General Gordon, 153; summons Congress for suppressing slave hunting, 157; his aims for prosperity of Congo State, 162; announces his sovereignty of Congo State, 165; his aim in Africa, 167; his subsidies to Congo State, 177; gives governing power to native chiefs, 179; and Christian missionaries, 183; British Baptist Missionary Society's address to, 222; his aid to Congo State, 260; his justice in the Congo, 273; appoints commission to inquire into alleged acts of ill-treatment of natives, 304; leads Belgian enterprise, 375—382

Leopoldville, Mission station at, 211

Lhuys, M. Drouyn de, 57

Liberal party in Belgium, 3, 18—46; and electoral reform, 357; administration from 1878 to 1884, 359

Liberalism, Belgian, 335—337

Limbourg, Coalfields in, 12

Lique Démocratique, 325, 327

Literature in Congo State, 245

London, Congress of, 1830, 55

Luluabourg St. Joseph, Mission station at, 205

Luxembourg becomes an independent State, 62

M

Maison du Peuple, 344, 345, 346

Malet, Sir Edward, on King Leopold II., 139; at Berlin Congress, 144, 146

Marx, Karl, 340

Matadi, Mission station at, 203, 204

Mayumbe country, Missionaries in, 211

Medical service of Congo State, 242

Mellaerts, Abbe, 327, 330

Meuse districts, Fortification of, 71

Military service in Belgium, Lightening of, 46

Ministry of Public Instruction, 39

Missionary stations in Congo State, Number of, 197

Missions Belge, 215, 219

Missions, Congo: Leopold II.'s influence on, 181—190, 192; labours of Pères Blancs d'Afrique missionaries, 190, 197; creation of Apostolic Vicariate, 192; labours of Pères de Scheut missionaries, 193, 203, 210—214; missionary orders in, 193; work and method of Catholic missionaries in, 195—200; labours of Sacré-Cœurs, 199—201; of Premonstrants, 201—203; of Trappists, 203; of Jesuits, 213—217; orders of nuns in, 217; statistics of Catholic missions, 220; commencement of Protestant missions, 220, 224; Baptist Missionary Society, 222; American Missionary Associations, 223, 224; Swedish Missionary Society, 223; Regions Beyond Missionary Union, 225, 226; statistics of Protestant missions, 225; missionaries and trading, 227; cheap sentiment of Protestant missionaries, 228; education of natives, 230—232

Missions en Chine et au Congo, 206

Moanda, Mission station at, 212

Moll Ste. Marie, Mission station at, 211

Mongolla district, Punishment of crime against natives in, 301

Moniteur, 58

Mpala, African chief, Death of, 117

Mpala district, Missionaries in, 198

Muata Yamvo, Slave hunting in, 101

Mullens, missionary, on slave trade, 100

Museum of the Independent State at Tervuren, 244

Mutilation: Its suppression in Congo State, 281, 282; of boy Epondo, 286, 292

INDEX.

Mutombo, Pania, Raids of, 206
Mutshifula, Chief, and missionaries, 207
Mutual Societies in Belgium, 368

N

Napoleon III.'s designs on Belgium, 57—65
National Congress of 1830, 21
National Debt of Belgium, 364
New Antwerp, Mission station at, 211
Neyer, Count de Smet de, 364
Nisco, Baron, 304
Nuns, Orders of, in Congo missions, 217

O

Old-age pensions, 369
Ouroundi, Arab rising at, 192

P

Palmerston, Lord, on neutrality of Belgium, 56
Pania Mutombo, Raids of, 206
Parliament, Belgian, 14—53; rejects proposal to institute personal service in army, 72 (*see also* Catholic party and Liberal Party)
Patronage Societies in Belgium, 319
Pensions, Old-age, 369
Pères Blancs d'Afrique, 192, 192, 193
Pères de Scheut, 192, 193, 203, 204, 210, 212, 258
Pius IX. and Liberalism, 36
Polygamy among savages, 217
Ponta da Lenha, Attempt to burn factory at, 277
Pope Leo XIII.: on Belgian Constitution, 38; on condition of Africa, 156
Pope Pius IX. and Liberalism, 36
Portugal: her pretensions in Africa, 122, 128—130, 134; appeals to Foreign Powers concerning Congo, 126
Postal service of Congo State, 240

Premonstrant missionaries in Congo State, 201—203
Primary education, 30
Protestant Missionary Societies in Congo State, 220—232
Prussia, Napoleon's proposed secret treaty with, 58

R

Raiffeisen banks, 327—330
Railways, Control of Belgian, 63
Railways in Congo State, Construction of, 234—238
Ramaeckers, Captain, Belgian explorer, 118
Rawlinson, Sir Henry, at Geographical Congress at Brussels, 105
Redemptorists, Missions of, 203
Reform, Electoral, in Belgium, 354—358, 360
Regions Beyond Missionary Union, 225
Religious teaching, excluded from Belgian schools, 39; restored, 42 (*see also* Missions, Congo)
Revue Générale, 198
Revue Politique et Parlementaire, 235
Rigby, Consul-General, on slave trade, 100
Riots, Socialistic, 363
Romée, Mission station at, 200
Ronslé, Monsignor Van (*see* Van Ronslé)
Royal Commission on strikes of 1886, 338
Rubber, Collection of, 173, 253, 268, 282, 299

S

Sacré-Cœur, Missionaries of, 199—201
Saint Gabriel, Mission station at, 199, 200
St. Luke schools, 324
St. Trudon, Mission station at, 205
Salisbury, Lord, 87
Sanford, General, appointed on International Association, 111; on

International African Association, 133, 138
Savings bank, General, 367
Schools, State, 30, 39; religious teaching excluded from, 39; religious teaching restored in, 42 (*see also* Education)
Schumacher, Dr. Edmund de, 305
Sciences in Congo State, 242—245
Secondary education, Law on, 25
Semenow, M. de, at Geographical Congress at Brussels, 105
Senne, River, Improvement of, in Brussels, 16
Slave hunting, in the Congo, 89—106; Congress for suppressing, 157
Slave trade, Association for Suppression of, 108—118; suppression of, 152
Slavery, Crusade against, 156
Sleeping sickness, Prevalence of, 210; in Congo State, 242, 243; ravages of, 299
Small-pox in Congo State, 242
Social legislation in Belgium, 314
Socialists, in Belgium, 337—355; and electoral reform, 357, 362; riots, 363
Society of Little Protectors of Animals, 317
Stanley, H. M., at Stanley Pool, 123; on Arab chieftains of Manyema, 155
Stanley Falls, Missionaries in, 199
Stanley Pool, M. de Brazza at, 123
Stanleyville, Mission station at, 200
State schools, 30; and Catholic clergy, 39
State universities, 32
Steamers on the Congo, 238
Stockmar, Baron, on policy of Belgium, 81
Storms, Captain, in Africa, 117
Straaten, Count Van der, on alcohol and native races, 145
Strauch, Colonel, 138
Strikes of 1886, Belgian, 338, 341, 346

Suffrage, Monetary, 22—24
Suffrage, Universal, Adoption of, 357
Swedish Missionary Society, 223

T

Tanganyika district, Missionaries in, 197
Tanganyika, Lake, Exploring station at, 116
Tax, Labour, in Congo State, 299
Taxation in Belgium, 364
Taylor's, Bishop, mission, 224
Technical education in Belgium, 322—327
Telegraph service of Congo State, 240
Telephone service of Congo State, 240
Timber trade in Congo State, 256
Trade, Belgian, 377—382
Trade in Congo State, Freedom of, 295
Traders, Barbarity of Congo, 278—280, 297, 301
Trades in Congo State, 196, 246—249
Trappists, Missionary order of, 193, 203
Treaty of London, 55, 69, 70
Tribunals in Congo State, 306
Trusts, Growing power of, 164

U

Uele district, Orphan schools of, 202
United States, and Congo State, 132; and negro question, 167
Universities, State, 32

V

Vaccination in Congo State, 243
Valette, M. de la, 59
Van de Weyer, M., on Belgian neutrality, 61, 70
Van der Straaten, Count, on alcohol and native races, 145
Van Ronslé, Monsignor, on Congo missions, 183, 187; on sleeping sickness, 210
Vandervelde, M., on strikes of 1886, 338, 341, 346; on co-operatives,

INDEX. 391

351, 353; on proportional elections, 361

Vermeersch, Father A., on labour laws, 312; on patronage societies, 320, 321; on St. Luke schools, 324; on Catholic guilds, 325; on Raiffeisen banks, 327; on Belgian creameries, 332

Vicariates in Congo State, 192—194, 197

Victoria, Queen, and Leopold I., 85

Vivian, Lord, on Congo State, 158

Volunteers, British, visit Belgium, 61

Votes, Plural, 357 (*see also* Reform, Electoral)

W

Waller, Horace, on slave trade, 100

Walloons, Characteristics of, 45; and union with Flemings, 374

Warecque, M., 337

Weyer, M. Van de, on Belgian neutrality, 61, 70

Wilmotte, M.: his description of Liberal party, 18; on educational system, 31, 33; on education law of 1895, 315, 323; on St. Luke schools, 324; on Belgian Liberalism, 334

Winton, Sir Francis de, 176

Wireless Telegraphy in Congo State, 240

Workmen, Act for benefit of, 46; fund for injured, 50

Y

Young, Lieut., on slave trade, 100